A SEASON IS A LIFETIME

THE INSIDE STORY OF THE DUKE BLUE DEVILS AND THEIR CHAMPIONSHIP SEASONS

Bill Brill
and
Mike Krzyzewski

SIMON & SCHUSTER
NEW YORK LONDON TORONTO
SYDNEY TOKYO SINGAPORE

SIMON & SCHUSTER
Simon & Schuster Building
Rockefeller Center
1230 Avenue of the Americas
New York, New York 10020

Designed by Levavi & Levavi
Manufactured in the United States of America
1   3   5   7   9   10   8   6   4   2
Library of Congress Cataloging-in-Publication Data

Brill, Bill.
A season is a lifetime: the inside story of the Duke Blue Devils and
their championship seasons/Bill Brill and Mike Krzyzewski.
p.   cm.
1. Duke Blue Devils (Basketball team)—History.   I. Krzyzewski,
Mike.   II. Title.
GV885.43.D85B75   1993
796.323'63'097565—dc20   92-35549
CIP

ISBN: 0-671-79811-1

Photo Credits
Cliff Burns/Duke University: 1, 2; Ron Ferrell/Duke University: 3; Jim
Midgett/Bradley Photographers: 4, 5; Bradley Photographers: 7; Chuck
Liddy/*The Herald-Sun*: 6, 8, 9, 10, 11, 12, 13, 14, 15, 16, 17, 18.

TO JANE, my wife, for her patience and encouragement; and to the employees at Dupac—Jane, Shirley, Carolyn, Kay, Rebecca, Carola, Gene, Aimee, and Dave—who kept me going.

—B.B.

TO MY MOM, Emily, who has given me a lifetime of love and support.

—M.K.

MY THANKS TO Donna Keane, Laura Ann Kidd, and Gerry Brown in the Duke basketball office; and Mike Cragg, Mike Sobb, Warren Miller, Richard Kilwein, and Paulette Rogers in sports information/promotions.

—Bill Brill

I HAVE LEARNED many things working on this book. Probably the main lesson is that writing a book is a team effort. The obvious team was basketball and myself; however, there were two other key members: my wife, Mickie, and Jeff Neuman from Simon & Schuster.

Mickie poured her heart and soul into the making of this book. Her thought and effort were evident at every stage. She was constantly reading and backing up everyone. Her ideas generated a better analysis of the season and a more in-depth look at our team. As always, she helped make me much better.

Jeff was brilliant. He helped me put in words what I wanted to say and made me think of things I didn't know I wanted to say. He also taught me about the English language, which I discovered had words I never knew before meeting him.

I would like to thank my Athletic Director, Tom Butters, for making the commitment to me and sticking to it.

Finally, a special thanks to my players, coaches, and support staff for working as an exceptional unit. Without their effort and cooperation, there would not be a book to write.

—Mike Krzyzewski

FOREWORD

Mike Krzyzewski

IT IS APRIL 20, 1992, the night of our annual basketball awards banquet. It's a gala affair, with over a thousand people in Cameron Indoor Stadium ready to dine at a sit-down dinner honoring the 1992 National Champions, the Duke basketball team. There will be awards for a variety of accomplishments, and we'll show videos on two huge screens. There will be two on this year's team: one high-lighting performances by each individual player, and another on the NCAA tournament. There will also be videos honoring each of the seniors, Ron Burt, Brian Davis, and Christian Laettner. The videos have become a tradition, and the seniors are anxiously waiting to see what my wife, Mickie, has come up with this year. She creates a special music video for each of the seniors: for Burt, the tune is the theme from "Greatest American Hero" ("Believe it or not, I'm walking on air . . ."); for Davis, it's "I'm So Excited"; for Laettner, it's "Unforgettable." The videos have become a great tradition for our program.

There will also be speeches. We don't bring in an outside speaker for the banquet; I will give one, and then each of our seniors will speak. Who can do a better job of capturing the true meaning of the season and their careers at Duke than they can? There is an unbelievably festive mood, and this will truly be a great celebration. We'll be raising banners to honor our ACC championship, our No. 1 ranking, Christian Laettner's retired jersey, the Final Four, and of course, the 1992 National Championship.

I still can't believe we won our second national title. But as happy as I am tonight, there is also some sadness in my heart. This will be the last time this particular team will be together. Each year when we have the banquet, I feel this mix of joy and sadness, because while we celebrate what we've done, we're bringing something special to an end. You see, to me, a season is a lifetime. It is born at the orientation meeting each year in early September when we first get the team together. The lifetime lasts only eight short months, and it ends every April at the awards banquet. What goes on during those eight months is incredibly fascinating to me.

When your life span is only eight short months, you're always aware of the pressures of time. There is simply no time to waste. We can't always take the nice, polite way of saying things to each other; we need to communicate in ways that are more direct than most people are used to. We can only do this if we learn to trust each other and to understand that we're not trying to hurt each other with our words, even when to someone outside our team they might seem destructive.

Destruction isn't necessarily a bad thing; it can be good if what you're destroying is immaturity, the fear of failure, jealousy, or a lack of commitment. What we have to destroy are those traits that lead an individual to put his own interests above those of the group. If we can minimize the amount of time we spend on elements like these, our season has a better chance of becoming a truly special one.

I always stress to my team the dignity of work. Work is a good word that society has too often used in a very negative manner. When we work hard at something, especially something we really enjoy, we feel good once the work is finished, and we're eager to work again so that we can feel good about ourselves again, and again and again. I try to get my team to believe each season that work is good. If we truly believe this, we'll come closer to developing our potential.

But while my ultimate concern is the team as a whole, I also have to be cognizant of the needs of each individual on our team. Somehow I must be able to satisfy these needs while meeting our group objectives. I must allow each individual to have the freedom to make mistakes and learn from these mistakes while our team develops.

If my players do work at a very high level, I have to give them the freedom to develop their full capabilities. When a player starts out in September, he is different from what he was in the previous season, whether he was in high school and is first coming into our program or is one of our returning players. I cannot assume who he is; I must allow him to show me who he is. I must also allow him to do this throughout the year. That's one reason I don't refer to players by a number for their position. What's a "3" anyway? A 3 isn't kind, it isn't smart, it isn't strong, it isn't brave. Grant Hill is all of these things; I would diminish him if I thought about him as a number in a diagram.

I believe it would be detrimental to each player's progress if I were to put him in a certain role right at the beginning of the season and keep him in that role throughout. It would be very much like putting a plant in a jar to see what would happen; of course it would only take the shape of the jar. But if I allow the plant to grow freely, it might grow to such an extent that twenty jars would not be able to hold it. The freedom to get better, to make mistakes, to learn from them, and to work hard —if these things are all put together properly, some truly unique things can happen individually and collectively during our eight-month lifetime.

As I get ready to listen to this year's seniors speak, I recall our banquet three years ago, on April 17, 1989. Our seniors that year were John Smith, Danny Ferry, and Quin Snyder. Those three had just completed a four-year career in which they won 117 games and were a part of three Final Four teams. I will always remember Quin's speech. His theme was "What Duke Basketball Means to Me." Listening to him, I had chills, I cried, and I experienced a great feeling of accomplishment.

Quin used eight words to describe his experience.

The first word was *commitment*. When I recruit a young man, I promise that I will give him 100 percent, and I expect the same from him in return. If we are to share common goals and achieve them, this pledge to each other is critical. We must give quality time to one another, both when it is easy and when it is hard.

One way we as coaches show our commitment to our players is that we don't bring in transfers or junior-college players in midstream. We're not like a pro team that makes a trade to fill an open position; our players come here for a four-year college experience. Sharing that experience is what helps bring our team together; I would be breaking faith with them if I brought in someone who hadn't gone through everything they had from the start. I've turned down some very good players who expressed interest in transferring to Duke—not because I didn't think they'd help our team as players, but because I want the players we recruited to know that we believe in them, and that our commitment to them is a meaningful one.

Our players show their commitment to us through their work. Their commitment and willingness to stretch themselves is crucial if we are to reach beyond our individual and group limits. In order to improve we must try new things. This will result in some failures. Mutual commitment helps you overcome the fear of failure because you always know someone is there behind you and on your side.

The next two words really go together: *honesty* and *integrity*. I have a policy on my team that when we talk to each other we must have eye-to-eye contact. I tell our players we can always deal with the truth; don't lie or cheat yourself or others. Being straightforward gets everyone on the same page quickly. Honesty helps develop in our individual and team character a strong sense of integrity.

This is where I would like to add a word to Quin's list: *trust*. A man of integrity can be trusted. We have to exhibit trust in each other every day. It happens at a team meeting when a sensitive issue is addressed and the player responds to what is said, not how it was said. It occurs at a time-out when we give instructions in a late-game situation and the players instantly believe what is said and don't ask "Why?" or "What about me?" It also happens when a player expresses himself, and I immediately believe he is sincere. The level of cooperation on our team increases tremendously as the level of trust rises.

Toughness was the next word. Any successful athletic team must be tough physically, but to become a champion, mental toughness is even more essential. I look at mental toughness as the ability to focus on one goal and not be distracted. When Bobby Hurley, for the good of the team, learns to show no sign of negative emotion during a game even when things aren't going his way, he is being mentally tough. When our team wins a huge game and must play the next day, putting a great accomplishment behind you to focus on what is at hand shows incredible toughness.

The fifth word was actually two words, *collective responsibility*. We are all accountable for the actions of our group. If something goes wrong or if we lose a game, we do not *blame* anyone. We take responsibility for it and try to ensure it does not happen again. When something goes right or when we win a game, we all take responsibility for it and try to ensure it *does* happen again.

In late February of 1989, we played a game in the Meadowlands in New Jersey on national TV against then–No. 1 Arizona. We were ranked No. 5. With one second to go in the game and Duke losing by two, Christian Laettner, then a freshman, was fouled. He had one free throw and a bonus. Arizona called time-out. On the bench I asked Christian if he was all right. He said, "I've got 'em, Coach!"

As my team went back onto the court, I felt good about Christian. He stepped to the line in a very confident manner. However, when he shot, he put too much into it. The ball was right on line, but long. It struck the back of the rim and bounced back to an Arizona player. Arizona won.

Christian did not move. However, everyone else on our team did. Before shaking hands with the Arizona players and coaches, everyone on our team rushed out to Christian. We all said, "It's okay, Christian. Don't worry. We win and we lose together." It was the best! I loved it!

Four weeks later in the same arena, Christian was our most important player in a win over Georgetown for the East Regional championship. One year later, also in the same arena, Christian hit a last-second shot against the University of Connecticut in overtime to win the East Regional championship again. Two years later in the Hoosier Dome, he hit two free throws that beat UNLV in the Final Four.

When we accept responsibility together, it sets the stage for the best things to happen.

Pride was the sixth word. Being a part of something that's bigger and better than you individually can help give you a sense of purpose that will let you accomplish things you never dreamed of. If we develop the first five words properly, this feeling of pride will grow and grow.

Quin's seventh word was *love*. Five weeks after Christian missed his free throw against Arizona in 1989, we lost to Seton Hall in the semifinal game of the Final Four in Seattle. After the game we returned to our hotel, and I met with the team in my suite. As I spoke to my players, I looked at my seniors, Quin, John, and Danny, and I started crying. Christian was sitting on the floor and looking up at me while I was crying. He seemed bewildered. Maybe he had never seen an adult cry before. It was difficult for me to speak, so I finally just said, "You guys go be with your families. We'll meet tomorrow and go over things. We're staying through the championship game to celebrate our season."

Later that night at about eleven P.M., I was watching tape with some of our coaches. There was a knock at my door. As one of the coaches opened the door, I saw that it was Christian. He was eighteen years old and had just lost the biggest game of his life that afternoon. As he entered, he said, "Coach, are you all right?" I told him I was fine. He sat down next to me, and as I was telling him he had a great year, he interrupted me. "Are you okay, Coach?" I reassured him that I was fine. As he was leaving the room, he turned and asked again, "Are you sure you're okay, Coach?" I will always remember his caring for me. It gave me one of the best feelings I have ever had as a coach, better than any victory.

The final word was *friend*. Quin said it was the word that meant the most to him, and it was the word that started me crying during my meeting with the team after the Seton Hall loss. I realized it was the last game Quin, John, Danny, and I would play together. It was over, and I told them that I would always be their friend. Ultimately, when a player finishes his career at Duke, I hope our relationship has developed to the extent that we have become good friends. It would be a shame if all we did was just win basketball games together. What a shallow thing that would be!

Quin's words are exactly the things that are important and exciting to me about coaching. I want to win games —you better believe I want to win games. But long after the games are forgotten, these are the things that last, the things that matter. So long as we have these things, we're winners, whatever the final score of our final game turns out to be.

The banquet is about to begin. I feel kind of sad. I guess I just don't want this season to end. When you have a team that reflects our beliefs as well as this one has, and you have the kind of success we had on the court—there's just no greater satisfaction. This year has been the best of my career. Let me share it with you, and maybe you'll understand why.

CHAPTER 1

"WE'RE GOING TO WIN the national championship."

Those were not the words that the discouraged Duke basketball team expected to hear from coach Mike Krzyzewski as the team bus pulled away from the Charlotte Coliseum.

The top-seeded Blue Devils had just been embarrassed, 96–74, by archrival North Carolina in the 1991 championship game of the Atlantic Coast Conference tournament. They had completely fallen apart against a team they had beaten twice in the regular season, including one week earlier in Chapel Hill.

Duke had fallen behind immediately. Blue Devil center Christian Laettner was called for a touch foul on the very first play. It was the worst thing that could happen, Krzyzewski knew, because if the officials called the game that close, Carolina's depth on the front line would put its big men in control. At 6-11, Laettner was the only legitimate force for the Blue Devils underneath.

The quick call against Laettner confirmed Krzyzewski's

opinion that the officials were uptight, even though the trio of Lenny Wirtz, Dick "Froggy" Paparo, and Gerry Donaghy was a veteran group. All had called national championship games.

"You can't call that," Krzyzewski bellowed at Wirtz.

After another UNC basket, Krzyzewski screamed out to freshman Grant Hill, "Grant, don't let him push you around. Box out. Don't let him go over your back again." Just 2:21 into the game, Wirtz called a technical foul for those remarks. "I wasn't even talking to you, Lenny," Krzyzewski shouted.

Paparo came over to the Duke bench and said to Krzyzewski, "Mike, control yourself."

"God damn it, I am in control. I wasn't looking for a T."

Coach K may have been in control of himself, but control of this game was another story. The harder the Tar Heels came at the Blue Devils, the more frustrated Duke became. Carolina led 49–36 at halftime and immediately extended its lead after intermission.

Laettner, the most competitive player Krzyzewski had ever coached, lost his cool. He constantly berated the officials, his remarks peppered with profanities, and finally drew a technical foul late in the second half. "That was the nicest thing I said all day," he said.

Carolina's players were laughing. King Rice was taunting Bobby Hurley, and Duke fell apart. Laettner and Hurley openly bickered on the floor. Duke had disintegrated.

Then Krzyzewski, the former Army captain, did an unusual thing. He stood up on the sidelines and remained standing for the rest of the game. Normally, he only stands to shout instructions, then sits back down. But now he wanted to divert the derision of the crowd away from his players and onto himself. In his mind, the game was already over and it was time to move on. If he could draw the taunts of the crowd away from his players, it would be that much easier for them to put the game behind them, too.

As he stood in front of the bench, he did another unusual thing: he looked across the court to where his family was sitting. What he saw was disturbing.

Mickie Krzyzewski, his wife and the mother of his three daughters, was visibly upset. Her sister, Donna Borman, had changed her seat in order to separate the eldest daughter, Debbie, a Duke sophomore, from her boyfriend, Brad Evans, a North Carolina sophomore. Debbie, perhaps Duke's most outspoken fan, was clearly distraught.

Before the game, Mickie had explained the ground rules to Brad, who was attending his first ACC tournament as a guest of the Krzyzewskis. "There is more going on here than just a basketball game," she said. "You are sitting courtside in the front row of the Duke section with the Krzyzewski family. There can't be any outward displays of support for Carolina, not as long as you're with us. This is family."

Debbie was already crying because her dad's team was getting trounced when Brad did the unforgivable. With the Tar Heels well in command, Rick Fox dunked and Evans clapped his hands together. "Way to go!" He didn't jump up. He didn't go crazy. It was a very quiet show of support for his school. But it was a big mistake.

Debbie elbowed Brad and they began to argue, so Aunt Donna separated them to keep things from getting worse. Mickie was furious. Middle daughter Lindy was being consoled by her best friend, Tracy.

"And Dad saw it because he was standing up," Debbie said, horrified.

Brad's suitcase was in the Krzyzewski family van, and he was leaving on vacation immediately after the tournament. With 2 minutes left, Mickie decided it was time to leave, not because she couldn't stand to see Duke lose, and not because everyone was so upset. "Let's go," she said to Donna. "I'm not going to give Brad the satisfaction of seeing his team win."

With the embarrassment of his team's performance and

the tense family scene fresh in his mind, Krzyzewski boarded the team bus. He walked to the back, where the players were waiting to be seriously chewed out because they had played so poorly. The message was unexpected, and completely positive.

"We're going to win the national championship," he said. *What?* The players looked at the familiar face, the straight black hair, the prominent nose, the sharp, piercing eyes. He looked at them again. He repeated, "We're going to win the national championship."

Krzyzewski had taken teams to four Final Fours in the past five years, including three in a row. He had learned something each time. He knew that it was necessary to have only positive thoughts. He also knew that nobody pumped up the head coach; it was his job to set the tone for everyone else. So Coach K was also talking to himself, setting his own thoughts to the task ahead of them. The words were for the team, but the message was for himself, too. Carolina was forgotten. It was NCAA time.

The team met the family at their dinner stop, the Sandwich Construction Company near the North Carolina/Charlotte campus. Krzyzewski stormed into the restaurant, looking for Evans, who was not there. But Brad was the topic of conversation at dinner.

Less than an hour later, the NCAA pairings were telecast on the big screen in the restaurant. Mickie took out a pairings sheet, her annual ritual, but her mind was still on the family scene at the Coliseum. The players watched the draw anxiously. They knew that if they'd won, they would have been placed in the East Regional, whose finals would be played in the Meadowlands in New Jersey. Duke had won its four East championships since 1986 and had lost just one game ever in that building. The Meadowlands was a home away from home; they had confidence there.

The East pairings came first. North Carolina got the No. 1 seed. Bobby Hurley was upset; his home was in Jersey City, where his father was the basketball coach at nationally prominent St. Anthony's, and he was counting on playing there.

The players had to wait until Duke was announced as the No. 2 seed in the Midwest. Their first opponent, in Minneapolis, would be Northeast Louisiana.

Freshman Grant Hill studied the bracket. It included Ohio State, LSU, Connecticut, and St. John's. It looked tough to him, especially after the events of the day. Hill decided Duke would get as far as the regional, which would be played in the Silverdome at Pontiac, Michigan, and then lose.

Graduate-assistant coach Jay Bilas was more upbeat. "I think it's a great draw," he said. Bilas played on Krzyzewski's first three NCAA teams in 1984–86, including the squad that won a record 37 games his senior year before losing, 72–69, to Louisville in the championship game. Now a law student at Duke, Bilas had a good feel for the NCAA tournament.

"Good, that's a good region," Krzyzewski said. He never worried much about the draw; when your goal is the national championship, you have to be ready to beat anyone in your path.

For Coach K, the purpose of the regular season was to get you ready for March. That's why you played tough games in February, to test yourself. He knows a team is judged by how well it plays in March.

Krzyzewski is a tough loser. Driven, intense, competitive, his ambition is to win. But while the Carolina loss was painful, it was already in the past. When he saw the pairings flash across the big screen in the paneled restaurant room, Coach K was immediately rejuvenated. "Way to go," he said to the team. "Number-two seed in the Midwest. You had a great season."

The gloom from the Carolina loss was gone by the time the players got back on the bus. It was time for the NCAAs to begin. March madness. The Duke players know that this is what the season is really all about.

The seating order in the bus was always the same. Max

Crowder, the trainer for thirty years, sat alone on the front row, right. Behind him sat Krzyzewski. In the next row was assistant coach Mike Brey.

In the first row on the other side was Col. Tom Rogers, a thirty-year Army veteran who was a special assistant to the athletic director, but his importance to Krzyzewski went far beyond his duties with the team. Colonel Rogers had been Bob Knight's first assistant coach when he coached the plebes (or freshmen) at Army in the 1960s. One of those players brought Colonel and Mrs. Rogers along with him to Durham when he became the Duke coach. Rogers was a pillar of strength and a great comfort to Krzyzewski, who often turned to him for advice or counsel.

Pete Gaudet, officially the part-time coach because he didn't recruit, but in actuality the number-two man, normally sat in the row behind Rogers. This time, Gaudet had driven back to Durham with his family because he had to arrange for film of Northeast Louisiana's games.

Assistant Tommy Amaker, who played for Duke, graduating in 1987 after playing in four NCAAs, was in the next row with Bilas.

Krzyzewski, as he always did, watched tape of the game they'd just played on his portable VCR. He wasn't looking at the action; he was studying the faces on the bench, the attitude of the players. Were they watching the game or relaxing with their thoughts somewhere else? These were the things he would discuss with them later. It was time to narrow the focus.

But even on the eve of the postseason, there were still the family concerns. Mike and Mickie called Debbie the next day. They wanted to talk about Brad; he had to understand that when he attended a Duke game with Debbie, he couldn't outwardly cheer against her dad. This was family. This was serious stuff. "Nothing is more important than family," they said. "If we were at a game where Brad was playing for Carolina against Duke, we'd root for him, not Duke. He's got to understand that."

"That was the beginning of the end," Debbie said later. She and Brad broke up that summer.

The Duke basketball staff always set high goals in the preseason, but there was room for reality. Not long after the Blue Devils had lost in record-breaking fashion by 30 points to Nevada-Las Vegas in the 1990 NCAA finals, assistants Gaudet and Brey talked about the season to come.

"You know, we ought to have a pretty good team this year [1990–91], but we'll be really good next year," Gaudet said.

Duke had lost three senior starters—center Alaa Abdelnaby, forward Robert Brickey, and guard Phil Henderson. They all were double-figure scorers. Abdelnaby was a first-round draft choice of the Portland Trailblazers.

What was returning would be Duke's youngest team since the recruiting class of '82, when Johnny Dawkins, Mark Alarie, and Bilas started as freshmen and David Henderson was the sixth man. Weldon Williams was also a part of that class. These players were the nucleus of the team that turned the program around and brought Krzyzewski to his first Final Four.

The current team was not as young as that squad, but the only seniors were Greg Koubek, an occasional starter, and Clay Buckley, whose college career had been seriously impeded by a chronic back ailment.

The starters usually were sophomores Hurley and Billy McCaffrey at guard, junior Laettner at center, and freshman Grant Hill and sophomore Thomas Hill at forward. Koubek, junior Brian Davis, junior Crawford Palmer, and freshman Antonio Lang all got at least eight starts as Coach K continually changed the lineup.

Throughout the year, Duke played like a young team at times. It played well but lost in the preseason NIT semifinals to a veteran Arkansas team seeking revenge for their loss to the Blue Devils in the 1990 Final Four. But Krzyzewski was pleased because, by winning their first two games in the preseason tournament, the team got to play four times before most others even started, including the semifinals and the consolation game in Madison Square Garden.

Georgetown outmuscled Duke in an ACC/Big East Challenge game in December at the Capital Centre, the Hoyas' home court, but then they won five straight before a stunning 81–64 shellacking at Virginia in the ACC opener.

Krzyzewski was furious after that game. When the team returned to Durham after the four-hour bus ride, he called for an immediate practice. Grant Hill's nose was broken by an accidental swipe from Lang in that workout, but the unusual workout got the team's attention. In the next game, Duke wiped out a good Georgia Tech team, 98–57.

There was one other discouraging loss, by 9 points at Wake Forest. But otherwise the Blue Devils played well, even in defeats at N.C. State and Arizona, the latter in double overtime. By the end of the regular season, which closed with a solid win over Carolina at Chapel Hill, the Blue Devils were playing their best basketball. Krzyzewski believed the team was better than last year's NCAA finalists.

All season long, the staff had felt that this was the best group of listeners they had ever had. "They're so young, they pay attention really well," Krzyzewski said.

But not always. In the ACC finals, the Blue Devils made the mistake of not understanding how hard Carolina would come at them. Now it would be easy to get their attention again.

Krzyzewski made a positive out of a negative. "This game put an exclamation point on things," he told his players. "If you suckers don't know now that you need one another, you'll never know." There was no need to yell at the team; this was the kind of loss that could actually help a team find its focus.

Gaudet arrived back at Cameron before the team and

called Hoop One Video in New Jersey to order tapes of Northeast Louisiana. They arrived Monday morning and the game plan was begun.

If there was one drawback to the pairings, it was that Duke would have to play Thursday morning at 11:35 (CST) in the Metrodome. Since the team didn't arrive home until late Sunday night and there was no official practice on Monday—"We just have to give them some rest," Gaudet said—there would be only one workout at home before the charter flight to Minneapolis on Wednesday.

Krzyzewski had Gaudet make up a 3-minute tape of Laettner against North Carolina. This was something Krzyzewski did often; he believed strongly in the power of videotape as a teaching tool. It's one thing to tell a player what he's doing right or wrong. When he can actually see it for himself, the image sticks and the lesson is brought home with that much more power. "Christian was mad at everybody," Coach K said about the Carolina tape. "It was a mortality check. He knew he couldn't beat North Carolina alone. But we've got to get his head straight."

Coach and player watched the tape together, but the conversation was one-sided. "Your look, the yelling, this whole thing," Krzyzewski said to Laettner. "You were bad, Christian, and that bothers me because you're not bad, you're a hell of a player, but if you do that in the tournament, you're not going to play. If you don't believe that, test me. I don't need us to beat ourselves."

Laettner looked his coach in the eye and said, "It will never happen again."

The team practiced on Tuesday. Gaudet was working on the practice plans for Northeast Louisiana, a small team from the Southland Conference that had a 25-7 record, including its last sixteen wins in succession. Meanwhile, because every week in the NCAAs was considered a two-game tournament by the staff, Brey and Amaker prepared scouting reports on Iowa and East Tennessee State, who were in the other half of the mini-bracket.

The later it was in the season, the less the team practiced. In March, practice rarely went longer than an
hour. By NCAA time, and especially for an opening game
against an unknown opponent, the staff concentrated on
what its own team could do. There was no time for exotic
game plans.

But the players were wary. The Carolina loss was still
on their minds, and they still expected to get chewed out.
They tried to read Krzyzewski's mood by what drills were
planned for the afternoon. But there was nothing unusual; for him, the Carolina game was in the past. Now it
was vital for the players to think only about the games in
Minneapolis.

Krzyzewski constantly pumped himself up by thinking, "We're going to win the national championship." He
told the other coaches, "Just because it's something we
haven't done before doesn't mean we can't do it. Getting
to the Final Four isn't enough of a goal. Maybe that's
what stopped us in the past. We have to establish a larger
goal."

Because the team was so young, their psyches were
fragile. But they were also suggestible. "We're going to
win," Krzyzewski told them. "But if we don't start playing
with enthusiasm, if we're afraid to fail, we'll lose the next
game."

Practice went fine.

Wednesday the team flew to Minneapolis and checked
into their quarters at the downtown Marriott. Mickie
praised the Krzyzewski suite as the finest they'd ever
stayed in. There was even a grand piano in the middle
(somewhat to the Krzyzewskis' regret; nine-year-old Jamie
woke them each morning by playing it when she got up).
The suite was part of their regular routine for all road
games. Mike held all his team meetings there, the better
to amplify the family atmosphere that was at the heart of
his program.

At the mandatory day-before media conference at the
Metrodome, the players continued to be questioned

about the "un-Duke-like" manner they had displayed against Carolina. "Getting our asses kicked by twenty-two points is un-Duke-like," Krzyzewski conceded.

Several writers wanted to know if the debacle had made it easier to face Northeast Louisiana. Krzyzewski grabbed the microphone. "We're already humble," he said. "I'm not sure Carolina ever does us a favor, so don't ask that question again."

The queries continued, especially concerning Laettner's technical foul.

"We're human beings, for Christ's sake," Coach K said. "These aren't machines out there. I'm glad every once in a while they show some frailties. It gives me a better chance to coach them."

The Blue Devils showed they weren't machines—at least not mercilessly efficient ones—at the start of the game against Northeast Louisiana, a team with only one player taller than 6-4. Duke was sluggish for the prenoon start, and the fifteenth-seeded Indians took a quick 19–13 lead. Duke was up 46–40 at halftime, thanks in part to a technical foul against Northeast coach Mike Vining with 12 seconds left, but Krzyzewski realized his team was too lethargic.

He knew they were going to win, but he didn't like the way they were playing. So Coach K put on a demonstration in the locker room normally utilized by the Minnesota Twins.

"He wasn't negative," Brian Davis said later. "He was just jumping up and down. He was enthusiastic. He wanted us to know we were not playing like this could be the last game of the season. He told us he'd give us his heart, if he could."

Krzyzewski picked up a five-by-four-foot chalkboard used by the Twins and smashed it to the floor. "Slam-dunked it," Davis said. That woke them up.

In the second half, the Duke bench took over. Davis had 13 points, 9 rebounds, and did a good defensive job on the Indians' star, Anthony Jones. Lang and McCaffrey also made major contributions. Those three combined for 38 points and 14 rebounds as Duke won going away, 102–73.

That night, after dinner, the team gathered in the Krzyzewski suite. The coach told his staff, "We've got to reinforce the feeling of the second half."

So Gaudet came up with another video. As the players watched, Krzyzewski was strictly positive. "These are the things you can do. You've got to go right after it. That's who you are."

The players saw themselves running and jumping, dunking and stealing, and doing it with abandon. When Grant Hill left the room, he was fired up. "I'm ready to play right now," he said.

Krzyzewski was satisfied. The team had reacted with enthusiasm. "They gave us an immediate response," he said to the staff. "I feel really good about the Iowa game."

The Hawkeyes, who had beaten East Tennessee State, were seeded seventh. They had finished 9-9 in the Big Ten, but Krzyzewski thought they were good enough to beat Duke if the Blue Devils didn't play well. He wanted his team ready to play an aggressive, active, enthusiastic game. At practice he told them, "Iowa is going to press you. We're going to break the press and get a lot of two-on-one and three-on-one breaks. I want you to visualize taking it right at Earl." Acie Earl, Iowa's 6-10 shot-blocker, was the last line of defense for the Hawkeyes.

The game plan included a couple of changes. Because Iowa was expected to press throughout, a trademark of coach Tom Davis's, Laettner would pass the ball inbounds; the 6-11 Laettner could see over any end-line defender and would be available as an outlet target if needed, and this would free up Duke's best finishers to attack the basket. Defensively, the 6-8 Grant Hill would team with Hurley to attack the Hawks' guards, hoping for turnovers.

Things worked to perfection. Hurley beat the Iowa press repeatedly. He wound up with 8 assists and just 1 turnover, and he shrugged off a couple of calls against him that would have rattled him a year before.

Hill helped get the ball down the court, and he also had a hand in many of Duke's dozen steals. Thomas Hill joined Grant in taking the ball to the basket. Duke was in command throughout. Even with no outside shooting attack, the Blue Devils jumped into a 44–29 halftime lead and finished off the Hawkeyes, 85–70. Duke's pressure defense forced 22 turnovers; as a result, the Blue Devils got 41 fast-break points, 6 breakaway dunks.

Grant Hill's contributions included 14 points, 6 steals, and 3 of the dunks. What's more, he became a true believer. "What happened is exactly what the coaches told us would happen," he said. "They told us to visualize attacking against the press, and we did. Iowa lives and dies by their press, and most teams don't attack Earl like we did. I'm surprised it was that easy."

Hurley had been eager for the game. Even though he didn't shoot well (1 for 6), he did his job by setting up those fast-break opportunities. "I really like it when a team presses me, especially a team with bigger guys," said the six-foot point guard. "If I stay low and dribble through the press, it's like those guys are cones or something."

Krzyzewski was pleased. "The kids felt great after the game," he said. "When you have a young team, and they have success doing what you told them to do, it helps. They believe in you more. They listen better."

The players were laughing and joking on the bus to the airport. That was where the family nicknames got started. Because it was the first week of the NCAAs, right after the ACC tournament, the Duke traveling party was small. Only a few parents were on hand and a smattering of fans.

Only Jamie, the youngest of the three Krzyzewski daughters, made the trip. Debbie and thirteen-year-old Lindy stayed at home.

On the bus, the players were laughing and kidding with Jamie, who became "Mo' Minutes," as in, "If you play with Jamie on the bus, you get mo' minutes."

Mrs. K was tabbed "Mo' Press," as in more publicity, while Lindy was nicknamed "Mo' Shots," no explanation necessary.

The statuesque Debbie, meanwhile, became "No Scholarship"—if you mess with Debbie, then . . .

Duke had won Minneapolis. For the regional at the Silverdome in Pontiac, Michigan, the schedule gave the Blue Devils a break; the two games would be on Friday and Sunday.

"We've got time to rest," Krzyzewski said. He knew the team was tired. The regular season had been grueling enough, and the ACC tournament was always tough. The turnaround time to get to Minneapolis was so short, there was no time to give the players some relief, a chance to relax.

The team had played some of its best defense of the year in the second half against Northeast Louisiana and the entire game against Iowa. "This team needed to know it could win even when it didn't play well offensively," Krzyzewski said.

Duke had begun the NCAAs with a 26-7 record; now, the number was 28-7. For this tournament, Krzyzewski had begun to use the record as a kind of mantra, though he wouldn't describe it that way. Time and again, maybe a dozen times during a game, he would try to banish any negative thoughts from his mind by repeating to himself what the record would be at the end of a win. 27-7, he told himself throughout the first half against Northeast Louisiana. 27-7. Then against Iowa, the refrain became 28-7. It was a deliberate effort to block the encroachment of any doubts, anything negative that might interfere with the proper aggressive, positive frame of mind he needed to have and wanted to communicate to his players. It helped keep him from getting too conservative, from being afraid of losing. It was a private technique that he shared with no one.

Duke's victory over Iowa had so impressed Sid Hartman of the *Minneapolis Star Tribune* that in a column the next day, he predicted the Blue Devils would not only reach the Final Four again, but that in 1992, with the event being held at the Metrodome, they'd return for a fifth consecutive time.

Not to be outdone, Jim Spadafore in the *Detroit News*, on the day prior to the regional semifinals, predicted Duke would not only get another crack at UNLV in the Final Four at Indianapolis but would win the game, 75–72. "Count on it," Spadafore wrote.

Back in Durham, Krzyzewski learned that Laettner had not been named the ACC player of the year. The award had gone to N.C. State senior Rodney Monroe. Coach K complained publicly that Laettner should have won. "Rodney's a great player, but Christian is the focus of our team, and we were eleven and three in the ACC and won the regular season. I thought Christian would win. I'm shocked that the vote wasn't close."

National media poured into Durham. Krzyzewski did not shy away; even during tournament time, players were not cut off from interviews. He considered it part of the maturing process. "If they make mistakes, that's okay. They have to stumble a few times to grow up. I don't believe in sheltering them. That's not the real world."

Because Duke would be playing Connecticut again, everybody wanted to talk to Laettner about 1990 and "The Shot." The previous season, at the East Regional in the Meadowlands, the fans had been treated to back-to-back miracles.

First, top-seeded Connecticut trailed Clemson by a point with just one second left, and the Huskies had the ball under their own basket. Somehow, Connecticut's Tate George managed to catch a full-court pass, turn and square up, and get off the winning jumper from the baseline that ended underdog Clemson's dreams.

Two days later, UConn was leading Duke, 78–77, with

2.6 seconds left in overtime. The Blue Devils had the ball out of bounds in front of their bench.

Originally, Krzyzewski had called for a play that would create a screen for a Phil Henderson jump shot. Laettner would throw the inbounds pass. But as the teams took the court, Krzyzewski spotted an opening. Immediately he changed the play. Krzyzewski told Laettner, then had to get the attention of Davis, who was being guarded by UConn star Nadev Henefeld. The coach called "Special," and Davis nodded. It was a play originally designed when Danny Ferry was the Duke star.

Afterward, Davis explained what happened. "Coming out of the huddle, I had nothing to do with the shot or the pass. I was just trying to get Hurley open. I looked at Coach and he'd already told Christian the new play."

Davis received the inbounds pass and promptly threw it back to Laettner, who split two UConn defenders and swished a double-pump jumper that sent the Blue Devils on to the Final Four. As the play developed, the other three Duke players were running a totally different play. "What's so funny is that no one else knew," Davis said. "If they had, I don't think it would have worked. It was so spontaneous."

So the subplot was set, at least in the minds of the media and fans. UConn coach Jim Calhoun wasn't buying. "Revenge is a waste of energy," he said. And Krzyzewski never gave a moment's thought to the revenge angle. He didn't focus on the past and neither would the players. Revenge was always a discussion of something that had happened before. Also, to want revenge you have to have lost; Coach K didn't like to remind his team about losses. Thinking about losing breeds losing.

The teams weren't at all the same. Duke had lost three starters. UConn was without two of its best players from the previous season, Henefeld and George. The Huskies were just 20-9 and had suffered through a six-game losing streak after starting out 12-1 against modest opposition.

They had lost in the first round of the Big East tournament.

UConn entered the NCAAs as a No. 11 seed and promptly thrashed LSU and Shaquille O'Neal, 79–62. Then they held Xavier to 50 points in a 16-point triumph that earned them their bid to the Silverdome.

But the Duke staff was confident. "Connecticut has had a hard time scoring all year," Krzyzewski said. "We've got to pay attention to Chris Smith, but they don't have anybody else to take up the offense. We may even play some zone."

A lifelong man-to-man advocate, Krzyzewski was villified by the media and even Duke fans his first couple of years for refusing to play zone, especially when he was using freshman starters. But he stuck to his guns; his teams learned to play tenacious man-to-man defense, and it became the Duke trademark.

Nearly a decade later, however, Coach K had mellowed a little. Some zone was okay if it made good sense.

Krzyzewski knew a lot about Smith, the Connecticut star. He had played on the U.S. World Championships and Goodwill Games team, directed by Coach K, with Laettner and Hurley on the squad.

Laettner's shot was a topic of conversation on that team. "Yeah, we joked about it," he told the media in Pontiac. "It was kind of like having the bragging rights for the summer. Chris would just laugh and say, 'You guys were lucky,' and, 'We'll get you next time.' It was all in fun; just goofing around."

Smith's only comment about it was, "The shot, I ain't talking about it."

Neither was Calhoun. "We've shown the team films of that game. But we never show the shot. It's X-rated. We do have some standards."

It was just the opposite for Laettner. "I've seen the shot, you know, a million times. But I've never seen the game."

The Duke staff concentrated on the Devils' offense,

seeking good shots against the Connecticut zone trap. Hurley, the distributor, would be the key man. "I know we can defend them," Krzyzewski said.

The atmosphere in Pontiac was far different from Minneapolis. The entourage had grown significantly. A lot more of the players' parents were on hand, as were all of the Krzyzewski girls. Mike's brother, Bill, a burly fireman from Chicago, arrived with his wife, Pat.

There was a definite contrast in the lodging, too. The group was staying in a "mom-and-pop" motel, just a couple of floors, and taken over completely by the Duke crowd. "I love it," said Mickie Krzyzewski. The family atmosphere was perfect.

When the families and friends wanted to gather, they met by the indoor swimming pool. When they wanted to eat, they strolled across the road to Denny's. What was lacking in ambience was replaced by hospitality. The Duke crowd was ready.

"The core group has expanded," Mickie Krzyzewski said. "More families are here. The distractions are greater."

The coaching staff and players liked the Silverdome. After Minneapolis, they weren't sure what to expect. Although the Blue Devils shot better than 50 percent in both games at the Metrodome, it was mostly on dunks and lay-ups, often after turnovers. They were just 5 for 18 from three-point range, including 1 for 9 by Hurley.

At practice in the Silverdome, Krzyzewski watched Bobby Hurley hit some shots from the outside. "The background's better than in Minneapolis, isn't it?" Krzyzewski said to him. The guard agreed. Another positive seed had been planted.

The game against Connecticut, like the one with Iowa, was over in a hurry. Koubek, still starting although he had only 9 points in the first two NCAA games, got the Blue Devils going with an offensive rebound of a Laettner miss that he turned into a three-point play.

Then Koubek went outside to hit a pair of shots behind the three-point line, and Duke led 14–4. "In the scouting report, we saw that they liked to press, then drop into a zone," he said. "Coach told us to be ready to shoot the outside shots because they would be there."

With a look of resignation, Calhoun admitted, "We thought one weakness we could exploit was their outside shooting. We let Duke jump on us. So goes that theory. If we played them again, I'd do the same thing defensively."

Duke's confidence in its ability to stop the Huskies was well-placed. By halftime, the Blue Devils were ahead 44–27. It was Iowa revisited. Thomas Hill had added a pair of three-pointers for the Blue Devils, who were 7 for 12 shooting at the "better" background.

The second half was ragged, with turnovers slowing down Duke, and UConn still having problems scoring. Smith, given special attention by the Blue Devils, finished with 5-for-18 shooting.

With 4:55 remaining and Duke solidly in control, Connecticut's Rod Sellers, frustrated and aware that defeat was certain, fouled Laettner and then elected to try and slam Christian's face through the Silverdome floor.

Laettner finally extricated himself and ran down the floor, smiling broadly. Krzyzewski immediately thought back to the session he had had with his star after the Carolina game, and the promise from Laettner that he wouldn't lose his cool again.

"I think the normal reaction would have been to swing back," Krzyzewski said later. "If that had happened, we'd have lost Christian for the next game. I'll always remember his not reacting. That's real discipline."

In the huddle during a time-out, Krzyzewski reminded his team, "Don't take anything personally, for Christ's sake. They're not as good as last year, and we're better. They're just frustrated. Stay cool."

Duke closed it out 81–67. Laettner finished with 19

points, while Koubek, averaging less than 6, had 18 in 30
minutes, his longest stint of the year. Krzyzewski stayed
with his hot shooter.

Duke was now just one step away from its fourth con-
secutive Final Four. Ahead was another Big East team,
St. John's, and again revenge was a potential motive. The
Blue Devils had rallied from a late deficit to edge the
Redmen last year in the second round at Atlanta, 76–72.

Seeded fourth, the Redmen shocked a lot of people by
crushing No. 1 seed and Big Ten co-champion Ohio
State, 91–74. "We were amazed at how well St. John's
played against Ohio State," Krzyzewski said.

The staff met and considered St. John's. "There's no
question we can defend them," Krzyzewski said. There
was no guessing game against a Lou Carnesecca team.
The Redmen preferred a patterned game. They would not
press.

The coaches agreed the key players were Malik Sealy, a
slender 6-7 forward with great instincts around the basket,
and point guard Jason Buchanan. "When he's out of
there, they drop off a lot," Krzyzewski said of Buchanan.
"He makes big shots."

Normally, the regional final was the worst game of the
year for Mickie Krzyzewski. She agreed with her husband
that there were no losers at the Final Four; there were
four champions and one ultimate champion. If you got
there, the season was an undeniable success. The real
tension was in the game that gets you there.

"Getting to the Final Four is so difficult," Mickie said.
"It can be a once-in-a-lifetime experience, and nobody
ever remembers who lost in the regional finals. If you lose
earlier, you just pack your bags and go home and say you
had a great year. But the regional finals, that's different."

For some reason, this time the atmosphere was different. So was the crowd, reduced from 30,461 to 25,634
because the Big Ten entry, Ohio State, was out. "It didn't
feel like a regional final," Mickie said. "There was no tension. I didn't feel any pressure." Unlike the previous three

years, when Duke had been the underdog and was playing the No. 1 seed for the right to advance, this time everyone expected the Blue Devils to win.

Duke's defense took St. John's out of the game early. Before it was over, the Redmen registered 26 turnovers, 8 by forward Billy Singleton. "They gang-defense you," he said.

Buchanan, the director of the St. John's offense, picked up two quick fouls, one of them a silly reach-in that caused Carnesecca to hide his head in his sweater. Then Buchanan drove for the basket, and Hurley shifted his feet, refusing to give the baseline. Buchanan pushed off. The whistle blew. He was called for charging, his third foul, and with over 12 minutes to go he was done for the rest of the half. It was, Krzyzewski said, "a big-time play. Bobby knew it was him and Buchanan."

Duke's lead built steadily after St. John's lost its quarterback, and the score reached 40–24 in the waning seconds of the half. The Blue Devils were holding for the last shot, but Laettner was called for offensive goaltending on Thomas Hill's miss. That stopped the clock with less than 4 seconds left. St. John's got the ball and Sealy got loose at the other end as Hill didn't react. The St. John's star hit a buzzer-beating jump shot. The officials signaled two points, but before the second half began, they changed their minds and awarded a three-pointer. It was the correct call, and the score was 40–27.

Krzyzewski thought back to 1986, when he had the best team in the country, but it tired during the NCAAs, and he didn't know how to help his players. Instead of being ahead by 16 or 18 points, Duke's lead was down to 13 because they were mentally tired. Hill had not reacted to Sealy's move as he normally would have; that was a sure sign. So the coach devised a plan. He didn't know if it would help, but he had to try.

In the locker room usually reserved for the Detroit Lions, Krzyzewski got on one knee right in front of Hill and screamed in his face. "What the hell is wrong with you? God damn it, don't you know you have Sealy? We're going for the national championship. God damn it, don't you guys realize that?"

Then he stood up and left. The players were left to themselves.

"Thomas can take it," Krzyzewski told the staff in the coaches' room. "I'm mad, but not as mad as I showed. But they're tired. They need to get their minds off how tired they are."

Before the team left the locker room for the second half, Coach K went right over to Thomas Hill. "Are you all right, Thomas?" They shook hands. Krzyzewski slapped palms with the others. He gathered his team. "We're going to Indianapolis. We need to kick their ass. If we can land the knockout punch right now, we're going."

The punch landed. Duke played like gangbusters for 10 minutes, starting the second half with a 10–1 run. The lead reached 22 points and the outcome was no longer in doubt. A lot of the fans headed for the exits.

But the adrenaline from Krzyzewski's outburst wore off. Duke made mental errors in the last 10 minutes, tired mistakes. So the game plan was changed, in a hurry. The Blue Devils were ordered to make at least five passes before any shot. The clock was their real opponent, not St. John's. "Sometimes you've got to do it, quit attacking," Krzyzewski said. "We were always in control." The final score was 78–61.

Buchanan made a trio of three-pointers in the second half and finished with 15 points before fouling out late. Sealy had 19 points, but shot just 8 for 19 against the constant harassment from Hill and Brian Davis. "Hill did a good job," Sealy acknowledged. "He bumped me around."

At game's end Laettner and Davis lay flat on the floor, their arms stretched in glee. Krzyzewski didn't like it. After the celebration, he chewed them out. "You planned that stunt. That was orchestrated. We don't do things that way."

The team cut down the nets, something they didn't necessarily do every year. Hurley was one of the last guys up the ladder, and afterward he walked around, a satisfied smile on his face, with the net hung around his neck.

Besides his defense, he had a game-high 20 points, including 4 for 7 on threes. All of the threes were in the first 12 minutes. "I just had so much confidence," he said. The background was just fine. He also had 7 rebounds to lead his team, although he was the smallest player on the floor. Add in 4 assists and 4 steals, and he was an easy choice for most outstanding player at the regional.

"He's a killer," Carnesecca said of the baby-faced kid from Jersey City. As for the Duke defense: "They seem to be always in the passing lanes. They took away our candy. It's not by accident that Duke goes to the Final Four every year."

But looming on the horizon was a team being called the best college basketball team ever: UNLV, victors over Duke a year earlier in the most lopsided NCAA final ever played. It would be a huge challenge for a coach who loved challenges.

For Bobby Hurley, the UNLV debacle was a nightmare— literally. A freshman in 1990, Hurley was sick during the Final Four. In the semifinal against Arkansas, he set what was surely an NCAA first, rushing from the court during a time-out because he had diarrhea. "I was so sick I was virtually useless," he said.

Of all the Blue Devils, Hurley appeared the most devastated after the loss to UNLV. It haunted him for months. During the summer, he had a recurring nightmare of being chased in a swimming pool by a pack of sharks. Sometimes he would jump out of the water, then wake up. Other times, he stayed in the pool. The sharks pushed a wave of water toward him, but they never attacked.

"Bobby, that dream is because you're thinking of Tark

the Shark," said Koubek, who was taking a class in dream analysis.

The dreams eventually stopped, and now Hurley was a confident player. In four games, won by margins of 29, 15, 14, and 17 points, he had 27 assists and just 4 turnovers.

"Bob has been great," said Davis. "If you look back at last year, it's pretty difficult to see this is the same person. From his demeanor on the court, his stats, his aggressiveness, he's just turned everything around. He's been the key guy for us."

"I'm definitely more mature," Hurley said. "Now I know how to take care of myself. I have a better mental attitude. I get the rest I need. I'm fresh, and that helps in the decision-making."

From the moment the St. John's game was over, the media pressed Krzyzewski about the rematch with UNLV. "I feel very happy," he said. "I don't know why people want me to feel sad just because we're playing Vegas. We're going to the Final Four. It is too bad we have to play Vegas, but it's a dream for these kids."

The team boarded the bus for the ride to the airport and the trip home. Immediately, Krzyzewski turned to Gaudet and started discussing game tapes. "We're going to beat those suckers," he said.

Seated two rows behind was Donna Keane, Coach K's administrative assistant. She heard the words, the positive statements. " 'We're going to win,' he kept saying. It was the most amazing thing I've ever seen. He was so confident. You could see the players believed him," she said.

Duke's record was 30-7. 31-7, Krzyzewski kept telling himself. 31-7. It was always on his mind. It drove him and encouraged him.

Bobby Hurley was a lousy loser. It wasn't something he'd had to deal with often. In high school, where he played for his dad at St. Anthony's, the team's record was 115-5.

Two of the losses were before Hurley joined the varsity his freshman year.

St. Anthony's won the mythical national high school championship his senior year, anointed by *USA Today*. The team went 32-0. When Hurley graduated, he left behind a 50-game winning streak.

Coming to Duke, which had just played in the Final Four twice in a row and three years out of four, Hurley didn't know what to expect. "I knew it was almost impossible to do. I worried that they might have used up all the Final Fours before I got there."

By his own admission, "I got a little carried away my freshman year. I tried to make too many passes past six-six guys with long arms." Part of his problem was his role on a team with three senior starters. Under Krzyzewski, the point guard was the leader on the floor from whom all action flowed.

Problems notwithstanding, Duke surprised most people by upsetting Connecticut in the East Regional finals and making the Final Four again. But the crushing loss to UNLV in the finals was difficult for Hurley to accept. His teams had won four straight state high school championships; he was used to the pressure of playing in the year's ultimate game. But losing was a shock, and losing the way Duke had was devastating. He had been sick and unable to contribute. He had felt overwhelmed on the court. He was determined never to feel that way on a court again.

His sophomore season, Hurley was more comfortable, more stable. He was still a young player, but it was a young team.

Still, there were moments of despair. The 81–64 loss at Virginia stuck out. "It was one of the worst days of my life," he said. "The four hours on the bus didn't help. I cramped out, and then we had to practice when we got back. I was wearing a blue shirt [second team]. That made me want not to lose.

"I always hated to lose, even in a pickup game. When you lose then, you wait forty-five minutes on the playground before you can play again. I'll do anything it takes [to win]."

Hurley had played well in the two games at Minneapolis, although he didn't shoot accurately. "Then something happened in Pontiac," he said. "I found my shot. I had the total game. I felt in control."

It was a confident Hurley who was anxious to prepare for UNLV. Then he read the *Durham Herald-Sun* and got mad.

Hurley's local newspaper ran a column written by Art Spander of the *San Francisco Examiner* after the Rebels had crushed Seton Hall to win the West.

"UNLV is unbeatable. Just send out the Rebels. Then send in the clowns. Duke may lose by only twenty this time."

Send in the clowns. Hurley cringed. Yet that was just the type of thing the Duke staff wanted. Never underestimate the value of a proper mental attitude.

Krzyzewski had started that train of thought as the bus from the Silverdome headed for the airport and the return to Durham. He told the players not to believe everything attributed to him that week. Normally a straight shooter with the media, Coach K said to the team, "I'm going to blow a little smoke Vegas's way. I'm going to talk about how awesome they are. But I want you to know, this couldn't be set up any better. We're playing our best basketball of the season. We couldn't ask for a more fun situation. This is a great opportunity."

That was the theme for the week: opportunity. The Spander column was greeted with quiet approval by the staff. "That stuff helps," Krzyzewski said.

Duke's companions in the Final Four included one very familiar team in baby blue. North Carolina had held off Temple in the East Regional final, making the upcoming games in Indianapolis a near obsession among the local population.

Not much business was conducted that week in the Raleigh–Durham–Chapel Hill Triangle. If you weren't a basketball fan, you had to be a visitor. Even the non-Duke and non-UNC fans were excited. It was the topic of conversation everywhere. It was the lead story on telecasts nightly. Stories about the Final Four ran on the front pages of the local newspapers. If war had been declared, it would have been on page two.

Duke would be going against the invincible Rebels, winners of 45 straight. UNC was matched against Kansas, a delicious pairing: Dean Smith against Roy Williams, who for ten years had been an assistant coach of the Tar Heels.

The perfect game in the eyes of the home-area public would be Duke against Carolina in the final. Later, Krzyzewski would say, "That would have been too much. Can you imagine what would have happened to the losers? People wouldn't have been able to go home again."

As soon as Krzyzewski got home from Pontiac, he told Gaudet to make highlight tapes of Hurley, Laettner, Grant Hill, and McCaffrey. "Make them all positive things," Coach K said.

Gaudet was a genius at creating highlight tapes—good or bad. These varied from 4 to 8 minutes and included the comments by the TV announcers: "Hurley's playing great defense," or "McCaffrey's on a roll," or "Grant Hill doesn't play like a freshman."

Krzyzewski and the players met individually to view the tapes. Twice. "They feel good about themselves," he told the staff. To accentuate the positive, when Coach K met with the players, he drove home a theme for each of them.

"Bobby, is Greg Anthony better than Kenny Anderson?" The tape showed Hurley in a great defensive posture, stifling Georgia Tech's superstar.

"Grant, you've got to guard [Stacy] Augmon. He's six-eight. You're six-eight. Only you weigh fifteen pounds more and he doesn't know it. You'll have the strength to move him around."

"Billy, you're going to get open. Bobby's going to get you the ball, and you're going to get great shots."

"Christian, work on those low-post moves. They can't guard you."

Tarkanian had already set the stage for the last approach. To the national media, he said, "We don't have anybody who can guard Laettner. He's not a center, he's a power forward." The Duke coaches agreed. They didn't think Tark would risk putting player-of-the-year Larry Johnson defensively against Laettner.

Krzyzewski was also doing a psych job on himself. He kept telling the players they were going to Indianapolis to win the national championship. He didn't want his players looking past UNLV, but rather right *through* them. They weren't an opponent to be feared; they were just another team between Duke and their final goal. "Think eighty minutes," he said. But he said that far more often to himself.

As crazy as the scene was throughout the state, and especially in the Triangle, there was no talk of North Carolina in the Duke basketball office. It would have been a distraction. Vegas was enough. The Rebels were overwhelming favorites. Even Mickie Krzyzewski didn't think her husband's team would win.

One of the first things Krzyzewski did after returning to campus following the Regional was to pull out the tape of last year's championship game. It was the first time he'd ever seen it.

"In all the years we've been married, that was the first time we'd played a game and Mike hadn't watched the tape," Mickie said. "He always watches the tape right after the game. He's terribly disheartened when we lose because he always thinks we're going to win. Always. It's like a shock to him when we lose. He thought we were going to beat Vegas in Denver. He'll watch the tapes because he wants to know why we lost. Once he understands the reason, then he handles it. He lets it go, and he goes on to the next game."

But having lost by 30, Krzyzewski couldn't bear to watch the game. During the summer and then the long season, he never found a reason to put that tape in his VCR.

Now he had to do it. And he was surprised by what he saw. While the margin had been 30 points, Vegas had really broken it open in the second half. If Duke had played just reasonably well, it could have been a 10-pointer.

What Coach K saw was a sick Bobby Hurley, with no zip, constantly picking up his dribble. He saw a tired team, one that had given its all in upsetting Arkansas in the semifinals, then had nothing left. And he saw a tired coach. "I looked hollow," he said. "There was no fire in me. I thought I was looking at a different guy."

He showed the team parts of the tape. He showed them that when they played their normal game, they held their own. He showed them that when UNLV challenged them, they backed down.

The players watched intently. "Bobby, is that the way you normally play?" he asked Hurley. The point guard already knew that answer. The players learned from watching the video that as great as UNLV had played, Duke had contributed heavily to its own defeat. The Rebels had put on the pressure and Duke hadn't responded.

Brian Davis understood: "When we lost to Vegas, I cried. That was the only time I ever cried after a game. It was because of the way we lost. We were scared; they took our pride. It was the worst thing that ever happened. They killed us. They kept killing us. They took our heart. I promised myself it would never happen again."

That was the attitude in practice all week: *it would never happen again*. Not revenge: we'll get even with them. Determination: we're going to play with our hearts.

Practices, as always in March, were short and snappy. "We're not going to have a huge scouting report," Krzyzewski told the staff. Everybody agreed. The game plan would be simple, and the primary focus would be on emotion. If the team played as hard as it could and lost, as everybody expected, then Krzyzewski could live with that.

By the time the team was given the scouting report, it was so simple it could have been used in a junior high school game:

1. Cut down on transition. Don't let Vegas run. That meant there couldn't be many turnovers. In 1990 there had been 21, and the Rebels conducted a fast-break clinic.
2. Eliminate second shots. Duke was not a particularly strong rebounding team. Vegas was, especially Larry Johnson and Stacy Augmon. They had to be kept off the offensive boards. "We can't give them cheap baskets," Krzyzewski reminded his squad.
3. Always know where Anderson Hunt was on the floor. He was the key three-point shooter, and Coach K didn't want a lot of open shots behind the stripe.
4. Make it as difficult as possible for Johnson. Don't let him go crazy. That required a change in philosophy.

Duke always made it a point to guard big guys on the high post. "It's our feeling that when they go out on top, they're not used to having somebody pressure them. When you go after them when they get the ball, it disrupts the offense. A lot of times you can force a turnover," Krzyzewski said.

But that would mean playing straight-up man-to-man, and there was no way Duke could do that against the 6-6, 250-pound Johnson. Koubek certainly couldn't handle him. Davis wasn't strong enough either. So the staff made a big adjustment.

The coaches gambled that UNLV wouldn't go to center George Ackles, even if he was open, because he was the fifth choice in their arsenal of weapons. Even if Elmore Spencer, a better offensive player than Ackles, was in the game, the staff agreed they couldn't afford to guard the center up high.

The plan was to keep Laettner inside the foul line on

defense, always sloughing back, helping out on Johnson. If it wasn't to be a double-team, it would at least be a man-and-a-half.

To gain something, you have to give up something. The staff agreed they'd much rather take a chance on getting beat by Ackles than by Johnson.

Practices varied from the past, even previous NCAA practices for Duke. No drill ran longer than 5 minutes. There were no harsh words. Everything was positive.

Krzyzewski elected to have the team practice at home on Thursday, then fly later to Indianapolis. "I think we've been getting to the Final Four sites too early," he said. "They have too much time on their hands."

So the team had its final practice at home. It started, as did the Wednesday session, with 5 minutes of dunking. Mike Brey could see the difference: "It's got them going. They love it."

The staff liked to allow the players some moments of expression on the court, which usually ended with a dunking session. Krzyzewski believed that practices could become too structured, so he had built-in periods, 5 to 10 minutes, when the team was on its own.

"They just have fun," he said. "Practices are usually built around the team concept. This is a chance to let them do what they want, to feel good about themselves. Their confidence level goes up. Right after that, they enthusiastically go to the next thing. It picks up their energy levels." With the Vegas game ahead, that was a good sign. The whole week had been dedicated to giving the team confidence.

The team charter for Indy left in the late afternoon. Mike and Mickie Krzyzewski had to go to an NCAA-CBS banquet that night. The banquets began in 1988 at Kansas City, which was the tournament's fiftieth anniversary. They continued every year after. It was always a major production, as each year the host city tried to outdo the previous host. The Final Four coaches were taken to the site in stretch limos. Video highlights of how each team reached the Final Four were shown. An original score provided the musical background. The banquets had become a particular favorite of Mickie's, who orchestrated the annual Duke banquet.

While the Krzyzewskis were at the NCAA affair, the team went to eat at St. Elmo's, a steak house close by the Hoosier Dome. Brey, Jay Bilas, and Col. Tom Rogers were with the team. The place was full, mostly with coaches. The team ate at a table right in the thick of things. A lot of high school coaches were there. Several of them came over to talk.

The players were having a good time. Krzyzewski was adamant that he wanted them to enjoy the atmosphere, and there was plenty in Indianapolis, perhaps the best place ever for the Final Four. Not only was the Hoosier Dome right downtown, with Market Square and its eating and shopping areas within walking distance, but Indiana was a basketball-crazy state, and that was apparent immediately. Indy loved basketball. Indy understood basketball.

Krzyzewski complained about the long distance between the team's lodgings at the Holiday Inn Airport and downtown Indy, where everything was happening. "I think the tournament committee should keep the teams downtown, so the players could absorb the atmosphere."

Krzyzewski's attitude was in stark contrast to that of some other coaches, who liked to be isolated. John Thompson took his team to Biloxi, Mississippi, sixty-plus miles away, when the Final Four was in New Orleans in 1982. But Krzyzewski wanted his players to feel as if they were a part of the tournament. He liked the downtown atmosphere. There also was a practical reason: it took a long time to take the team to practice, to eat, and to the many interview sessions.

Tarkanian obviously didn't agree with Coach K on this. From the moment his team arrived on Wednesday there were DO NOT DISTURB signs at their hotel. They left their rooms only for a closed practice at North Central High, where the windows at the gym were taped over. Students strained outside to get a peak at the defending champions. A handful of youngsters hid out in the locker room, but they were thwarted because UNLV arrived dressed for the practice. All attempts at autographs were denied.

"We're just trying to stay focused," said Augmon. "The fewer distractions we have, the better we can concentrate on the game we have to play."

Meanwhile, Brey gave the Duke team 90 minutes after dinner to explore Market Square. Some of the players made a rock video. Marty Clark stayed with the coaches because he was on crutches, having sprained his ankle that afternoon in Durham. Backup center Crawford Palmer pulled a book off a shelf in the restaurant and sat down to read. Brey reported to Krzyzewski that everything went well. "They're loose," he said.

Friday morning, when most coaches would have huddled with their assistants for further fine-tuning, Krzyzewski went to the hotel where most of the coaches from around the country were staying. The National Association of Basketball Coaches holds its convention in conjunction with the Final Four every year, and as chairman of the Legislative Committee, Krzyzewski was in charge of a meeting to discuss volatile issues that were going to be voted upon at the 1992 NCAA convention. The meeting lasted two hours.

Later that night, sipping a beer in the media hotel, William and Mary coach Chuck Swenson, a former Duke assistant, said, "Mike wanted all the coaches to get involved in what's going on. He's been on them a lot to become interested in the affairs of the NABC. This meeting was critical. He wanted them to see that if he could spare the time when his team was playing, they could get involved, too."

Krzyzewski had long been concerned that the NABC had little voice in NCAA affairs, and he was determined to do whatever he could to change that. Then he joined the team at the Hoosier Dome.

Final Four Friday is always fun, but in Indianapolis the atmosphere was better than ever. Some thirty thousand fans, many of them school kids playing hooky, came to watch the four teams practice.

Each team got 60 minutes, timed precisely on the scoreboard clocks at either end of the arena. North Carolina was first, and the most excitement was created when seven-foot freshman Eric Montross came onto the floor. A hometown boy from Lawrence North High, he had spurned the beloved Indiana Hoosiers and Bob Knight to attend school in Chapel Hill. He was greeted with a chorus of boos.

Carolina and Kansas, with their look-alike drills, practiced conservatively. They shot, rebounded, and ran. There were few frills.

UNLV did the same. There was an air of arrogance about the Rebels, befitting their status as the kings of basketball. They had been through all of this before. They were veterans. Their youngest player, Anderson Hunt, was a month older than Duke's oldest, Greg Koubek. Ackles was nearly twenty-four. Greg Anthony was twenty-three.

Grant Hill was eighteen years five months old when he joined his teammates in the dunking parade that took up the first 10 minutes of the Duke practice. Krzyzewski loved the dunking routine, which got the adrenaline flowing. "It gives the guys a good feeling about the court, and it gets the fans going. Sometimes the fans at Final Four Saturday can be different. But this is like a dress rehearsal. I like having the electricity during the workout."

Even when somebody missed a dunk, the crowd cheered. The joint was rocking. Krzyzewski stood under the basket and smiled. He could see the excitement in his players' faces.

"This is the way the crowd is going to be tomorrow," he told the team. "This is the third straight dome you guys have played in, and you've played great in the other two.

That's a huge advantage for us. You understand about the backgrounds and the crowds."

A big team meal on Friday night had become a team tradition. All the coaches' families, including young children, attended. It was strictly lighthearted, with everybody involved. They ate at the Orleans House, and there was plenty of banter among the players. Krzyzewski, who could trade barbs with anyone, felt good about his team, which was loose and confident. The week of practice had gone well, and he was certain they were ready to play. "We've got a shot at this thing," he said to his coaches.

All week long in practice, Krzyzewski made one point over and over with his team: UNLV hadn't been tested all year. If Duke could keep the game close going into the final few minutes, the Devils would have the edge.

On Tuesday, at the first practice, he said in the locker room before they took the court, "Fellows, they haven't been in an end-of-game situation. Just think how many we've been in. We know how to handle it. We can be better than them for two minutes. If we put them in that situation, we have an advantage. That's a huge advantage."

Then, Friday night in the team meeting back in the hotel suite after the dinner, Coach K left his players with one last reminder: "There will be a point in the game tomorrow where they'll look you in the eye, and what they see will determine the outcome."

Because Duke and UNLV was the featured game for CBS, it was the second game of the doubleheader. Among all coaches, Krzyzewski probably complained the least about starting times. He understood television's role, and his team was on TV as much as anybody's. Still, he hated second games. "It's different from a regular nine-o'clock game. You're not sure when you're starting, and there are so many other distractions."

The Duke team arrived on Saturday at the Hoosier Dome, where 47,100 fanatics were in attendance, while

Carolina was playing Kansas. It was one thing not to talk about the Tar Heels all week; it was another to ignore the fact that they were actually playing. That was too much to ask.

In the locker room, there was a large TV set tuned to the game. Carolina was favored. The Duke players, in an upbeat mood, watched the game.

Krzyzewski brought along the tapes Gaudet had made for Hurley, Grant Hill, McCaffrey, and Laettner. He showed them again in the coaches' dressing quarters on his portable VCR. Laettner's was intentionally scheduled last.

"Christian, do you want to see your tape again?" asked Krzyzewski.

"Coach, I don't need that damn tape. Let's just play."

Krzyzewski was thrilled. That was exactly the response he wanted. Laettner was sending a message to his teammates: they wouldn't have to worry about him. He would have a big game. As far as Christian was concerned, the preliminaries were over.

The Carolina game neared its conclusion, with Kansas coming from behind to take a safe lead. Then, in the final minute, official Pete Pavia called a second technical foul on Dean Smith, the Hall of Famer, who became the first coach ever to be ejected from a Final Four game.

There was bedlam in the arena. Nobody was certain why the technical was called, and even CBS—for its billion bucks—wasn't going to get to interview Pavia. UNC assistant Bill Guthridge had to be restrained from going after the official as Carolina headed for its locker room in the bowels of the huge dome.

It was time for Duke to take the floor and warm up. But just as the players were ready to leave, Krzyzewski called them back and seated them.

He had a sick feeling in his stomach. Carolina was out, and Smith had been ejected; no matter what happened to underdog Duke in the second game, it couldn't be as devastating as what had occurred to its biggest rival. All week he had told his team, time and again, that the idea was to play 80 minutes. Now something he had no control over, a UNC loss, could create a different mind-set for one or all of his players. He felt a sudden, huge fear. All week long, everything had been positive, with everybody tuned in to playing two games. Now there was the possibility that some of the players might feel that it was all right to lose, since Carolina had lost. Krzyzewski moved instantly to stop that train of thought.

"Do any of you feel that since Carolina has just lost, there's no way they can be better than you, even if you lose?"

There was some nodding among the players: Davis. Koubek. Krzyzewski understood. It was a natural reaction. But it was counter to what they had emphasized all week. A team can't win the national championship if it has a way to rationalize losing.

"First, it's okay that you had that feeling," he told them. "The second thing is, flush it. Let's go kick their ass."

Davis huddled the team in the wide runway that leads onto the court. "No backing down," he said. "Give it everything you've got. Let's leave our blood on the floor."

It had taken a good part of the season to establish the chain of command. But now everybody knew. "We're not the captains," Davis said, "but Christian and I are the leaders."

Only the Duke coaches and players thought they could win. The media was certain UNLV was destined to take its place as the greatest college team of all time. Now, because of the stunning ejection of Smith, most of the press corps missed much of the second game. Writers and broadcasters were busy trying to find out why the technical had been called on the Carolina coach. There was no air of urgency in the interview room about the nightcap; UNLV was playing, therefore the result was a foregone conclusion.

For the second time in his young college career, Grant Hill was a nervous wreck. The first time had been against

Arkansas in the preseason NIT, when he played in Madison Square Garden in just his third college game.

The first play in any basketball game is rarely significant. But this one was. Hill, enormously gifted but perhaps the youngest starter in Final Four history, got the perfect beginning. On the opening tap, the ball went backward toward Anderson Hunt. Before he could grab it, Hill swooped in, stole it, and scored an easy lay-up.

With Laettner and Hill scoring inside, Duke ran off to a 15–6 lead and the crowd was buzzing. The Blue Devils were not backing down.

The coaches told all the players, "They're going to go after Bobby. So help him out." Hurley, the perceived goat of the '90 title game, when he was 0 for 3 from the field with 5 turnovers, was playing with confidence.

The game plan was working. Tarkanian was right that he didn't have anybody who could guard Laettner. Grant Hill, his butterflies calmed, was leaning a body on Augmon, who hadn't been defended all year by another 6-8 guy. And Laettner was able to help a scrambling Koubek on Johnson.

The UNLV guards, Hunt and Anthony, were playing sensationally—perhaps too well. The Rebels, used to going with whatever worked, weren't even looking for Johnson as much as they might have.

The Blue Devils led 41–39 with 90 seconds left before halftime. But Grant Hill missed a scoop lay-up, and Hunt promptly scored an easy lay-up at the other end to tie it. Hurley, driving the middle, threw the ball away on a miscommunication play. The Rebels held the ball until 10 seconds remained, when Anthony banked in a lay-up for a 43–41 lead. Duke compounded the mistakes with another turnover, and UNLV almost scored again before the horn.

Krzyzewski was upset with the ending: "We were horrible." He told the team, "There's no way we can win by being dumb. We played nineteen minutes of great basketball and then we went into mental arrest. If we just try and play physical against them, and not smart, it just isn't going to happen."

A year ago against UNLV, the game had still been close until a collapse right before halftime pushed the deficit into double digits. Coach K had been determined it wouldn't happen again, but it had, though not to the same degree.

Vegas had gotten back in the game after going to its amoeba defense. The previous year, the Rebels had killed Duke with a straight man-to-man. Using the amoeba that early was a sign that their man-to-man defense wasn't working. That was a good sign for Duke.

The crowd at halftime was making that noise of anticipation that comes when you see the unexpected, and you aren't sure it's going to continue. It was a great half, but was that just setting the stage for a giant letdown?

Duke answered the question immediately. Because of the way the team ended the first half, Krzyzewski felt it was imperative to begin the second half with a sense of structure. He wanted the ball in the hands of his two stars. Hurley took the inbounds pass that started the period, and Laettner set a screen near the foul line extended. Christian then rolled right, took the perfect bounce pass from Hurley, and scored an uncontested lay-up. Laettner now had 22 points, and the message had been firmly delivered.

Thomas Hill scored and Duke led 45–43. The Rebels regained the edge, but could never pull away. UNLV couldn't pressure Hurley because Grant Hill and Laettner kept helping out with the ball-handling.

The Duke players could sense it: UNLV was beginning to feel the pressure. The Rebels expected the underdogs to go away, and they wouldn't.

Hunt stole the ball, one of just 14 Duke turnovers, and dunked. Then he turned to where the Vegas fans were seated in a crowd that was otherwise pulling for the underdogs. He raised his arms in an effort to get more support. The Rebels, the supposed best team of all time, were asking for help.

About 5 minutes into the half, McCaffrey undercut Hunt as he went in for a lay-up. Hunt went down hard and got up mad.

On the next sequence, Augmon retaliated. He threw an elbow and got caught. Intentional foul. Three and a half minutes later, Hunt was going hard for the goal and Hurley, making a slight effort to get to the ball, tackled him. It was the sort of foul you'd expect in the NBA play-offs, not from the fresh-faced kids from Duke.

There was a lot of shoving. Hurley wasn't called for an intentional foul, but Johnson got in the last shove and was charged with a technical. All the messages had now been clearly delivered. Duke was tough. Duke was sticking around.

The Blue Devils took the biggest lead of the half—5 points—when Koubek put in a jumper following Johnson's T. But UNLV came back. The lead changed on seven straight scores before UNLV went up 3 on a lay-up by Hunt.

Then came a key play. Anthony, the team leader, had 4 fouls. But he drove for the basket anyway. Davis was in his way. They collided hard. The whistle blew—charge. Davis jumped to his feet, his arms held high in celebration.

"I knew he'd try and take over. They were in trouble. Because of who he was and who they were, I didn't know if it would be a block or a charge," Davis said later. Anthony had fouled out with 3:51 left.

Earlier in the half, Davis had driven for a lay-up and when challenged, changed his shot and missed. "Dunk the son of a bitch," Krzyzewski yelled. The next time he got the opportunity, Davis dunked and screamed at the bench. "Yeah, there it is." After drawing the Anthony charge, he screamed again.

But UNLV still led, and when Ackles tipped in his own miss with 2:30 left, it was 76–71, and some Duke fans were prepared to accept condolences and a moral victory.

Not Bobby Hurley. UNLV was back in the amoeba, designed to take away the three-pointer. But Hurley got open and didn't flinch. With 2:14 left, he made a three, and now it was 76–74. "I'd been looking for that shot for three minutes," he said. Coach K called it the biggest play of the game. "It was a gutsy, winner play and he nailed it."

Panic set in with the Rebels. Hunt, who scored 29 points, was forced into the unexpected position of primary ball-handler. UNLV was having a hard time getting off a shot. Augmon forgot about the 45-second clock, and for the first time all season, the Rebels didn't get off an attempt. Davis raised his arms to the bench again. Krzyzewski's words were coming true: with the game close in the final minutes, Duke was in familiar territory, while UNLV was facing the unknown.

Grant Hill drove, then passed neatly to Davis, who made the tying lay-up and was fouled. He made his free throw, his fifteenth point coming off the bench in just 21 minutes, and shockingly, Duke led, 77–76.

Johnson was fouled on a rebound with 50 seconds left. He had scored just 12 points, half his average. He missed the first attempt. Krzyzewski screamed at the team, "No lane violations." Hurley reminded them. Johnson missed again. But Thomas Hill stepped in the lane too soon. Violation. Johnson got another try and tied it at 77.

Krzyzewski called for Duke's delay offense. "If you get something for the basket, go to the basket," he shouted. Thomas Hill did. The lefty shooter drove hard from that side, drawing the defense to him. It was a good shot, with 15 seconds left, but it bounced off. Laettner was in perfect position. Right in front of the basket, with three Rebels rushing at Hill, he rebounded. As he turned to shoot, he was fouled by Evric Gray, playing for the foul-plagued Ackles.

There were 12.7 seconds left. Time-out. Krzyzewski kept thinking about Laettner's freshman year when, against Arizona in the Meadowlands, he was fouled at the buzzer but missed when he could have sent the game into overtime.

Krzyzewski looked at his star. Laettner was smiling. "I got 'em, Coach." It sent a chill up Coach K's spine. "This is the biggest moment of his life, and that sucker is smiling," he thought.

The strategy was simple enough. "We're doubling Hunt," Krzyzewski said. "He can't get the first pass." With Anthony out, Hunt was the only experienced UNLV guard. He was also a three-point shooter, and that would win the game no matter what Laettner did.

The best free-throw shooter in tournament history made it look simple. He swished them both, Duke led 79–77, and when UNLV couldn't get the pass inbounds, the Rebels took another time-out.

The extra minute changed nothing. Hunt was still double-teamed. So the pass went to Johnson, who dribbled up the right-hand section of the floor, all the way to the three-point line. In his postgame interview, Tarkanian said he wished Johnson had taken the shot. But Laettner was there.

"I might have blocked it," he said. "He's six-five and I'm six-eleven. I started to jump in the air, like you do when a guy shoots, and then I knew he wasn't shooting. But I was there. At the least, he would have had to elevate the shot."

The ball was passed to Hunt. Time was running out. He spun, then took a desperate shot from out where the pros would shoot the three. "I saw the angle all the way," Krzyzewski said afterward. "I knew it was off-line."

The ball bounced deep, touched first by Thomas Hill, then claimed by Hurley. The buzzer sounded. Duke had done the unthinkable. It had beaten the unbeatable. There would be no more talk about UNLV being the greatest team ever.

Hurley leaped into Grant Hill's arms. There was a

short-lived celebration on the floor, while the fans were going berserk. Duke radio announcer Bob Harris was screaming, "It's the greatest upset in Duke basketball history!"

But there was Krzyzewski, palms down, instantly reminding his team that the job wasn't finished. Even as he was interviewed on CBS, he grabbed Laettner tightly around the wrist. "We've got another game to play."

The players reacted almost immediately. For the most part, they suddenly stopped celebrating, recognizing their coach's message. All week long the theme had been "eighty minutes." There were 40 left to play.

Hurley rode on Clay Buckley's back as he left the court, slapping palms with fans. But once he got under the stands, he yelled, "We still have one more, we have one more; I feel great, but we have one more."

Mickie Krzyzewski had gone to the game in a mellow mood. "I felt absolutely no pressure to win." Then, when Carolina lost, it was, "Now there's even less pressure. Whatever we do now is okay."

She tried to reassure Mike's mother, Emily, who had come in from Chicago. Emily always got upset at the games.

When the game ended, Mickie couldn't get her breath. She hyperventilated. Just as she could breathe again, Mike's brother, Bill, picked her up, tears streaming down his face. "I'll always remember the way he looked," she said later.

In the locker room, the coaches congratulated the players. Krzyzewski was satisfied with their attitude. "They're saying the right things."

He told the team, "We've gone to the Final Four so many times. You can say we'll be here again, but it's so hard. This is our time!"

The team arrived back at the hotel and walked into a mob scene. Wildly delirious people, in varying degrees of sobriety, were everywhere. The players had a hard time moving. Coach K had never seen a sight like it. Now everybody was a true believer. "It was as if they had seen Santa Claus and the Easter Bunny," he said.

The crowd was just reacting normally. They had seen one of the great games in college history, and one of the more memorable upsets. But if they kept talking about UNLV to the players, the emphasis would be on the past, not the future, which was Kansas. Krzyzewski knew he had a tough job ahead, getting his team's mind on the game to be played. As far as the fans were concerned, they had already achieved the impossible dream. There was just one problem: there were still 40 tough minutes left.

The team came to his suite, and Krzyzewski sent them on their way. He told them to go be with their families, their friends. They could enjoy the moment.

The staff, however, had a game to prepare for. They pulled their usual all-nighter, watching tapes and formulating a game plan. Krzyzewski decided that "we've got to keep it simple. We're better than Kansas. Not much, but we're better. Let's not let Duke beat Duke."

Mickie, meanwhile, had joined Emily, the other Chicago Krzyzewskis, and her sister, Donna, for a postgame celebration. Emily and Donna decided to chug a beer. Mickie, a light drinker at best, joined them. She got smashed. She even tried playing Quarters, a drinking game, with Debbie.

Finally, she knew she had to return to her room. She got on the elevator. She was alone. It stopped on the next floor. Bobby Hurley got on. In her state of intoxication, Mickie thought swiftly. Or so she thought. "I don't want him to know I've been celebrating." So the mother hen of the Duke basketball brood rode the elevator with the star guard and acted as if she didn't know him.

The elevator stopped. Mickie stood still. "Uh, Mrs. K, I think this is your floor," said Hurley.

Mike arose after a brief nap Sunday morning. He was headed to a breakfast where he would be honored as the

NABC coach of the year. Mickie asked him to check and see if the top of her head was still attached.

Mike looked at her. "Mickie, don't try and drink with my family. You don't have what it takes."

Following the obligatory interviews with the media for himself and the starters, Krzyzewski got on the bus headed for practice and sensed immediately something was not right with his team. "They're sauntering instead of walking. They've had their asses kissed all night."

Marty Clark and Christian Ast were wearing Indiana Jones hats. Coach K sent Brey to the back, quietly, to tell the players: "Get rid of those damn hats." After that, things were a little quieter.

In the locker room, Krzyzewski let the team have it with both barrels. "Everything you said yesterday was bullshit. I don't like the way you're walking, talking, anything. You should go watch Vegas tapes because there's no way you can beat Kansas. Go back to the hotel and watch tapes and let the fans kiss your ass."

He sent the players out. They huddled together on the court for 5 minutes. Finally, Krzyzewski walked out on the floor and looked at his team. He studied their faces. "I knew we were going to win then," he said later. The team had the proper mind-set back.

He called them together. "We're national champs as long as you keep this focus, and not the way you walked in here."

Practice was terrific.

The staff was concerned about physical problems. Hurley had played all 40 minutes. But he had done that before. Laettner had also played 40. "I'm not tired," he insisted, but in Duke's scheme, Laettner had to cover more ground than anybody, from end line to end line, and the corners as well. Krzyzewski knew his star had to be weary.

Monday night, in the national championship game, senior captain Greg Koubek took some of the pressure off Laettner in the opening minutes against Kansas. Before

Christmas, after not playing at Oklahoma, he had almost quit the team. Now he was starting in the NCAA finals. He made the game's first basket, a three-pointer from the side. Then he made another goal.

It was 5–1, and the Blue Devils were on a fast break. Hurley threw a lob pass to Grant Hill, only it was too high. It was headed for the middle rows of the stands. Hill went up, and up some more. He caught the ball somehow and slammed it. Even Billy Packer gasped while doing TV analysis.

The play made every highlight film. The picture was in *Sports Illustrated* and numerous newspapers. But pictures couldn't do that dunk justice. It wasn't just how high he soared, but the roar of the audience afterward. More than 47,000 voices joined in a crescendo of disbelief.

Kansas couldn't catch up. Every time the Jayhawks got close, there was McCaffrey, hitting an open jumper. He finished 6 for 8, 16 points, and made the All-Tournament team although he didn't start either game.

Laettner was nursed through the game by his coach. A minute or so before every TV time-out, Krzyzewski substituted Palmer so his star could get a little extra rest in addition to the 2 minutes of TV breaks. It worked to perfection; Palmer's line in the box score may have showed no points or rebounds, but his contributions were much greater than box scores measure.

Laettner's legs were rubbery, and he had a hard time guarding his friend Mark Randall. But if Christian couldn't get many shots, he could still make free throws —a dozen straight.

Down 39–34 just before halftime, Kansas was holding for the last shot, but turned it over with about 15 seconds left. Krzyzewski inserted his three-point shooters. Laettner came out because he was tired, but Hurley, McCaffrey, Koubek, and Thomas Hill were all on the floor. Hurley made a strong penetrating move and passed out to Hill, who hit a three. Instead of a possible 2- or 3-point lead, it was 8. It was a huge play, Hill's only basket of the game.

McCaffrey was hot in the second half. He started a 13–4 run that broke it open with a three-pointer.

Kansas went into a 1-3-1 zone. Krzyzewski had set up a play for just that situation. Hurley spotted Davis for a dunk. On the bench, the coach was pleased. "It absolutely worked. You're lucky when something you said comes into being."

The score was 61–47 with 8:30 to play. "Don't let Duke beat Duke," he had warned them before. Now he did it again during a time-out. "No technical fouls. No quick shots. No turnovers. Take your time." The clock was Duke's opponent, not Kansas.

Kansas didn't quit, and a couple of turnovers helped cut the deficit to 70–65 with 35 seconds left. Time-out. Krzyzewski reminded his players in the huddle, "There's one time-out left. Don't do anything dumb."

Kansas was gambling on defense. Hurley was double-teamed. Pressured bringing the ball up the floor, Thomas Hill was still behind the midcourt line when he took Duke's last time-out, just in time—the clock read 0:25. One more tick with the ball in the backcourt would have meant a turnover. Hill had made a great play before half-time, and now a smart play.

They came back on the floor. Krzyzewski saw Kansas overplaying. He tilted his head to Grant Hill, who was making the inbounds pass. Hill gave Davis a look, and Davis nodded. The pass was deep; only Davis was there. He dunked with emphasis.

After nine Final Four appearances, five under Krzyzewski, there would be no more talk about Duke not winning the Big One, or about Krzyzewski the bridesmaid. It was 72–65, and the Blue Devils had led every second. There were no monkeys to be seen on anybody's back.

What's more, other than the UNLV game, Duke had dominated the NCAAs. The last three games in the Regional were over by halftime. The Blue Devils shot better than 50 percent in every one of the six games.

Laettner was the MVP, his 18 points and 10 rebounds against Kansas following the 28 points, 7 boards against UNLV. Hurley, who played all 80 minutes of the Final Four and finished the NCAAs with 43 assists and 10 turnovers, could have been selected as easily. There would be no nightmares this time around. "They were the most special games of my career," he said. "We did some incredible things."

Before the final, Mickie Krzyzewski had been even more nervous than usual. Though she was so calm before UNLV, now it was different. "We've come this far. We've got to win."

So when it was over, she and the three girls rushed to hug Mike. The court was a madhouse. After she spoke to her husband, she retreated to the stands to watch. She had eyes only for Mike. "He looked so mellow, so satisfied."

"I was so fulfilled," he said. "There was so much inside. All I could do was smile."

Everywhere he looked on the court, he saw someone special: his former players, Tommy Amaker and Jay Bilas, who had been on the losing side in 1986. The veteran trainer, Max Crowder, who had worked all of Duke's previous eight Final Fours, none with a championship. He summed up the moment simply: "It's the best feeling in the world."

After the ceremonies at the Hoosier Dome, the team arrived back at the hotel, which was swarming with deliriously happy fans. Everybody had to buy a T-shirt. The beer flowed freely into the night.

The staff and a few close friends gathered on the sixth floor to celebrate. Tom Mickle, ACC assistant commissioner and a former Duke sports information director, stood on a table and sang the school fight song. Former players dropped by to join the party.

An emotionally drained Krzyzewski stayed in his room,

where he shared the joy with his family and his closest
friends from his boyhood days in Chicago.

In 1990, his mother had tried to console him after the
UNLV game: "That's all right, Son, you'll do better next
year."

Stunned, Krzyzewski replied, "But Mom, we just
played for the national championship." That became one
of his jokes during the season. Whenever he had a speaking engagement, he related that story.

Now, hours after his greatest triumph, a laughing, smiling Emily Krzyzewski reminded her son, "See, Mike, I
told you that you'd do better this time."

CHAPTER 2

WITH HIS TEAM ON TOP of the basketball world, Mike Krzyzewski had reason to feel a deep sense of satisfaction. Duke fans everywhere were beside themselves with joy. But the coach's own feelings were more complex.

"Fans don't understand what it's like for a coach," Krzyzewski said. "You don't get to enjoy things the way they do. For them, it's a game, an event. For me, though, it's a responsibility. Every minute of the game, every moment that leads up to the game, you're trying to think and plan and prepare yourself and your players for anything that might happen—and that means putting some of your own emotions aside if they won't help you reach your goals. And it's hard to let them take over again even after you've won.

"Sure, there's a feeling of accomplishment, but as far as enjoying it goes . . . I didn't get that great feeling everyone else had from the Vegas game until weeks after. It wasn't until I looked at the tapes later that I really got caught up in it, when I could feel, hey, we really did something special. When the team got together after the game, when we met for the ceremonies at Cameron, I felt really proud of them and what we'd done. But as a coach, you always have to look ahead, and even after winning the final, you can't break the habit. What's next? How do we get to the next goal? I started thinking about it right away."

Within days of returning to an ecstatic Durham and the celebrations that followed, Krzyzewski was already planning ahead to 1992. With Laettner, Hurley, and the Hills returning, Duke was certain to begin the season ranked No. 1. Krzyzewski knew that everybody would save its best for Duke; his team was going to be a target every time out. They would have to be ready for the challenge.

Krzyzewski had been involved with USA Basketball for years, coaching the team in the World Championships and Goodwill Games. He was on the player-selection committee. He liked his players to participate on the various international teams in the summer; he was convinced that college-age players always needed new challenges, and that taking the summer off wasn't a good idea. They would just play basketball anyway; he wanted them to play with a purpose.

Laettner was the key. He was an all-America and had been voted the most outstanding player in the Final Four. He had played internationally in the past. It was important that Laettner play on the Pan-American team.

In thinking about the season to come, Coach K analyzed what UNLV did after winning its championship. Their star players had ignored requests to play in international competition. "I know. I tried to recruit Larry Johnson for my international team."

He wanted his players involved. Rather than worry about burnout—"They're only nineteen, twenty, twenty-one years old, they play basketball every day anyway"— he preferred that they keep playing and broaden their horizons.

"There are three reasons why guys don't play in the summer. They have a job that pays so much money they can't afford to quit; they have to attend summer school for academic reasons; they don't want to do it."

He had some control over the third factor. In mid-April, he met with Laettner in his office. Krzyzewski didn't want Christian to be satisfied with his accomplishments. Satisfaction was a potential weakness for his team. The coach wanted his star to seek additional goals, and the Pan-Am team could provide that. Moreover, he realized, how could he ask all the other team members to play if Laettner didn't?

"I don't want to play, Coach," Laettner told Krzyzewski.

"Christian, I understand that you're tired. Is that why you don't want to play?"

"Yeah. I'm exhausted."

"Well, you ought to be tired. It's been a long season. But look, don't make a decision now, when you're tired. Christian, you played in Buenos Aires last summer. Don't you think Stacy Augmon and Larry Johnson could have helped that team? Don't you think they could have improved if they played on that team? But they didn't come.

"What you ought to do is take four or five weeks off, get away from the game a little, and then you'll want to start playing again. That's right around the time the practices will be starting. Believe me, you'll want to play then."

Laettner immediately agreed with his coach. The message was clear and pointed: UNLV's stars had taken the summer off and they had lost in the NCAAs. Coach K knew Laettner would do anything to keep that from happening to him.

There may never have been a collegiate sports star as complex as Christian Laettner. His appearance was as deceiving as his image. Though he was movie-star handsome, with piercing blue eyes, his choir-boy looks masked a competitive nature that far exceeded that of the typical athlete.

As a child, Laettner got an early baptism in competitiveness. He would always be called Christian because his brother, Christopher, four years his senior, was already Chris. The younger Laettner learned the hard way from Chris Laettner and his friend Mike Taylor, who were the kings of the playground. They taught all the younger kids that lessons on the basketball court would be learned through combat. Nepotism wasn't permitted, and youth was no excuse. "Going through four or five years, losing against them every day, makes you hate to lose, especially when they rub it in and laugh at you."

Laettner responded well to his brother's tactics. But along with the basketball lessons came a fierce drive to prove himself to anyone who might doubt him. Laettner was obsessed with proving himself, and the teams he led, to unseen (and sometimes imagined) critics. It was a feeling that drove him to some remarkable accomplishments.

He always had an overwhelming belief in his ability. In the third grade in Angola, New York, his teacher wrote on his report card, "Shows too much self-confidence." Nothing changed in the next thirteen years. "If I told you how confident he was, you wouldn't believe it," said roommate and best friend Brian Davis. "Where do you go after arrogance?"

Laettner's concern was with winning, in life and in sports. He was always eager to test the unknown. He was never concerned with popularity; what he craved was recognition. "There's never been a time where I want to be a regular student because the spotlight on us or on me was too much. No, never. I want as much as I can get."

Athletically, that meant cherishing the games that posed a personal challenge, that presented him with someone more highly regarded than he was. That's why the home game with LSU and Shaquille O'Neal was his favorite of the previous season. Laettner knew he wasn't the physical talent that O'Neal was, but that had never been his concern. Being the more effective player was.

Laettner embarrassed Shaq. He went outside and drove

past him repeatedly. He outscored O'Neal 24–15 and out-rebounded him 11–10, and most important to Christian, Duke won easily by 18 points.

The situation against UNLV was much the same, al-though the game was of much more importance, and Laettner didn't go head-to-head against player-of-the-year Larry Johnson. But mostly because he outscored Johnson 28–13, Duke won its biggest game ever.

Laettner's boundless curiosity carried over into his pri-vate life. He and Davis, who is black, and another black roommate lived in Bragtown, a highly integrated middle-class section of Durham. Laettner said, "I consciously said to myself, 'I don't want to be protected.' It's impor-tant to live in the real world and not alienate the people of Durham. Duke and Durham, they're very separated. We're like an invading school, a lot of rich, white kids. You shouldn't build up barriers anymore."

Privately, Laettner did far more than most to improve racial relations. "Black-white, Durham is lacking. Every-one won't admit it, but I talked more at the black schools than anyone. That doesn't make me out to be a saint."

Certainly his teammates would never make that claim. There were tensions on the Duke team throughout the past season. There were times when some players weren't on speaking terms with teammates—off the court. But the occasional friction with Laettner rarely affected the Blue Devils in practices or in games.

Laettner treated his teammates the way his brother had treated him. After all, it had worked for him, hadn't it? In practice, Christian was toughest on the best players. He knew that he had gotten better because his brother had been hard on him, so the players he criticized were those he felt could most help the team. Wasn't that fair?

Grant Hill got the Laettner treatment right away. It took some time before Hill understood him. In the fall of '90, before practice began, the players worked out in old Card Gym. Hill arrived burdened with the credentials of being a prep superstar, plus the weight of being the son of a football Hall of Famer, Calvin Hill.

Hill had everything. Laettner understood that. So when they scrimmaged, "Christian dunked on me," Grant said. "Then he talked a little trash. I didn't play too well the rest of the way, the rest of the week. I really questioned myself. But I ultimately got the confidence.

"He's limited athletically. He's not that fast, he can't jump that high. So he had to be a little weird, a little cocky. That's a big front. He's a sweet, caring guy, but he gains his strength from that front. He thinks he's a bully, a tough guy."

Laettner loved Grant Hill. He marveled at Hill's pure talent, while Hill admired Laettner's willingness to take risks. "He loves to take that last shot. He wants that pressure. He's the most competitive person I've ever been around."

Laettner overcame the doubters all along the road in the only way he knew—he won. When he was a teenage basketball player, he played at the Buffalo YMCA, the only white kid among a group of inner-city blacks, the better to learn the game. "They doubted me then," he said. "They said the only reason I was any good was because I was big." To Christian, "big white kid" in the black man's game was always a stigma to overcome.

The son of a schoolteacher and a father who worked for the Buffalo newspaper, Laettner attended the Nichols School, a prestigious private school in Buffalo. "It was rich, upper class. I wanted to learn about things. I wanted the things that seemed glamorous." He felt comfortable in the Y and at Nichols, perhaps because he had to prove he belonged in both places.

In his freshman year at Duke, he missed the front end of a one-and-one against Arizona in the Meadowlands at the final buzzer. Two conversions would have sent the game into overtime. Four weeks later, in the same building, he outscored the more publicized freshman Alonzo

Mourning, 24–11, and outrebounded him, 9–5, as Duke won the East Regional against top-seeded Georgetown. He had accepted the challenge.

Being conventional was never his concern. "I don't go to the frat houses. They're mostly white, and all they do is stand around and drink. I'd rather go somewhere and dance."

He liked Prince and read Stephen King, who contacted Laettner after hearing of his interest. His bedroom was plastered with posters of jungle cats, tigers, panthers, and a billboard dripping blood, publicizing King's *Pet Sematary*.

Laettner's heroes were men who were considered to be the best: Wayne Gretzky, Jack Nicklaus, Michael Jordan. He wanted them to win all the time, every time. "The greatest people are those who perform. Magic, Bird, Jordan. They got to the pinnacle. You've got to be the ultimate to be considered a legend."

Laettner wanted, someday, to be legendary. That meant giving your all, but that wasn't enough. It took winning. You were judged by whether you won, and he wanted to win—at all things. He would go into the freshman dorms to find Marty Clark, just to beat him at Ping-Pong. When the players went bowling, he won. When he played the piano, he had to do it better than others.

In his sophomore year, Laettner wanted to room with Davis. "We'd gotten along," he said. "I walked into his room. I was scared. I didn't know if he would say yes. I was in the closet, combing my hair, when I asked him." Davis and Laettner became the closest of friends.

As much as he handed out, Laettner could take it. He craved respect, and the way to gain that respect, to answer the doubts he was convinced were still out there, was to be the best, and to take the trash and the jive as well as to give.

"Sometimes the best way to handle him is 'God damn it, you asshole,' and then you get his attention for two weeks," said assistant Pete Gaudet. When the coaches got serious with him, Christian listened.

Laettner was a leader, and he went about it his own way. He liked Grant Hill, but he was hard on him "because he was young and great," said Laettner, and he wanted to hasten the maturing process.

He was hard on Hurley, who had never been treated like that before. Tough in his own right, just as anxious to win, Hurley realized that Laettner's badgering made him miserable but also made him better.

"We almost never had a problem when playing," Tony Lang said. "We put everything behind us. We all wanted to win, and Christian knew how. And we knew that he knew."

Laettner didn't mince words during practice with anybody he felt could make the team better. "Quit being a pussy," he would say to freshman Cherokee Parks.

Or he'd say to Lang, "You're being a wimp."

He also liked to plant a seed with a comment. To Thomas Hill: "You used to take it to the basket." Or to Grant Hill: "Why don't you dunk?"

Hurley and Laettner weren't particularly friends off the court. Other than at team functions, they rarely saw each other. "But I think that shows a level of maturity, that it never bothered the way we played or practiced," Hurley said. "Christian's toughness, his ability to say anything to any guy on the team, that made us very strong. He sacrificed some of the camaraderie with the guys. He sacrificed himself by making us pissed at him, because he knew that made us better."

Krzyzewski watched Laettner mold the team. He knew Christian's bedside manner wasn't gentle, but he wanted his leaders to lead. A really good team couldn't rely on its coaches to motivate it; it needed players who would demand from their teammates all they had to offer.

Coach K knew, too, that the role Laettner chose helped him motivate himself. If he was going to dish out criticism, he had to perform. If Laettner didn't play so hard and so well, the players would never have accepted his verbal abuse. "We trust him to do what's right for the team," said Marty Clark. By allowing Laettner to do it his way, Krzyzewski didn't have to worry about his star's performance.

The person Laettner respected most of all was Krzyzewski. Even when the coach was screaming at him, he didn't mind; Coach K was a winner, and the star player had no doubts about that.

Brian Davis was a different case. Unlike his roommate and best friend, he had not been highly recruited out of high school. Through hard work and total faith in his ability, he had made himself into a good player.

While he and Laettner were different in many ways, they were alike when it came to leadership. Although Koubek and Buckley were the co-captains of the '91 team, down the stretch, as the team headed toward Duke's first national championship, the leaders were Laettner and Davis.

"Brian and I are mature," Laettner would say to his teammates. "You're babies." The roommates liked to present that image, and they enjoyed talking tough to one another.

Davis was always a man with a plan. During the summers in his first three years at Duke, he worked on Wall Street and Capitol Hill. He talked about going to law school—immediately after graduation if pro basketball didn't work out, or later after his sports career was finished.

Combative, competitive, aggressive, and articulate, Davis meshed easily with Laettner. It wasn't just that he and Laettner liked many of the same things; they had similar ideas about life. Even their numbers were similar: Davis, 23; Laettner, 32.

Laettner was the tall, handsome, white superstar. Davis was black, 6-7, one of the few players on the squad who wasn't a high school all-America. But that never worried him. He was accustomed to people questioning his talents, telling him what he couldn't do. That merely got the juices flowing.

In high school at Bladensburg, Maryland, Davis was as good a student as he was an athlete, maybe better. Modestly recruited, especially after missing eleven games with injuries his senior year, he was signed by Duke because Krzyzewski appreciated his toughness.

Basketball would be his ticket, but it wasn't his sole interest. "My heroes were never athletes," he said. There were a variety of them: political leaders, religious leaders, CEOs. Davis liked people who had been successful because of their minds more than those who relied on their physical skills.

"You want to be accepted for more than basketball," Davis said. He and Duke were a perfect match. He enjoyed the university's academic prestige. He resented the popular assumption that student athlete was an oxymoron. "Other schools talk about graduating," he said. "We do it. Come to Duke and finish in four years. That's part of the deal. That's what I was looking for. I know what life holds for me."

Always the activist, Davis was a member of the 21st Century Commission for African American men. He was on the dais when Dick Gregory told the audience, "You are a slave for the white man. If you don't get your degree, then you've been taken advantage of." When it came time for Davis to speak, he looked at Gregory and said, "Thank you, I won't be a slave."

Davis had seen enough in his boyhood to know that education was the path to success. "The way you don't forget where you came from is to graduate," he said. "A lot of guys are not doers if education is not the most important thing to them."

Davis enjoyed his leadership role on the basketball team. It was Davis who spoke to the team in the hallway prior to the UNLV game. The year before, Duke had simply been meek and hadn't fought back when the Rebels turned up the pressure.

"We didn't realize how much the game meant," Davis said. "We died before we cried. When we got back a second time, I realized, this may be the last time. I didn't think in terms of win or lose. If we had any heart, we'd play as hard as we can. The one thing I wanted to get across to everybody, when it's over, no matter what happens, we had to say to ourselves, we played hard."

He wanted to become a better player, to prove everybody wrong, to show that a guy who had averaged just 5.2 points in his first three years was good enough to play in the NBA.

Essentially a driver and defender, Davis worked hard on his jump shot. He had trouble with the three-point line, consistently hitting it with his toe as he shot. But he worked diligently, reaching the point where he no longer had a red light from the coaching staff if he was open on the outside.

The politician in Davis was a benefit to his career. He understood the way things were done, even if others didn't. He could take abuse from the coaches in practice. It wasn't that he didn't have an ego; he did, a big one. But it was his roommate who was the star, the heartthrob, the focus of the opposition. It was his job, Davis believed, to do what he could to help his team win, and that meant fitting into the slot that best displayed his talents.

Being the tough guy came easy. "It's societal," he said. "Politics never leaves sports." Brian Davis was, most of all, a politician.

Those two inseparable friends would be the leaders of the next team. But Hurley also figured into the equation, and so Krzyzewski wanted to make sure Hurley kept his competitive edge through the summer as well. Bobby had played fantastic basketball during the NCAAs. The offense and defense always started with him. Hurley was the hardest worker Krzyzewski had ever coached, a player who led by example on the court rather than through words in practice or in the locker room.

After meeting with Laettner, Krzyzewski called Hurley into his office. Bobby was one of four Duke players who had an invitation to the Pan-Am trials in Colorado Springs, but the schedule for that team conflicted with a family commitment Bobby had already made.

Krzyzewski understood that, but he wanted to make sure that Hurley played internationally during the summer. That was fine with Bobby; he would be delighted to participate in the World University Games in England on a U.S. team coached by Seton Hall's P. J. Carlesimo. It would be like old home week for Hurley, the Jersey kid, to play under New Jersey's most prominent coach.

Krzyzewski had planned his team's summer well. He had assured himself that Laettner and Hurley, who would be the floor leaders next season, were playing at the highest level of competition. And he knew that the rest of the team would follow their lead. The only people who didn't play in the summer were Kenny Blakeney and Erik Meek, both injured.

Laettner didn't have to take part in the Pan-Am trials, but was placed on the team along with the Hills, who were both selected on the basis of their play at Colorado Springs.

Freshman-to-be Cherokee Parks and Marty Clark were set to take part in the Olympic Festival in Los Angeles. Then Parks would join Lang on the Junior National team, which was to play in Edmonton, Alberta. Davis was picked to play for the NIT All-Stars in Europe, while Christian Ast was a member of the German under-twenty-two squad.

Krzyzewski liked the fact that his players would get to travel and see different cultures. They also got the obvious basketball experience, often against veteran international teams that knew all the tricks.

"I don't mind them getting roughed up, knocked around a little bit," he said. "That way, when they get back, they understand they have more to learn. They work harder in practice."

One of the more unfortunate players was one of the two not in uniform during the summer. Erik Meek, a 6-10, 240-pound recruit from Escondido, California, was out jogging in early June when he was struck by a hit-and-run drunk driver. Meek suffered serious leg and shoulder injuries, the worst being a damaged calf. But he was fortunate to be alive, and doctors were certain that he would have a full recovery. Meek had to attend his high school graduation in a wheelchair, but he was eager to rehabilitate and assured the coaches he would be ready to play in the fall.

The national championship paid immediate dividends on campus. In recent years, NCAA-licensed paraphernalia had become a major business. But the situation at Duke was ridiculous. It was weeks before things got back to normal at the campus bookstore. Everywhere around Durham, the uniform of the day was some kind of a Duke T-shirt.

"The national championship was worth about two million dollars in additional revenue," said Jim Wilkerson, associate director of Duke University stores.

Donna Keane thought she was prepared for all this. Keane had been Krzyzewski's administrative assistant for nearly a decade. "The first year, I hated it," she said. Then she began to develop a relationship with the players, and inevitably, their families.

"I have a great relationship with mothers," said Keane, who had her own teenaged daughter and a son who had just graduated from college. "I'm about their age. I can understand their concerns. Some of them will just call to say hi and ask if I've seen their son lately."

Keane became an extension of Krzyzewski. She often

made decisions on what happened with his time. She learned, over the years, who had access to Krzyzewski, "who gets through on the phone and who doesn't."

She knew how her boss thought, how concerned he was that things not change now that Duke was on top, and how aware he was of the public's interest in his team. While it seemed impossible even to address the thousands of requests that came in, nobody was turned down flat. At the least, fans always received team pictures.

Keane thought she was prepared for the demands that would follow the NCAA title. "I didn't think it would be that much different. We'd always gotten so much recognition. I thought it would be a breeze."

Instead: "I was overwhelmed in a flash. There was so much joy and excitement in winning."

Things were hectic enough on their own, but then Krzyzewski made a mistake. Actually, he made the same mistake several times. Aware that there was no way he could sign enough autographs, whenever he spoke to large groups of people, Krzyzewski told them, "Bring your stuff to the office and we'll get it signed." That created instant chaos.

Day after day, lines formed at Cameron in the narrow hallway that leads to the basketball office. Krzyzewski always insisted on being accessible, but this was absurd. "We're crippled," Keane said.

Two rooms were filled with basketballs, T-shirts, hats, and Final Four programs. Anything people brought, the basketball office accepted. Worst of all, each item had to be recorded and labeled.

There were so many basketballs that ball racks were brought over from the equipment room, and all were promptly filled. There weren't nearly enough. The office was under siege. It was hard just to move around because of all the material. Finally, in an act of desperation, the remainder of the basketballs were moved to the Hall of Fame room.

That created a strange scene. The basketball office was

located halfway down the long hallway; the Hall of Fame room was at the end. Students working in the business office were recruited, and they rolled basketball after basketball down the hall to their new storage site. It looked like a perpetual-motion bowling alley.

In trying to anticipate what the office might face, Keane called Indiana, Kansas, UCLA, and Carolina, schools that had won NCAA championships, for advice. "I didn't get the feeling it was all that crazy," she said. But it was at Duke.

There was such a volume of items that a number of things disappeared. Keane and the others working in the office had the unpleasant task of calling the fans and telling them their mementos were gone.

Especially distressed were the people who had brought Final Four programs, which Duke couldn't replace. Instead, those people got a media guide and an apology.

To handle the massive number of requests, the team was assembled in the Hall of Fame room, two players to a table, and signed autographs for hours until writer's cramp set in.

Basketballs were passed down, table by table, like an assembly line. Then the shirts, the hats, the programs. The players hated it, but there was no other way to get it done. Eventually, most of the items were signed. Some of them weren't picked up until late in the summer. By then, there was serious attrition, especially with the basketballs.

In another new phenomenon, fans stopped by from all over just to spend a moment looking around Cameron. The ancient Duke gym was now a basketball shrine. Not atypical was a family from West Germany who were in Florida on vacation. They watched the title game on TV, ended the trip on the spot, and drove to Durham just to see Duke.

Visitors would stroll slowly down the hallway leading to the office, stopping to gaze at the various team pictures that lined the wall from end to end. They would all come into the basketball office, to be greeted by Keane. They all had a story to tell about being Duke fans. Keane saw the joy on their faces when they talked about Duke and the basketball program. "That's fun," she said. "I enjoy that."

Mail was always heavy in the basketball office, but after the team won the NCAA, it arrived daily in bins. Keane called for help. She needed assistance just to open the flood of letters. "I need more people," she said. "I should have hired somebody."

Almost everybody got some kind of response. Keane read it all. The letters were divided into three categories: kids got team photos. Adult mail was handled with a fan response letter, all of them individually signed by Krzyzewski. To the people he knew, he dictated a personal note. Callers who said they knew Coach K or went to school with him or were in the service with him were listed separately by Keane. Every few days, he would go over the list. Often, he would reply, "Who are these people?" or, "I don't know them." As Krzyzewski's fame grew, so did the memories of the people who wanted to get in touch with him.

Even with Duke's success throughout the season, not all of the mail was positive. When Laettner unloaded his string of frustration-born profanities during the Carolina game in the ACC tournament, it distressed some fans.

One letter on the subject came from a woman in York, South Carolina:

> It is always sad when a halo breaks. That was what I felt when I read about Christian Laettner's conduct. I am glad I was away from the television when it occurred, and I wish I had not read the article.
> Basketball has always been my favorite sport, and Duke has always been my team. I was not fortunate enough to attend Duke, but I have always taken vicarious pride in the victories of the basketball team. Perhaps it is unfair to assign bigger-than-life status to people one has never met, but I have always thought Duke players were a cut above all the rest; Duke players have always been the class act of the game

of basketball, just as you are the class act of coaches. Since Danny Ferry left, Christian Laettner has been my shining light—the epitome of what an all-America athlete should be —the ideal that children would do well to emulate—the young man I would like to have for a son. To say I was sickened by the newspaper articles would be making an understatement.

I understand frustration. I understand justice. I understand giving your heart and soul and every ounce of effort to a losing cause. I know the Blue Devils are only human.

I only wish to remind Christian and all the players that people are watching. Some are children who are imitating a hero. Some are parents who are seeing the ideal child. Some are peers who are wishing they could be like Christian or Bobby, or one of the others. People in the spotlight have a responsibility, whether they want it or not, because everyone is a hero to someone. As it says in the Bible, much is required of those to whom much has been given. Christian Laettner has it all: good looks, a healthy body, a good mind, athletic prowess. He has the responsibility to use his attributes for good.

My balloon has burst. I have learned a valuable lesson. I will not idolize another player. That is sad because there are just too few Tommy Amakers and Danny Ferrys in the world. Duke will always be my team, but Christian Laettner is no longer special.

The letter struck a nerve with Krzyzewski. He was aware of Duke's status and image. He had spent considerable time downplaying the heroic nature people attached to the players, and he constantly reminded the media and fans that the players were not perfect, and nobody in the program ever thought they were.

Krzyzewski found a few warts acceptable. He wanted players to learn through experience, and that included mistakes.

In a response to the letter, Krzyzewski wrote:

I think it is important for you to understand that the youngsters playing for us are young men, eighteen to twenty-

two years old, who are human beings and not perfect people.
They will certainly make their mistakes.

Danny Ferry and Tommy Amaker also made their mistakes while they were players here at Duke. Maybe you didn't see them, but we did. I must say that every one of our players has made many more positive actions than negative ones. However, when they make mistakes, you can be sure that corrective action is taken.

Christian has been an excellent representative for Duke University. He is under a lot of pressure and usually responds in an outstanding manner. He of course did not do that during our ACC tournament game with North Carolina. He understands this and hopefully, he will learn from it.

I would recommend that in the future, you never put a halo around any of the young men. They are human beings and should be treated in that manner. I am pleased that you have also learned a lesson from this, in that you will not idolize another player.

I agree with that 100 percent. They are people just like you and me. You made reference to the Bible. You also made a statement that Christian Laettner is no longer special. I would like to remind you that forgiveness is one of the greatest gifts a human person can show. It is also good to remember that all of God's creations are special.

But for each negative letter received, many positive ones arrived. One of the best came in late May from Rick Madden, research associate in Duke's Department of Biological Anthropology and Anatomy. Madden had been on a six-week field trip to Patagonia.

Little news from back home reaches Argentina, unless it is of global significance. We learned that Stormin' Norman blew away his opponent from the local papers. It took a telephone call back home to reveal that Duke and UNC were among the group of eight in the NCAAs. . . .

On the day of the semifinals, we reached the southernmost point of our itinerary. High in the Patagonian Andes, above the beech forests, in the rock and snow, we were collecting fossil mammals. . . .

On a lark, we scanned the shortwave bands. A very faint, but definitely familiar sound, CBS basketball. With all the atmospheric interference, we could catch only every other word. "Fox . . . ball . . . court . . . Carolina." Holy shit. Carolina made the Final Four. With intense listening and interpretation, we followed the fate of Carolina. Some hokey evangelical station broadcasting out of Indianapolis with some unimaginably strong-wattage nuclear-power-driven transmitter was carrying the CBS feed, bringing the good word to the most remote corners of the Judeo-Christian honkey world. Carolina out of it, CBS announced the next matchup, "buzz, crackle . . . and UNLV," that's all we heard. Turned it off, too tired and disinterested to listen to UNLV wax some other college team.

On Monday night we were in a small hotel much farther north in Esquel, Chubut Province, on the return leg of our field trip. After pizza, we tuned in the evangelicals for the last good word, and again, the familiar CBS play-by-play, only this time the reception was better and we could make out every word. JESUS CHRIST, DUKE IS IN THE FINAL. The implications were immediate; we had missed the greatest basketball game of our lives. But we weren't going to miss another. I ran about town looking for someone with a dish, on the hope that we could tap into a visual. No dice. We settled for the audio. Beers and Duke b-ball in Patagonia, it doesn't get much better than this.

Krzyzewski understood what had led to the outpouring of support from all over the nation. "We slew Goliath. That captures the hearts and the emotions of the country. Duke is a private school. I don't think this would happen with a big state school. People from any state can identify with Duke. They remember what that team did against Vegas.

"It's just the way things happened. The whole nation watched Christian hit those two free throws. Then they saw Bobby Hurley, a little kid, in Grant Hill's arms and riding off the floor on Clay Buckley's back. You identify with that. It's not only that we won, but that everyone can identify with one of them: the big, good-looking guy with the size and the talent, or the gritty little guy who just plays his heart out. It's not that simple with either of them, but that's how it looks, and a lot of people identify with those images."

There were other rewards for winning. The team made trips to the state legislature in Raleigh and to the White House. There was a celebration in Durham. Krzyzewski was overwhelmed with demands on his time. He and his family were insistent that they wouldn't change, but much to their dismay, they found that their lives had changed, and not for the better.

"With the people who really knew us, everything was like it had always been," said Mickie. "But sometimes people we had been friendly with turned real cold to us. It was like they thought that we thought we were better than they were, and we weren't thinking anything of the kind. And on the other hand, some people started treating Mike like he was some kind of demigod. It irritated me that people were forming their opinions of us because of seven points in a basketball game.

"After we won, it was like Mike and the boys on the team became objects. People would just come up to them, and if they asked for an autograph, maybe in the middle of dinner when you really didn't want to sign right then, and you said no, they thought they could just say something rude right to your face. It was like we didn't have feelings anymore—we were no longer people.

"When he won the national championship, it was like Mike had won this big green hat. He could waltz around with it, and he was proud of it, and everybody could see it and wanted to touch it. But they couldn't see him anymore, just the big green hat, and he could never take it off. And the worst thing is that everything we worked towards, and everything we wanted, all of Mike's efforts —they were all going towards winning another one of those damned hats."

Krzyzewski saw those changes and knew there was nothing he could do about them but to be himself and ride them out. But in looking at them as a coach, the biggest problem for him was that everybody was celebrating an event that was in the past. He was already planning ahead. Nobody had won back-to-back championships since UCLA's seven-year run ended in 1973. He knew that Duke would have a chance to win again, just as UNLV had the previous season.

Krzyzewski knew that most people believed Duke would not win in '92 because UNLV had not been able to win in '91. If Vegas couldn't do it . . .

Coach K thought Vegas was a great team. But he thought the Rebels hadn't prepared themselves properly for the task of repeating. UNLV hadn't tested itself with its schedule. Since the Big West was not a strong league, the team was rarely challenged during the season. "I think that hurt them," he said.

Krzyzewski was determined that that wouldn't happen to his team. He knew the ACC would be strong as always, but familiarity was a problem. The coaches and players knew each other so well that while the games might be wars, it was difficult to learn anything new about your team from them.

Krzyzewski knew he would have a veteran team that could stand up to some adversity and benefit from the challenge. So he devised a nonconference schedule that was the most difficult any of his Duke teams had ever faced. The key games were all on the road. They would play St. John's in Greensboro as part of the final ACC/Big East Challenge, a made-for-TV event that Krzyzewski enjoyed. (The ACC coaches liked it; much of the Big East group didn't, and the series was ending a year before its contract expired.)

Duke also had a game at Michigan before Christmas. The Wolverines had recruited the nation's top freshman class, and one of those recruits was 6-9 Chris Webber, who had been pursued avidly by the Blue Devils. That game was on December 14, just before exams, and Coach

K considered it a perfect place to take a break. He knew that with almost everybody playing in the summer, it would be a long grind from the opening of practice on October 15 until the holidays. The Michigan game would end the first segment of the season.

There was a rematch with LSU, set for February 8 in Baton Rouge, part of what would be the toughest stretch of road games Coach K had ever scheduled: within eleven days, Duke would play at North Carolina, LSU, Georgia Tech, and N.C. State. The Tar Heels were always talented and would be the No. 2 pick in the ACC. Shaquille O'Neal had talked about playing Laettner again almost as soon as the 1991 game in Durham ended. Georgia Tech was always a hard place to play, and Duke had not won in Reynolds Coliseum in Raleigh in four years.

"I'm scheduling us to lose," said Krzyzewski, who considered February the month to test a team, to get it prepared for the tournament schedule in March.

He added an additional test, a March 1 game at UCLA. The Bruins were the favorites to win the Pac-10 and had all their star players returning. Coming just a week before the end of the regular season, that game would serve as a good final proving ground for Duke.

Intersectional games were rare at that time of the year, when conference competition was at its peak. But this was part of the master plan. Krzyzewski wanted to win another championship.

"I'm not afraid to lose," he said. "We must continue to be hungry. We need to be put in tough situations to see how we'll respond. You can't account for everything. There's some things you just can't coach. You just let those things happen, like injuries. You just deal with them."

Being No. 1 in the polls was never a goal. "It never will be," he said. "The only time it matters who's number one is at the end of the year. Our goal is to play well, to improve. Our goal is to place our team in a position to get a bid to the NCAA with a good seed. We don't want to peak too soon. The schedule will knock us back some. That's good. It will make us better."

The master plan was in place. It was time to start preparing for the hurdles to come.

CHAPTER 3

THE INITIAL TEAM MEETING FOR '91–'92, the only one permitted by the NCAA prior to the opening of fall practice on October 15, was held in the locker room at Cameron on September 3. The coaches and eleven players were there. A couple of faces were missing.

Shortly after winning the NCAAs, Billy McCaffrey came into Krzyzewski's office and told the coach he was planning to transfer. It came as a surprise. Even his roommate, Hurley, didn't know of Billy's plans. McCaffrey and his parents apparently felt his only chance to play pro ball would be at the point, and with Hurley around, he wasn't going to get many minutes there.

The news broke on ESPN shortly after the team banquet. The staff felt that if Dick Vitale had not gone national with the report prematurely, perhaps McCaffrey would have stayed. He was concerned about his playing time, even though he had been Duke's second-leading scorer and played the third-most minutes, behind Hurley and Laettner. But Thomas Hill was the starter by the end of the season. McCaffrey talked to several schools and eventually wound up at Vanderbilt.

Crawford Palmer, who would have been a senior, might have remained at Duke had Coach K been able to redshirt him and get him enrolled in graduate school, but that couldn't be worked out academically. He transferred to Dartmouth, from which his father and brother had graduated. Crawford was looking for a chance to play, and with incoming freshmen Cherokee Parks and Erik Meek added to the list of big men, it looked as if his opportunities would be even more limited.

The ostensible purpose of the meeting was orientation; the players were given the notebooks in which they would keep their scouting reports, and pocket calendars, which noted important dates and included all of the coaches' home telephone numbers. The calendar for the next three months included dates for the team picture, when recruits were being brought to campus, the annual clinic for coaches, the Blue-White scrimmage, and the two exhibition games.

But the real purpose of the meeting could be found in Krzyzewski's comments to the team, comments that would set the tone for the whole season to come. "We're not defending a national championship," he told them. "We are *pursuing* a national championship. I better not hear the word *defend* from any of you guys!"

Krzyzewski had had a whole summer to think about the task of repeating as national champions. Why didn't teams that won win again? He knew from experience that every time you went to the Final Four you learned something useful that made you better prepared the next time around. Why didn't winning follow from winning when it came to the ultimate win?

The whole idea of defending a national championship was built on two false premises, he realized. The first was assuming that a team could be the same for two straight years. It can't. It's not just a question of who graduates or who transfers; the question went far deeper than that.

Krzyzewski believed that each college team had its own identity, its own life cycle within a single season. Even when a team had its stars returning, as Duke would, the changes that come from being eighteen to twenty-two years old make the players completely different from year to year. High school all-Americas could become stars or bench warmers; lightly recruited kids could grow and develop into top pro draft picks. That was the fun of coaching college players; they were still growing up, physically and emotionally, and every year was a new challenge. It was very different from pro teams, where the same adult players return year after year.

"A season is a lifetime for a team," Krzyzewski has said. "The names may be the same, but the players always are different. Two weeks down the road for these kids is the equivalent of ten years. And after you finish the final game, the team, that team, is dead, it's over. The next season will have a life of its own."

But there was also something wrong with the idea of *defending* a national championship. When you defend your house or your country, you're trying to keep someone from taking it away from you. But nothing could ever take away the championship Duke had won. It was won —over and done with. Thinking about defending something keeps your mind in the past and puts you in a defensive frame of mind. To win something—for the first time, for the second time, for the hundredth time—requires thinking aggressively, to go after it, to pursue it, to take it. Krzyzewski knew that right from this opening meeting he wanted his players thinking aggressively, about the title they were going to take, not about the one that no one could take away from them.

"We are not defending a national championship," he repeated. "We already won that. Nobody can take that away from us. We are pursuing a national championship this year."

The players understood. Coach K talked to them about Vegas. He had thought about UNLV during the summer and was convinced the Rebels hadn't prepared as well as they could have for a try at their second title. He believed UNLV had defended its championship. And Duke had taken it away.

There were routine orientation matters to discuss as well. The coaches went over the preseason schedule: mandatory conditioning Monday, Wednesday, and Friday; optional on Tuesday and Thursday. Weight lifting Monday, Wednesday, and Friday. Mandatory breakfast daily on campus, starting that day.

The players were reminded about their schoolwork. Coach K praised them for having had their best semester last spring, when the team might have been distracted by the lengthy NCAAs. Nobody flunked a course, and there was just one D, even though they had spent most of March on the road. It showed that when there was a solid plan and the players stuck to it, they could do the work.

Coach K didn't believe in setting a lot of rules for the team. That went back to his days in the Army, where he felt there were far too many rules you had to live by. "Rules get in the way of leadership," he said. "They just put you in a box, and sooner or later you're going to wind up in a situation where you want to do something else but you have to go along with some rule you've made up."

There was only one firm team rule, he told them: "Don't do anything that is detrimental to you because that will be detrimental to the whole team." That gave Krzyzewski the flexibility to make the call about whether something was detrimental or not; he realized that what is detrimental to a freshman may not be to a senior. Missing a team bus might be okay if the circumstances were extraordinary; if you have a rule against it and you decide to ignore it, that just undermines the trust your players put in you. That flexibility both fostered and reflected the trust and rapport Krzyzewski has with his teams.

Krzyzewski reminded them of the responsibilities of being Duke basketball players, especially now that the public focus on them would be so much sharper. "Things

are different now. People are going to make demands on
you. Always be courteous."

He repeated the opening message. "We're not defending anything. We're pursuing a championship. Pursuit's
more fun."

Freshmen Parks and Meek met the first week with Duke
vice president Chris Kennedy, the academic adviser and
also the school's NCAA compliance officer. Kennedy's
initial message never varied: "Use your time differently
than in high school."

Most students wanted to do the same things they had
done in their high school days because that had worked
for them. "We dislocate them from that concept," Kennedy said.

School was a shock for freshmen. "It compares to the
first day of practice," Kennedy said. "That's when they
really find out that everybody is a good player. As freshmen, they learn about the competition in the classroom,
and how they must handle it."

All players were given a chart to fill in, showing not only
their classes but also their basketball schedule. The idea
was to make them realize where the available hours were.
"I tell them that regular students may have more empty
boxes in their charts, but they should still have sufficient
time to do the work. It's just a matter of understanding
when that time is, and planning ahead," Kennedy said.

Typical was the situation Greg Koubek faced last
spring. Koubek, a senior on target to graduate in four
years, had a major paper that was due on the Thursday
after the NCAA championship game. While he had no
way of knowing Duke would make it to the finals, he also
knew it was possible, so he planned ahead. He started the
paper two weeks before the Final Four and had it finished
before the team left for Indianapolis.

Kennedy had some suggestions for the athletes. He ad-
vised them always to do the hard work before practice

whenever possible, instead of trying to do it at night when they would probably be tired. "They're not used to thinking of daytime as study time," he noted. That changed in a hurry.

Kennedy went out of his way to discourage them from cramming, trying to do a lot of work in a short period of time. It was never a good idea, but especially not for young athletes, for whom injuries and fatigue can come out of nowhere and mess up that well-planned eleventh-hour study session. "We talk about time organization. If you have a paper due on October eighteenth, you don't start on it October sixteenth. You get started a couple of weeks ahead and go in short bursts."

Duke was a prestigious private school. But Krzyzewski and his staff resisted the elite tag at every opportunity, and the squad represented every segment of society—as did the school, whether outsiders realized it or not.

Academics at Duke posed a unique challenge to its athletes. They were competing at a school where the grade point average of the student body was 3.1. Over 93 percent of the students graduated in four years. The graduation rate for athletes was the highest in the nation among the 286 schools in Division I that awarded scholarships. The latest figures showed that 99 percent of all athletes, forty-two of the forty-three who matriculated in 1985–86, graduated, virtually all in four years.

Duke required thirty-four courses for graduation, a recent jump from thirty-two. Most students—and athletes —took four courses per semester, which meant they needed two more eventually. A number of Duke players attended summer school, but not after their freshman season. Krzyzewski liked his freshmen to go home.

The first year in college was always the longest. Coach K felt his freshmen needed to go home, to reestablish family roots. "It's been a traumatic time for them, and they've changed a lot. They need to show their families who they are now."

He believed the greatest change in the relationship between parents and sons came after that first year and the reunion. The players had adjusted to being away from home and had matured. Now the parents could witness the results of that maturation process.

To succeed at graduating its athletes Duke began early, right from the start of recruiting. Krzyzewski and his staff not only had a feel for which players would fit in on the squad, but for whether or not they could handle the academic pressure. "The people who get in are the people who can get through," Kennedy said.

Another factor was that Duke players never hear the word *eligibility*. Most athletes are disciplined about striving for goals; the staff tried to keep them from settling for too little. "They learn how not to get a D," said Kennedy. "Our main message to them is not to settle for a C. We're constantly on them to reach for more than that."

In Coach K's twelve years at Duke, two players, Greg Wendt and Bill Jackman, graduated elsewhere. Palmer and McCaffrey would presumably make that four. Alaa Abdelnaby graduated six months late, in December. Robert Brickey and Phil Henderson had not received their Duke degrees. Everyone else graduated in four years with their class, despite the intense pressure they faced in their sport and the time spent away from campus during the NCAAs. Much of that success came from working closely with the faculty. Because Duke is a small school (6,200 undergraduates), the classes are usually small, and professors can see who's in attendance and who isn't. Duke charters a plane for its long road trips, so that a squad member who had played at Clemson the previous night can be on hand for an eight or nine A.M. class the next morning. No one was looking for any special privileges in those situations.

Planning ahead was essential. The players were reminded to tell their teachers of their schedules, when they would have to miss class, and what they planned to do to get the material they would miss.

Additionally, Kennedy considered "conversation in the locker room" vital to the academic success of Duke athletes. "When the younger players see that the older guys are concerned about graduating, that there is an atmosphere of academic interest, it's beneficial," he said. They could see that it wasn't just their coaches, or their academic advisers, who were thinking about classwork. Their peers took it seriously. It was not unusual for a player to send a paper by facsimile when the team was on the road. The players took their books with them; they often did their assignments in motels or on the team plane.

Beginning after the sophomore year, Kennedy encouraged the athletes to attend the first session of summer school. Because most of the team went to summer school after both their sophomore and junior seasons, the typical Duke player entered his senior season ahead academically. That enabled most players to carry relatively light class loads in that second semester. It didn't hurt that the last semester coincided with the NCAAs.

Another unique aspect of the Duke program was the family influence. Mickie Krzyzewski was vitally involved, from the moment a player was being recruited until he graduated.

The Krzyzewski daughters not only were fans but the Duke players became like big brothers to them. They would come to the girls' school plays or recitals; Jamie, the youngest, would have vicious Nintendo tournaments with the players in the game room of the Krzyzewski home. (Cherokee Parks would become "Cheat-akee" to her after one particularly pitched battle.)

Mickie orchestrated a number of activities that made Duke different. The postseason banquet was an elaborate celebration and got bigger and better every year. Mickie was in charge of the videos, with the help of Raleigh TV photoessayist Jay Jennings. They produced extraordinary videos of the team, with emphasis always on the seniors. Mickie selected the music, and the videos were shown to an audience of several thousand who came to Cameron to pay tribute.

Mrs. K was also the administrator for the summer basketball camp, during which sixteen hundred youngsters learned the game under the tutelage of Pete Gaudet and a large staff of counselors. The camp was always sold-out, and Duke didn't even need to advertise. Mickie's tasks were incredibly time-consuming, coordinating the arrival and departure of four hundred campers and their counselors over a four-week span. Day after day, she was on hand at eight A.M. and rarely left before midnight. With so many youngsters there were always numerous problems to solve.

Lindy and Jamie Krzyzewski were on hand every day, as Debbie had been before them. Since the upperclassmen on the squad were usually in the first semester of summer school, they came into constant contact with the Krzyzewski women.

Players could, and would, call Mrs. K with any problem. She could be like a nurse or just a friend, happy to listen. In one memorable example, a player on the 1986 team came knocking on the Krzyzewskis' door after midnight on their second night at the Rainbow Classic in Hawaii. Mike answered the door, but the player asked to speak to Mrs. K. "She's already in bed," Mike told him, "but okay."

The player walked on into the bedroom and sat down on the bed. "Mrs. K, I need some advice," he said. "I'm in love."

"You're in love? Who are you in love with?" Mickie asked.

"A girl I met here in Hawaii."

Mickie groaned inwardly, but looked compassionately at the earnest young face. "Look, we just got here yesterday. I promise you, you're not in love with her. It's the palm trees, the warm weather, the beaches. Go to bed, get some sleep, and I promise you everything will be okay in the morning."

The player did in fact recover from his "tropical fever," and Duke's resident den mother had helped ease another crisis.

Mickie attended a majority of the road games, traveling with the team except during the ACC tournament. In the postseason, the children were also on hand as much as school schedules permitted. She believed just as strongly in tradition as her husband. Each year, before the final home game, the family would invite the seniors out to a nice restaurant for a reflective, fun-filled evening. When Coach K talked about a family atmosphere for his team, he meant it. The Krzyzewski women were always involved.

Having gotten their instructions from their coach, the Duke players had scrimmages almost every afternoon in Cameron. That was fun; they got to try out on each other the moves they'd developed during the summer competitions. Practice could get tedious. Playing games never did.

Venerable Cameron wasn't air-conditioned, and on occasion the heat was stifling. In some ways, that just added to the appeal and the playground atmosphere: all the better to sweat and shove and swear and do your thing. As usual, Laettner was the focal point of most of the scrimmages, which the coaches were forbidden by NCAA regulations to watch.

Krzyzewski disagreed with the rule. "I could help my players more if I could watch. I'm not talking about coaching. I know the rule is intended to prevent coaches from working their players too hard by making them go year-round. But that isn't really an advantage anyway. You show me a coach who's working his team to death in practice, and we'll beat him every time because his team will be worn-out."

All Krzyzewski wanted was some common sense. At least let the head coach watch the scrimmages. "You're on the road recruiting for most of the preseason anyway, but when you're home, you should be allowed to watch. Again, I'm not talking about coaching. If there's any concern about that, have the compliance guy sit with the coach. Have Chris Kennedy sit with me to make sure I don't coach.

"As a coach, I'm responsible for my players, on and off the court. I can tell a lot about a player by the way he handles himself on the court. If somebody is having trouble with academics, or has a problem with his girlfriend, I can tell something's wrong by the way he plays. If he's sulking, if something has happened to him over the summer, I know it right away. If I could watch, I could help them. It's a bad rule."

Coach K also knew that at the age of his players, physical development came rapidly. They could mature into adults almost overnight. He expected that they would be stronger, even taller than they had been on April 1. He wanted to see what they had learned, basketball-wise, during all of that summer competition; to see his players in action, to see how different they were from the last time they played for him.

If he could have watched, he would have seen some fierce games, usually with NBA players Johnny Dawkins and Danny Ferry participating. Dawkins, of the Philadelphia 76ers, was the college player of the year in 1986. Ferry, who won the award in 1989, was a member of the Cleveland Cavaliers. Both were among the elite few who had their numbers retired at Duke.

Laettner was most often compared to Ferry; both were big white players with a great shooting touch from the outside. Laettner loved going head-to-head with Ferry in those workouts, especially shooting three-pointers from the wing, knowing Danny wouldn't come all the way out to guard him. Left alone, Laettner could shoot threes as if they were free throws.

Occasional visitors dropped by. One Friday, Wake Forest star Rodney Rogers was on hand to see his close friend Grant Hill. Durham-native Rogers, a burly 6-7,

240-pounder, liked most of the Duke players, but not Laettner.

During the pickup game, Laettner shoved Hill, who fell, hurting his wrist. Grant left the floor and stood talking with Rogers. Laettner came over and said, "Quit faking it." Then he shoved Hill.

Rogers was shocked. "Why do you let him do that? You can't let him push you around," he told Hill. "If he does it again, I'll knock him out for you."

Hill calmed his friend down: "That's just Christian being Christian."

That was Laettner's method. He would shove to see who would shove back. "I tried to explain to Rodney that Christian was different," Hill said later. "He's so different. He only gets on the people he really admires, the ones he thinks can make us better."

Hurley had difficulty accepting that approach at first. Especially in his freshman year, Laettner's tactics really bothered him. Once, during his sophomore season, Hurley went to Krzyzewski and complained. "Tell Christian to quit getting on me all the time. I don't deserve it."

Krzyzewski replied, "You tell him." Hurley did, which was what Laettner wanted in the first place. He respected the players who stood up to him. But that was a lesson everyone had to learn on his own.

Hurley usually played on the same team with Laettner in pickup games. While Laettner and Davis were the team leaders and co-captains, Hurley was the field general.

More than anything, Hurley was a winner. He was the least likely looking great player. The deep-sunken eyes, the pale skin. Even his size—six feet, barely; 165 pounds, maybe.

Playing for his father at a high school with so many bigtime players, Bobby understood the recruiting process better than most kids. When it came time for him to go through it, he and his father carefully made out the recruiting list. He was considered the second-best point guard prospect in the country, behind Kenny Anderson.

Hurley had been a lifetime North Carolina lover. "Once, in my junior year, Dean Smith came to see me play and that was really a big deal. That meant something to me. I had always watched Jordan, Perkins, and Kenny Smith play. But at that time, I was just a fan."

Choice of a college was a different matter. "In the summer, we asked all of the coaches I was considering, 'If I were to decide tomorrow, would you stop recruiting point guards?' Everybody said yes except Carolina. They were still involved with Kenny Anderson. I pretty much scratched them off my list."

Hurley made unofficial visits to Villanova, St. John's, and Seton Hall, "schools that were nearby, that I already knew a lot about."

Then he made the trip to Durham. "The visit was the whole thing for me. So much of what I knew was the Big East. I didn't know that much about Duke. I wanted to get away from home, and that was the perfect distance for me. I could fly home in a couple of hours, drive it in eight hours. And the guys in the program seemed like good guys."

Of course, there was Krzyzewski. "I knew how well he got along with the players. There were a lot of similarities with my dad."

Krzyzewski accompanied Hurley back home to Jersey City. "Coach K had his home visit, and that day I committed. My parents were a little surprised at first, but my mother always wanted me to go to Duke. The academic reputation, she liked that part of it."

Hurley was Duke's point guard from his first day of practice. Krzyzewski just gave him the ball and told him to run the team.

The first season was difficult, even though Hurley set a school record with 288 assists and Duke reached the NCAA finals. But his petulance, his whining at the officials, drew the derisive chant of "Hurl-lee, Hurl-lee" almost everywhere Duke played.

Hurley had some growing up to do. He was away from

home for the first time. "I had to adjust my life. There wasn't someone to make my meals or do my laundry, or make me do my homework. My mom always did that. It was definitely a problem."

There were basketball problems, too. Hurley was the point guard on a team with three senior starters. "They dominated the team. In the past, I'd always felt I was in control. My freshman year, I didn't feel that way."

There also was a matter of self-doubt. "Right away, I was on the floor against Syracuse, playing against Derrick Coleman, Billy Owens, and Stevie Thompson. I was in a little bit of awe. The whole season was pretty much ups and downs.

"There were always signs I could play at this level, like the time I played against Rumeal Robinson and Michigan, but mentally, I wasn't always able to handle it. The hostile crowds did get to me a little bit. I was able to block it out somewhat, but the taunting, it may have made me lose control of my emotions a little bit. I'd go after officials, I'd complain more than I usually did."

Hurley didn't shoot well as a freshman, just 35 percent, and he had too many turnovers. "I tried to make plays that weren't there. I made things tougher on myself."

He did everything he could to blend in on campus. "The first couple of months were the easiest. Nobody knew who I was, and I guess I don't look much like a basketball player. I never wanted to be looked on as a superstar."

The next season, operating in a backcourt with fellow sophomores Bill McCaffrey and Thomas Hill, Hurley raised his scoring average from 8.8 to 11.3. "And I was comfortable. My assist-turnover ratio was much better. I felt I belonged." Still, not all of Hurley's problems went away. The abusive crowd cries were not so frequent as in his rookie season, partially because the Duke fans now chanted "Hur-lee" as a sign of support and approval, thereby lessening its effect when he played on the road.

But there remained that petulance, and the coaching staff knew that it was counterproductive. So Pete Gaudet produced a tape of Hurley in February of '91. There was an exclusive showing—Coach K, Gaudet, and the point guard. What Hurley saw made him cringe. The tape showed him whining, arguing, moaning, shaking his head, pouting after an errant pass.

"The point was to show him what he looked like," Gaudet said. "Our team gets its cue from him. When Bobby gets down, they get down. When he's up, they're up. We wanted him to understand how important his demeanor was to our team."

Hurley was not a talker on the floor. His face spoke for him. When his look was the look of confidence, it helped everyone. When it wasn't there, it was a negative for his teammates.

"I needed to see the tape," said Hurley, whose court actions during the Final Four were beyond reproach, while his game reached new heights. "I had been getting away with stuff and slipping into bad habits. I needed to stop doing those things, and seeing myself doing them really helped."

Hurley was not the most vocal of players. But his determination and hard work in practice gave the other players confidence. He had the look of a winner, and his teammates recognized it. He was the team's hardest worker in practice.

Now he was established. Anderson had gone to the pros. So had Chris Corchiani and John Crotty, other tough ACC competitors. Hurley might not look like the best point guard in the nation, but he was.

When the time came to begin practice, Krzyzewski repeated the theme he'd touched on a month and a half earlier. When a member of the media asked him about defending the championship, Coach K responded, "We aren't defending anything. We won the championship last year. That banner is up. Nobody can take that away from us. We're pursuing the championship this year."

At one early practice, Krzyzewski talked to Brian Davis, with the team listening. The words were addressed to the co-captain, but the message was for everybody.

Coach K lectured Davis on the potential danger of spreading himself too thin. He wrote on the blackboard: captain, player, student. "This is all you need to worry about being," he said. "These must be your main priorities. You've got to ask yourself if anything that you're doing is keeping you from focusing on them. Things have changed for all of us. There's a lot of demands on our time. We need to be sure nobody tries to do too much. Brian, you're trying to do too much."

Davis had his hands in so many things. He was involved with the black men's organization, he was socially active, he talked regularly to school kids. "Those things are all right in the summer," the coach said. "But now you need to get on with your responsibility."

Krzyzewski got his message across to the whole team. Davis may have been the focal point, but that was one of the ways Krzyzewski used his senior leaders. He knew Davis was tough enough to understand that and take the criticism.

"If you're playing well, leading and doing well in school, you can do other things," Davis said. "I didn't think I was doing anything wrong. We had just won a national championship. But he wanted to humble everyone."

Humbling Davis and Laettner would take some doing, especially since Krzyzewski admired their leadership qualities. "This team will be dominated by Christian Laettner and Brian Davis. They have their own leadership style. Maybe it's not what mine would be. But leaders have to be given the opportunity to lead."

Krzyzewski talked with his captains: "You have a huge responsibility. You're players, but I need you also to be part of the coaching staff." There were roles he wanted them to take on without the other players necessarily knowing it came from the coaches. If Coach K thought some players were going to the weight room individually instead of all going together, he could mention it to Laettner. Then Christian would talk to the team. "We're not working hard enough in the weight room. We're going as individuals, not as a team." Then he'd lead the way.

When the players griped about the food on the training table—and every team everywhere gripes about the training table—Coach K called on Laettner and Davis. "You come up with a menu that's better. You tell me what you like." Either the players as a group would agree on something different, or they would understand, through their captains, that the griping was without reason. Either way, they were involved, and a lesson was learned.

Krzyzewski put a lot of thought into teaching leadership as well as basketball. Sometimes when the team was screwing up in practice, instead of stopping things and straightening it out, he'd go silent and let it run. He wanted his captains, who had been there long enough to know how everything was supposed to go, to sense that things were wrong and to set them right on their own. He knew there would be some potential problems along the way; he knew that not all of his players responded well to Laettner's pointed criticism. "Some of them won't appreciate it. If it gets too extreme, I'll have to step in." But he also knew the risks were worth taking because a team that was smart and knew how to correct its mistakes was going to be very tough to beat.

The previous season, when he had a young team that needed to learn a lot of basketball, practices were hard and long. Things were changed now. Except for Parks and Meek, who was still hampered by his summertime injuries, this was a veteran team. "We're not going to practice long," Coach K said. "We'll go hard when we go, but we'll keep it short."

The focus of the coaches was simple: worry about Duke. Don't worry about the other guy. You probably can't do much about them anyway. That meant getting the team as prepared as it could possibly be, and then accepting what happened. If you did everything you could and still lost, well, so be it. Just go on to the next game.

That also meant not getting carried away with any one victory. That stuff was for fans. Volunteer coach Jay Bilas recalled what happened his sophomore year, when Duke upset No. 1 North Carolina, with Michael Jordan and Sam Perkins, 77–75, in the ACC semifinals. The Blue Devils supporters went bonkers.

"I'll never forget the score," Bilas said, "because the next day, they already had bumper stickers out. I thought, 'That sucks.' They had deified the other team. I hated that." Duke lost the next day, to Maryland, in the championship game.

"I think Coach K gets us to move on to the next thing," Hurley said. "He doesn't let a loss go by without talking about mistakes, but then we move on. You have to be able to handle the success of winning, to win the big game and still be able to concentrate on the next one."

Now the job was to forget last season completely and concentrate on the task ahead. "Part of coach's personality is to go on from one thing to the next and not let the last thing drag you down so that the previous thing affects your future," said assistant coach Tommy Amaker. "I've heard him say over the years, 'Hey, go on to the next play.' I may come down and throw the ball into row F. You want to show your negativity and disbelief in your body language. Then you hear him say, 'Go on to the next play.' "

Krzyzewski knew he had a good team. He had always been candid with the media; when he had good teams and good players, he said so. He wasn't the type to poormouth his chances. "We're good," he said. "We can be very good. I just have to keep reminding them they aren't as good as they're hearing."

By now, a plethora of basketball magazines were stacked high in the bookstores and newsstands. Duke wasn't a unanimous No. 1, but the Blue Devils were never picked lower than third, and usually then only because of the Vegas Syndrome: if UNLV couldn't repeat, then Duke won't, so let's choose somebody else. Indiana, UCLA, and Seton Hall all got support.

Laettner was closer to being a unanimous pick—as a cover boy. He was on the front of *Sports Illustrated*'s basketball issue. He was also on the cover of at least eight other magazines. Hardly any Shaq. No Alonzo. Almost all Christian.

There wasn't any question the Blue Devils had a good team, but one thing they lacked was depth. Who said they had everything as practice began? Not Krzyzewski.

Duke lacked bodies. The transfers of McCaffrey and Palmer left them with just eleven scholarship players, one of whom, Meek, was already injured, so the team was only an injury or ailment away from having too few players to scrimmage. Krzyzewski turned to the student body for help. On the evening of the first day of practice, October 15, the team held a tryout in search of a walk-on who could contribute.

The madcap evening at Cameron produced Ron Burt, a 6-1 guard from Kansas City who was a senior engineering major. Burt was not exactly an unknown, and if there was a favorite going into the series of frantic 5-on-5 scrimmages, he was the man.

Burt roomed with Mark Williams, the senior basketball manager. He had been given advance warning that the team would be looking for at least one more player in the fall, so he had groomed himself all summer, athletically and academically, to accept the challenge if offered.

He was one of three members of the intramural champion Dream Team among the thirty-seven contenders who played a series of shirts-and-skins games before an enthusiastic audience in steamy Cameron. Watching with amused expressions were the champs themselves, alternately cheering or laughing after each unusual play. Variety was the buzzword for the evening.

During a lay-up drill, one guy almost lost his oversize purple shorts, to the amusement of all. A writer for the school paper ordered one of his fraternity pledges to serve as his water boy. Then there was the Kamikaze Kid, who went for the ball with such enthusiasm that it didn't matter what was in the way. "He had more collisions tonight than Richard Petty had in his whole career," said Krzyzewski, displaying some unanticipated NASCAR knowledge.

The physical conditioning of several of the prospective Blue Devils was in question. One, unfortunately playing on a "skin" team, displayed an excess of it, a potbelly that drew considerable attention from the onlookers. The overall look was not enhanced by his goggles.

"There are always ten percent or so who know they aren't real candidates. They just want to play in Cameron," Krzyzewski said. "That's okay. A number of them came over and thanked me for letting them try. The guy who was the worst player out there came up to me and said, 'Thanks, it was a big thrill.' I thought that was neat."

Burt was clearly the player that Krzyzewski wanted. He fit the criteria perfectly. He knew all the players. They were comfortable with him. He was twenty-one and mature enough to take his role seriously, not some thrill-seeking teenager who was looking for a seat on the bench so he could wave to his friends in the crowd.

Burt, who had attended prep school in Maine, was not a bad player at all. He was a legitimate point guard, a good athlete who could work hard defensively against Hurley. "I wouldn't be afraid to put him in the game for a minute to give Hurley a break," Krzyzewski said.

So Burt went from a star on the Dream Team to a bench warmer on his own dream team. Burt also filled another role: as the walk-on, the automatic last guy off the bench, he would be the victory cigar for the Cameron

Crazies. When they would yell, "We want Burt," the game figured to be well in hand.

Krzyzewski had a message for the fans about Burt. "Don't treat him as a walk-on. Treat him as a player. There's a purpose for Ron Burt. He's an important part of our team."

There were very different demands on the two freshmen who were trying to fit in. While Meek had doctor's clearance to join the team for practice, he was still rehabilitating and didn't project to play that much. But Parks had more than held his own in the fall workouts. "Cherokee really looked forward to coming to school," said Tony Lang, who played with Parks in the summer. Parks played well in the scrimmages.

Laettner had kind words for Parks's progress, which the coaches couldn't assess for themselves since they couldn't watch any of the workouts. His only criticism to them was that Parks was too unselfish. "He won't shoot the ball. We're like, 'Cherokee, shoot the ball, you're open.' "

"I keep forgetting that Christian is a lottery pick and one of the top players in the nation," Parks said of his daily sessions against Laettner. "When he does something, I'm just like, 'Damn. I wish I could do that.' Then I realize who he is."

Parks was on display in the annual Blue-White scrimmage on November 2. The crowd that overflowed into the creases and corners of Cameron was rocking from the start, eager for the season to begin. Basketball was the students' passion.

The starters played for the winning Blue team, but the crowd was interested in Parks, the lone newcomer to see action. Meek did not play because of a minor leg injury, suffered during practice. Cherokee slapped the ball away from Laettner, and the Crazies cheered. He scored 6 points, but more impressive to Coach K was his rebounding. Six of his 9 were on the offensive end.

"I walked out on the court and said, 'No way,' " Parks said, referring to the size and enthusiasm of the crowd. "I just remember looking at the floor because you feel every-body's looking at you. It was all kind of a blur."

"Cherokee, if he performs like that with the key players, will fit in really well," Krzyzewski said. "He's constantly on the offensive boards. That's something we didn't have last year, a consistently good offensive rebounder. Maybe he can do that for us."

Two weeks later, Parks made an official debut in Duke's first exhibition game, against High Five America. He scored 17 points, 2 fewer than Laettner's game-leading total, on 8-for-9 shooting, and added 7 rebounds.

Parks and Laettner worked well on the floor together, although generally Krzyzewski was displeased with the team's halfcourt offense. "We can give our offense a couple of different looks, but we've got to recognize what we look for with each of them," he said. "If we have two big guys in the game, we're going to look for certain types of shots. If we have one, we're going to look for other types, and we didn't do a good job of that."

Parks was the center of attention after the game. He was the new piece in the puzzle. "That's what Coach Krzyzewski wants me to play, big," he said. "It's about making everybody notice you—notice your presence. It's about not being a girl out there. It's about being a man."

Parks admitted Laettner was free with his advice, and his criticism. "Christian talks to me a lot and he doesn't beat around the bush. If I'm doing something wrong, he lets me know about it. One thing I've been working on, for example, is to have no wasted moves. Make 'em all count. Christian does that so well. I need to do a better job of getting out on the wing and denying the ball. I have to get out there and defend and not worry about getting beat, knowing someone will rotate behind me to help out."

Krzyzewski was pleased with Parks. "He did a good job tonight. Our kids love playing with Cherokee."

Thomas Hill became the first casualty of the season when he suffered an ankle sprain during the exhibition. It made the addition of Ron Burt to the squad even more important.

The final exhibition was against a Soviet Select team a week later. This wasn't the same as playing the Soviet Nationals, as they had in the past, but NBC telecast the game anyway. Playing without Hill and Lang, Duke won easily, 90–70. Parks, in a starting role as Duke opened with the big lineup, scored 19 and had 8 rebounds. He was 8 for 11 from the field and blocked 4 shots. One reverse slam after an offensive rebound had Cameron buzzing.

But it was Hurley who showed the new look of the offense. The playmaker turned scorer with 22 points, including 2 three-pointers. "With Christian, Cherokee, and Grant playing on the baseline this year, it's opening a whole lot of things up for me outside. My first two years, my main job was to pass the basketball. This year, we need me to shoot the ball a little more from the outside because people are playing me to pass."

Grant Hill thrilled the crowd with one of his stunning dunks en route to his own 22-point game, and he said more should follow. "This year I'm just going to go for it and see what happens. I think toward the end of last year, I showed my abilities more. I'm going to go out there and try to be a spark on the court."

Hill had played the role of the learner as a freshman. But the spectacular dunk against Kansas in the title game had shown his capabilities to a national audience. He was ready to become a star as a sophomore.

The NCAA had instituted a new twenty-hour weekly limit for involvement with an individual's sport. It was aimed at coaches who had three-hour practices or never gave their players a day off. The rule also required one day a week away from the sport.

Duke had no problems fitting into that schedule. The normal week included eighteen or eighteen and a half hours devoted to basketball. Practices were not long, and they could be cut shorter if Coach K wished. In the preseason, Sunday was usually the off day. That would change somewhat to accommodate the schedule, which included Sunday games the last four weeks of the regular season.

Krzyzewski always made up his practice plan the night before. He kept each day's schedule in his notebook, which was similar to the ones used by the players. The staff met each morning; Donna Keane would join the coaches in the conference room, where they would discuss any business or recruiting matters. Then the coaches would make the practice plans among themselves.

Coach K would break down various segments of the day's schedule, telling everybody how he wanted a particular segment to be taught. Although Krzyzewski had a young staff, it had been with him a long time.

Gaudet was Mike's assistant at Army and had been at Duke since '83. Brey was in his fifth year. Amaker had played for Coach K before becoming a coach. Bilas, the volunteer who was in law school, was also a former Duke player. They understood their boss. He didn't have to explain in great detail how he wanted practice to go.

"We have a feel for how he wants things done," Brey said. The daily meetings could be over in a few minutes or last as long as an hour.

If the team had played a game, Krzyzewski would discuss it with the squad before practice began. Often, they would watch some tape in the locker room. Duke was one of the few programs that utilized film as well as tape. "When we want to teach, we use film because it shows the entire court," Krzyzewski said.

The videos were used for a variety of purposes. It might be to show highlights from practice or to watch a team they didn't even play do something the Duke coaches thought was especially good. If Duke had worked on a play during practice—say, a side out-of-bounds situation —the next day the TV would be brought to the floor and the players could see how they had performed. The staff also watched for bench scenes and other player reactions, including how attentive the players were during a huddle.

Gaudet kept a tape on each player, mostly of positive things. Often, the players would come in and ask to view their personal tapes. If the team had not exceeded the twenty hours of practice permitted by the NCAA, a coach or coaches would watch the tape with the player. Otherwise, they would take it home with them. Gaudet had everything cataloged on computer, so he could instantaneously pull up a specific situation for a player or for the staff.

On the court, while the players were doing their stretching exercises, the staff might huddle, and Coach K would reiterate specific things he wanted to work on. Gaudet and Bilas worked with the big men, while Brey and Amaker were at the other end with the perimeter players. Coach K was the overseer at both ends. If he saw something he wanted to discuss, he would move in. Perhaps because he was a guard at Army, he was more likely to have something to say about what was going on with the outside players.

One of the strengths of the Duke practices was the individual workouts. Players would drill with their position coaches for 20 minutes before the team began its overall workout.

Individual instruction often began with a video. Krzyzewski would have Gaudet pull together a tape of, say, all of Marty Clark's minutes in his last three games or scrimmages. Then the tape would be shown to Marty, and he could see what it was that they wanted him to work on.

The players responded well to the videos. When they saw themselves making a particular mistake time and again, there couldn't be any argument. They could see what they were doing wrong. It also worked to reinforce what they were doing right. Usually, it would be a particular offensive move or defensive posture that had been emphasized in practice. When the player saw that it worked when he did it properly, it not only made him feel good but made him want to work harder.

One aspect of practice never varied: the team always practiced free-throw shooting after running sprints or at the end of practice. The point of practice was to get ready for game conditions, so it made no sense to practice free throws when you were fresh, since you were hardly ever fresh when you shot them in a game. Coach K wanted his players to be used to shooting free throws when they were tired.

Free throws were an important weapon for Duke, and it was no accident. Over the course of the '91–'92 season, Duke shot nearly twice as many free throws as its opponents and made nearly two hundred more than their opponents *attempted*. It wasn't just that they were a team that attacked the basket; there was a definite strategy that created their advantage in this area.

Krzyzewski analyzed free throws every bit as much as he analyzed other aspects of the offense and defense. When the NCAA changed its rules to award two free throws for any foul from the tenth foul on in a half, it was generally seen as a way to try to cut down on deliberate fouling at the end of a game. Krzyzewski realized, however, that it was every bit as much a strategic opportunity as the introduction of the three-point line a few years earlier.

If Duke got its opponents into the penalty situation early in a half—a team shoots one-and-one on nonshooting fouls after the seventh foul of the half—they deliberately changed their offensive set. They attacked the basket even more than usual, trying to drive the other team up to and past the ten-foul mark. From there on, every little touch foul was two shots. This created an enormous advantage for the Blue Devils.

They were just as aware of the foul situation on the other end of the floor. If there was a danger of getting into the penalty situation early, Duke might change the way it picked up in its man-to-man defense, or even switch to a zone, just to avoid the team foul trouble. Every player, on the floor or on the bench, was expected to be aware of the team foul situation as well as his personal total. A player could get pulled for committing a dumb foul even if it was his first, if it put the team at or over the limit. "We're always aware of it on the bench," Krzyzewski said. "Our players pay a lot of attention to it; they'll give someone recognition if they do a good job of staying away from fouls in tight situations, and they'll get on someone for doing something wrong. The whole area of fouls and free throws—it's a major, major factor for us. It's really a key part of our philosophy, and it's a subject you just never, never hear anyone talk about."

Krzyzewski had a good feel for his team. He knew when they were tired, when they couldn't be pushed harder, even if there was more ground to cover. He always kept in mind the big picture; it was a long season, and what happened any day, or even in a particular week, wasn't nearly as important as what the goal was for March and April.

By design, the preseason had not been that difficult. Coach K knew his players had stayed sharp by playing through the summer. He wanted the squad to have fun in November and December, to enjoy the games.

As far as he was concerned, the season would start after Christmas. He thought his team might be good enough to be 5-0 by then, but even if it lost, it wasn't going to bother him. He didn't want the team to defeat itself, to get anybody hurt or sick for when the season really started after the holiday break. The opening games would be an opportunity to see the players in competition.

Coach K wanted to see his guys play.

C H A P T E R 4

DUKE'S PRE-CHRISTMAS SCHEDULE matched the lightest since Krzyzewski became the Duke coach. East Carolina, Harvard, and Canisius figured to be easy. St. John's, in Greensboro, figured to be a good test, and the finale for this period at Michigan was intriguing and potentially exciting.

Unlike college football schedules, which are locked up years in advance, basketball schedules leave a coach lots of room for careful tailoring. As late as the end of spring or the beginning of summer, it was usually still possible to arrange a nonconference game that would suit your needs. The light early schedule made sense for a veteran team, one that didn't need to be pushed yet. Krzyzewski knew the capabilities of his stars. He was eager to see if Lang was prepared to take a major step forward as a sophomore, and he wanted to see Parks in action. The next three weeks would let him watch his players, particularly his bench, see how they developed, and make determinations for the real season that would begin with the ACC schedule. The team would then have sixteen days before its next game—an unusually long break.

When the players came back after Christmas, Coach K figured they would be anxious to play, though not yet in top game condition. That's when they could go all out, and the staff would have a better idea of what to work on.

Laettner and Lang were sidelined for the opener against East Carolina on November 25, just two days after the game with Soviet Select. The last three times ECU had visited Cameron, the margins of defeat were 38, 49, and 43 points. This loss was more modest, 103–75.

Parks started in Laettner's place, contributing 16 points and 8 rebounds in 20 minutes despite being in foul trouble. He was 5 for 5 from the floor.

The other player who benefited from the absence of Laettner and Lang was Clark. The 6-6 sophomore scored 17 points and added 5 rebounds and 4 assists. He hit both his three-pointers. "Marty has the ability to hit the open shot, which we definitely can use," said Hurley, who led the Duke scoring with 20 points.

"I definitely think I can stick the open shot," Clark said. With McCaffrey and Koubek gone, Duke was looking for more three-point shooting. Krzyzewski said it was a case of Clark's recognizing his opportunities. "If he's out there with a team of some of our starters, he probably won't be defended as hard as those starters. Some people are going to play off him, and if he can hit the shot, rebound, and play defense, it's going to make us just that much better."

Harvard was the next sacrificial lamb. Academic peers, the schools were worlds apart in basketball. But the Crimson enjoyed the game, and Krzyzewski preferred it to some non–Division I opponent. It offered a chance to do some more teaching.

This time, it was a zone defense, which was not Coach K's forte. There had been times in the past when it was necessary to play a zone, and he wanted his team to get some experience with it. "We played it horribly," he said after the 118–65 victory. "I was glad to see them play us in a zone because it's tough for us to simulate it in practice since our kids don't believe in it."

The most impressive thing to Krzyzewski was how hard his team played against an obviously outmanned opponent. Laettner, who had been a doubtful participant, not only started but was diving on the floor for loose balls. "It's up to the captains to set an example," he said. "Brian does a good job of getting everybody excited. Intensity is an important part of our team. If you're not out there playing as hard as everybody else, you'll definitely hear about it."

Harvard coach Frank Sullivan got enough of a look to satisfy him. "I felt we saw the best team in the country. What impressed me most about Duke was how they were focused, both as individuals and as a team."

That also pleased Krzyzewski. "It would be easy for our team not to be ready to play tonight. Our team didn't do that. They were more than ready to play."

Parks was 6 for 6 from the floor and scored 15 points, one of eight men in double figures. He led the team with 6 blocked shots. In his first two varsity games, he had not missed in 11 tries; counting the two exhibition games, he was 27 for 31.

The preliminaries were over. Now it was time to take the first test. The Blue Devils bused to Greensboro for a meeting with St. John's, the preseason favorite in the Big East and a team that Duke had beaten the past two years in the NCAAs.

Dave Gavitt, then the commissioner of the Big East, and ACC commissioner Gene Corrigan had created basketball's first Challenge series in 1989. In a made-for-TV extravaganza, the two powerhouse conferences would play eight games in four nights, all carried by ESPN. Krzyzewski and his compatriots in the ACC loved the format; to Coach K, it was an early opportunity to test your team against a legitimate opponent. A loss certainly wouldn't be fatal, as Duke had proved the past two years

—the Devils were 0-2, having lost to Syracuse and Georgetown.

But the Big East coaches, led by John Thompson, were opposed. So the series was ending, and the Duke–St. John's game in the Greensboro Coliseum would be the finale.

Jay Bilas feared the Redmen: "This is going to be our first test. We can lose."

St. John's was ranked No. 7 in the nation. Rarely has the gap between first and seventh appeared so wide. For 27 minutes, it was a chasm.

Grant Hill started the game with a slam, one of three for the night. With less than 3 minutes off the clock, Laettner's three-pointer made it 12–2.

Duke was doing everything right. Hurley placed a defensive blanket over Jason Buchanan, the St. John's playmaker. Buchanan, humbled by Hurley in the Midwest Regional eight months before, finished with 1 field goal and 7 turnovers.

The Blue Devils had the lead up to 16 points in a hurry, saw St. John's cut it to 8, then finished with a Hurley-Laettner flurry that made it 48–30 at halftime.

Befuddled St. John's was a step slow on defense, grabbed away, and got called for 16 fouls that resulted in 22 free throws by intermission. For the game, Duke made 38 of 44 free throws.

By halftime, the old coliseum was humming. The sellout crowd of 15,786 was having a hard time believing what it was seeing. In the first week in December no team should look that good.

The first few minutes of the second half saw more of the same. Grant Hill made one of his 4 steals and it was time for a thunder jam. Dick Vitale, doing the game for ESPN, screamed, "Showtime, baby."

St. John's, a veteran team with senior stars, took a timeout. With 13:45 left, the humiliation factor had reached 68–37.

Seated on the bench, Bilas couldn't believe what he was seeing. Duke was making great play after great play. "Whoa," he thought to himself.

At the time-out, while Coach K talked to the team, Bilas looked across the huddled players at Amaker, with whom he shared an office. Their eyes met, and Bilas arched his eyebrows: "Whew!"

"That segment was scary," Krzyzewski admitted. "I started doing some things to break the momentum." From a coach's viewpoint, the rest of the game was perfect. Krzyzewski tried a number of combinations of players, some of which hadn't even been used in practice. Without saying so, he called off the execution. It served no purpose to win by 40. A team could pay a price for that, especially against a good team such as St. John's that they might face later in the NCAAs.

The coaching staff hadn't done anything to make the team that good that early. It wouldn't even necessarily be helpful in the long run. "It would be like starting a mile run like a one-hundred-yard dash. You don't want that much success too early," Krzyzewski said later. So he put on the brakes.

That, combined with a righting of the sinking ship by Lou Carnesecca's team, led to a big St. John's rally. The Redmen were, after all, not some handpicked patsy. Malik Sealy went wild offensively, Duke got sloppy with the ball, and St. John's suddenly got a lot of second shots. With less than a minute to play, the lead was down to 8 points at 89–81 before the Blue Devils scored the final 2.

"We learned how well we can play and how badly we can play," Coach K said after the game.

It was one of the most deceiving 10-point games ever. Privately, Krzyzewski was pleased. He had seen how good his team could become. And his players had gotten a dramatic lesson in what could happen when they lost their focus. The St. John's rally would actually help him to teach. St. John's scored 44 points in the final 13 minutes.

Carnesecca wasn't fooled. "They have a great orchestrator. Mike designed a wonderful team. Their game is not complicated, it's simplistic. But greatness is simplistic. They are ten to fifteen points better than last year's team."

The next day, Bilas kept getting calls from friends in California who had seen the game on TV. "What was that? That was something special."

"Can you believe it?" he replied. "I can't ever remember watching anything like that. It was frightening."

There was only one real negative. Cherokee Parks, who had played so well since the start of the exhibition season, suffered a high ankle sprain and played just 9 minutes, during which he scored 9 points. Parks would be sidelined until after Christmas, and his freshman season would never be the same again.

The next day, Duke flew to Buffalo for what would turn out to be part game, part happening. The featured entrée was Christian Laettner and buffalo wings, in Erie County, where they were both beloved.

The invitation to the party had been issued four years previously, when Canisius coach Marty Marbach wrote to Duke, North Carolina, and Virginia, finalists in the Laettner recruiting sweepstakes, and invited the lucky winner to please bring Christian home. Krzyzewski accepted the offer, getting a pair of home games with Canisius in the bargain.

Laettner was big enough in Buffalo before the November 25 *Sports Illustrated* was published. But that just enhanced the following for Duke's golden boy; Christian on the cover set a lot of young hearts atwitter.

Buffalo hadn't seen much big-time basketball since the days of Bob Lanier, a generation before. The all-time local attendance record for college basketball was 13,558, set when Notre Dame brought hometown boy Keith Robinson to play against St. Bonaventure in 1987.

By the time the Duke plane arrived, an hour late because of a snafu with the luggage, more than sixteen thousand seats had been sold for the game at Memorial Auditorium, popularly known as The Aud.

Laettner was fired up. "I'm excited not just because Buffalo fans can see me play, but also so they can see Grant Hill and Thomas Hill and Bobby Hurley and my teammates. I'm proud of my team, and I think if all Buffalo could see us play, everybody could say to themselves, 'I saw the national championship team play.'"

Then there was Laettner the resident chef. He had spent years telling his teammates that they had no idea what real Buffalo-style chicken wings tasted like. "I always talk about chicken wings," he said. "Whenever we go out of town, restaurants will say, 'We have Buffalo chicken wings.' They'll come out, and they're horrible. They try to bake them and you don't bake them, you deep-fry them."

How big was Laettner in his home area? At the airport, there was a press conference televised live, carried by all the Buffalo stations. The hometown hero received mementos from County Executive Dennis Gorski, who proclaimed this "Christian Laettner Homecoming Weekend."

The autograph seekers were on hand when the team arrived at the hotel, but there was nothing extraordinary about that. The mob scene would come the next day.

While the Duke players were dining Friday night, and Laettner was pointing out the difference in the quality of the buffalo wings, Bob Fitzgibbons scored a record 54 points for the Nichols School. The old mark had been 46 points—held, of course, by the weekend visitor.

When the team was ready to leave for the game on Saturday, the bus had not arrived. Trainer Max Crowder was furious. When the coaches and players came outside to make the short trip to The Aud, they discovered Max, his face beet red, and the elderly female driver engaged in a war of words.

Krzyzewski attempted to break it up. "We need to go to the game," he repeated several times. "Let's just go." Eventually, everybody was aboard, and the still-grumbling driver took off—the wrong way up a one-way street.

The Aud was the home of the NHL Sabres, a hockey arena. Canisius did not normally play games there. While the Griffins were in one hockey locker room at the end of the building, designed so the skaters could enter the ice from behind the goal, the Duke dressing room was in the middle of the concourse.

To get to the floor, the players had to walk half the length of the building along a public mezzanine. Their path to the floor was lined on either side with young autograph seekers. The target of their affection was Laettner, but any Duke player would do.

The game itself was routine. What was astonishing was what came after.

The crowd of 16,279 was almost nonpartisan, more interested in Laettner than any of the specifics of the 96–60 Duke victory, achieved with 66.7 percent shooting. The audience saw the unselfish Laettner taking only an occasional shot, scoring just one basket in the first 19 minutes. There was no need for him to score as Duke jumped to early leads of 13–2 and 32–12. Laettner finished with 19 points, 6 assists, 5 rebounds, and 3 blocked shots as some forty relatives watched with pleasure.

The basketball part of the evening belonged to the Hills. Thomas made 9 of 10 shots and scored a career-high 26 points; Grant, playing extensively at point guard when Hurley got three early fouls, had 16 points and 10 rebounds and just missed a triple double with a career-high 9 assists. "We wanted to show the people of Buffalo how Duke plays basketball," he said.

The rest of the night belonged to Laettner. When the team returned to its dressing area, security police were patrolling two portable walls placed along the mezzanine, designed to keep the fans at bay. Wave after wave of youngsters shoved at the walls, slowly pushing them in. They were seeking autographs from everybody, anybody, but mostly from Laettner.

Duke promotions director Mike Sobb did his best. He handed out schedules, then team pictures. That pacified the crowd until one kid yelled, "These aren't even auto-graphed."

"We've got to take Christian up to the floor," said his mother, Bonnie Laettner.

"Bonnie, we can't do that. If we do, we'll never get him out of here," answered Sobb.

With help from the police, the team left The Aud down a back stairway located near the dressing room. As they neared the main floor, there was nobody there. Suddenly, as if by magic, fifty or so screaming kids appeared.

The players left through large doors in the middle of the building. They were approximately two hundred feet from the waiting bus, and they could see thirty or so people waiting for them. Laettner stopped to chat, sign an autograph or two, and was suddenly engulfed by a much larger crowd. Several hundred people had been standing by the other side of the bus.

The police had to hold the crowd back. Parks, who sat out the game because of his ankle injury, became the substitute autographer while the team inched its way to the bus. The chant grew louder and louder: "Christian, Christian, Christian."

When the team arrived back at its hotel, there was another large gathering. As Laettner got off the bus, a young girl, perhaps thirteen, put her hands to her face and began shrieking, "Oh, my God, there he is!"

Laettner's hero Prince would not have created a greater stir. "Damnedest thing I've ever seen," Sobb said. This was a taste of the kind of crowd reaction that would follow the Blue Devils throughout the year.

That night, the Duke team attended a reception at Nichols. The hosts were expecting 200–250 people. More than 350 showed up. Laettner spent most of the night mingling with the crowd, thanking them for their support.

A much smaller group, including Crowder, Sobb, orthopedic resident Tee Moorman, Jr., and radiomen Bob Harris and Mike Waters, had a quiet dinner.

"Big game Saturday at Michigan, Max, number nine

hundred," Sobb said. Canisius had been the 899th straight contest on the bench for Crowder.

Max was feeling poorly. "Yeah, if I make it," he said.

Crowder didn't make it to Michigan, missing his first game ever in almost thirty years as a trainer. He had been diagnosed with cancer. He had briefly worked in construction as a youth and got some asbestos in one lung. The condition flared up in the early eighties, but not previously during the season. Now he would have to have the lung removed at Duke Hospital.

Crowder's importance couldn't be measured by numbers, although those were astonishing. He had been with the team to nine Final Fours and witnessed more than six hundred victories.

He had become a legend in the most unusual way—by never, ever, changing. The youngest of ten children, Crowder graduated third in his high school class in Cherryville, North Carolina, but the family didn't have enough money for him to go to college. So he worked for several years, then entered the Army in 1954 and served three years, saving enough money to attend college after he was discharged. He went to Gardner-Webb Junior College in 1958, transferring to Duke in 1960.

Crowder's room at Duke was 302 Card, at the top of a dark flight of stairs in the old gym that adjoined Cameron. The room became part of the Crowder mystique. Virtually nobody was ever permitted to visit. Nothing mysterious, Max insisted; there was just one room and a bath and no place for visitors.

A lifelong bachelor, Crowder left that room after twenty-eight years to move into a two-room apartment at 202 Card, one floor below. Max was never more than a couple of hundred yards from work.

He became the cotrainer after his graduation and was elevated to head basketball trainer upon the death of Bob Chambers. In 1978, he became the head athletics trainer, from which he retired in 1988, staying on only to handle his beloved basketball team.

Jokester, surrogate father, resident nutritionist, Crowder didn't have the academic credentials associated with his position. But that meant nothing to the people connected with the basketball program.

In the early seventies, when Carl James was the athletic director at Duke, Crowder was considered to be in a vulnerable position.

"They were ready to fire him," said Bucky Waters, then the basketball coach and now a vice president/fund-raiser for Duke Hospital. "The logic was that Max wasn't really trained as a trainer. The feeling was there were others more qualified, those who had their master's in physical therapy. It was a tough financial time, and if cuts were to be made, Max would be the one to go.

"I recall standing up at a meeting and stating that I didn't want to hear about educational values. I said I didn't need a trainer who could do a frontal lobotomy because we had one of the great medical centers in the world a par five away from Cameron. I said that Max was going to be my trainer or they could find a new basketball coach."

Crowder inspired that kind of loyalty from all his bosses. That included five basketball coaches.

What remained of his hair was red. He had a bushy mustache and often wore a cowboy hat. He was the brunt of more players' jokes than anybody could imagine, but he gave as much as he took.

As to the less than luxurious accommodations in Card, Crowder said in 1988, "I'm not sure why I've stayed up there. A number of times, I've considered having a place in Durham, but for some reason, I never did. I guess it just wasn't always convenient."

Quin Snyder, who played on three of Duke's Final Four teams, said, "Max is like a base. It's kind of a constant in your life. Coaches have changed, players have changed, uniforms have changed, but Max is always there."

Crowder was around so long that he served as trainer

to Jay Buckley in the early sixties and to his son, Clay, nearly thirty years later. "When you come back, you look for Max," Jay Buckley said.

Crowder handled the travel plans for the team. He chose the hotels where the team stayed; a good restaurant was the primary criterion. Max loved to eat, but it was vital that his boys have the best food.

When Crowder was unhappy, which was often during games, his face got as red as his hair. He was the resident bench jockey. "I just loved to watch him rip the referees," Snyder said.

When Duke wanted to endow a scholarship in Crowder's name, 145 former athletes raised more than $125,000 in a hurry. On October 10, 1988, Cherryville held Max Crowder Day. He was given the key to the city of five thousand.

There was no way to know it on this night in Buffalo, but Max had spent his last game on the bench. On May 28, six days after his sixty-second birthday and a month after his induction into the Duke Hall of Fame, Max Crowder died. Things on the sidelines wouldn't be quite the same without him because there was nobody at Duke who could remember when he wasn't there.

The first segment of the season would end with the Michigan game. If the games themselves hadn't been testing so far, the feeling among the staff was that the sixteen-day break would be welcomed by everybody. But first there was Michigan to deal with.

The team arrived at the airport in Ann Arbor, and Gaudet decided it was time for a lesson in human behavior. On the surface, Gaudet was the least likely of the staff to be a practical joker. The elder statesman at forty-nine, he had coached five years with Krzyzewski at Army and succeeded him when Mike moved to Duke. After two seasons at West Point, Gaudet coached a year in Kuwait before Coach K called again in 1983. The tag of "part-time coach" was merely a measure of NCAA interpretations. Only two assistants could recruit, Brey and Amaker; the third assistant was considered a part-timer, but nothing could have been further from the truth.

Gaudet handled much of the video work, did all the advance scouting, and drew up game plans. He also ran the summer camp for Krzyzewski. Still, compared to the youthful Brey, Amaker, and Bilas, Gaudet was the gruff elder statesman. "Wrong," said Grant Hill. "Coach G is a real joker."

As the team awaited the arrival of its luggage, Gaudet called an impromptu meeting. He tossed a one-dollar bill onto the rotating conveyor belt and told the players to watch what happened. As the George Washington made its methodical way around, an elderly lady scooped it up, held it in her hand, and looked around. Seeming somewhat embarrassed, she dropped the bill back on the moving beltline.

The dollar disappeared behind the back wall, reappeared on the other side, and was promptly picked up by a male passenger, who stuffed it hurriedly in his pocket. The amused players broke into laughter. They thought so much of Gaudet's lesson in amateur psychology that it was tried several times later on, always with a different result.

On one occasion, Grant Hill put a dollar on the belt. When it went behind the wall, the players were betting an airline employee would grab it. Instead, it came back on the other side, placed alone in one of the large crates used to transport luggage.

Michigan would be no laughing matter the next day, however. In 1990, North Carolina's recruiting class had been anointed by the pundits as the greatest of all time. Just twelve months later, the same experts were saying the Michigan freshmen were even better.

While only Eric Montross started regularly for UNC as a freshman, four of the five Michigan freshmen would open against Duke. All five of them had started two nights

1

2

With 12.7 seconds to go in the game, this Christian Laettner free throw broke a 77–77 tie and gave Duke its stunning win over UNLV in the '91 NCAAs.

Brian Davis exults as he takes the ball to the basket in the final against Kansas.

A true sign of community support greeted the Krzyzewskis on their return from Indianapolis.

The Krzyzewski family: Lindy, Jamie, and Debbie in front; Mike and Mickie in back.

The 1992 Blue Devils: front row, left to right: manager Mark Williams, Marty Clark, Bobby Hurley, Brian Davis, Christian Laettner, Thomas Hill, Kenny Blakeney, manager Suzanne Gilbert; back row: Mike Krzyzewski, Mike Brey, Max Crowder, Antonio Lang, Erik Meek, Cherokee Parks, Grant Hill, Christian Ast, Jay Bilas, Tommy Amaker, Pete Gaudet.

Cherokee Parks overcame freshman difficulties to play some productive minutes in the '92 NCAAs.

The Hills are alive on defense as Thomas (12) and Grant (33) combine efforts against James Terrell of UNC-Charlotte.

Co-captains and best friends Laettner and Davis start to celebrate their ACC tournament championship.

9

Krzyzewski and his starters (Laettner, Grant Hill, Hurley, Davis, and Thomas Hill) await the start of a game at Cameron.

Tough defense by Davis and Lang contributed to a long dry stretch for the Campbell Camels in the NCAAs.

Bobby Hurley plays
tough defense
against Jon Barry of
Georgia Tech.

11

Grant Hill slams one
home against Florida
State at Cameron.

12

An ecstatic Laettner and Grant Hill wound up at the bottom of a pile of bodies after Laettner took Hill's pass and hit the shot that beat Kentucky.

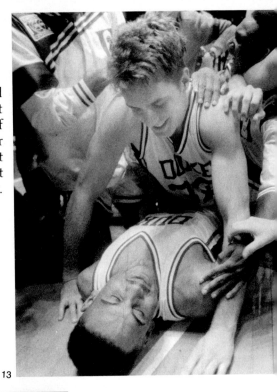

13

Bobby Hurley's face-off with brother Danny in the Seton Hall game left him in what he described as a "no-win situation."

14

Davis is helped to his feet after sustaining an ankle injury against Indiana.

15

Krzyzewski gives instructions to Marty Clark, who played a critical role in the victory over the Hoosiers.

16

17

Laettner and Chris
Webber battle for the
opening tip of the '92
NCAA finals.

Laettner and Thomas Hill
embrace in celebration of
the 71–51 win over
Michigan.

18

before against Eastern Michigan. The Fab Five was born. But against the Devils, guard Michael Talley started in place of Jimmy King.

Krzyzewski was aware of the danger of an upset. The best of the Michigan rookies, Chris Webber, had been recruited hard by Duke. The Blue Devils were one of the finalists, but the Detroit native elected to remain near home.

At 6-9 and 240 pounds, Webber was a scoring and rebounding machine. "If we had gotten him, we would have had the best college team of all time," Krzyzewski said earlier. "He's that good."

Even without Webber, Duke was good enough. But the Wolverines had additional weapons. Chief among them was an unusual point guard, 6-8 Jalen Rose, son of former NBA great Jimmy Walker. In some circles, Rose was considered to be the greatest tall point-guard prospect since another 6-8 guy played for neighboring Michigan State— Magic Johnson.

The other Wolverine freshmen—Juwan Howard, King, and Ray Jackson—had all been highly recruited players in high school. They weren't bashful, either. Words were flying fast and furious. Howard wore a Duke hat. "It's my psych thing," he said. Webber wanted to see how he matched up with Laettner. Michigan was No. 18 and unbeaten against the likes of Detroit Mercy, Cleveland State, and Chicago State.

More than just the lineup had changed at Michigan, as Mickie Krzyzewski discovered when she talked with coach Steve Fisher's wife, Angie, as the teams warmed up.

"Steve was so impressed with the atmosphere at Duke last year that we've changed things here," Angie Fisher said. "We've moved the student body down to the floor, just like you have them."

The minuscule Duke following was seated directly behind the bench, just like the visiting fans in Durham. Crisler Arena had been Cameronized.

The Michigan pep band, seated courtside, played

loudly and incessantly the famed fight song "Hail to the Victors." There was a definite feeling of electricity.

The crowd of 13,609 was in a rambunctious mood. When the band stopped playing, a drumbeat started and the students, in unison, mocked their opponents. In Cameron, to the drum accompaniment, the student body yelled, "Let's go Devils." At Michigan, the words were significantly altered to "Fuck the Devils." It didn't stop all afternoon.

In the early moments, the Wolverines showed their youth. They had ball-handling problems even in their easy victories; now they were having serious difficulty against Duke's man-to-man.

The score reached 37–20, and it was looking like another Duke runaway. "Then we got a little sloppy," Hurley said later. "We rushed shots, our defense faltered a little bit, and we let them back in the game."

The margin was down to 10 points at halftime, and when Michigan went on a 14–0 tear early in the second half, the home team was suddenly ahead, 55–54, and the decibel level at Crisler was at an all-time high.

Duke couldn't stop Webber throughout the game, or Rose once the Wolverines began their comeback. Webber finished with 27 points and 12 rebounds, while Rose scored 18 and handed out 6 assists.

Trash talk followed as easily as trash cheers, and later, Coach K acknowledged it. "They're young; they're going to say a few things. But we said a few things, too. That's stupid. I tell my team all the time, 'Talk to Duke. If you start talking to somebody else, your head's not in the right place.' "

Whether the yapping had anything to do with the action was debatable. That Webber did was obvious. With 1:40 left, Webber hit a three-pointer with Grant Hill in his face. That gave the underdog Wolverines a 73–68 lead, and the crowd was going bonkers, sensing a stunning upset.

Enter Hurley. Months before, against UNLV, the tough point guard made the biggest three-pointer in Duke history. It came with his team trailing late in the game by 5 points and preserved their hopes of victory.

The margin was the same this time, but it was even later on the clock. Just 12 seconds after Webber's three-pointer, Hurley came off a Laettner screen that freed him from Rose's long arms and swished his own trey. It was 73–71. "We needed to do something quick, to stop the crowd," Hurley said.

Webber made a foul shot; Hurley made two. Then Rose hit a pair at the line and it was 76–73, Michigan.

Webber had been superb. But he was still a freshman, and he made a rookie mistake. As Hurley was firing away on another three, Webber leaped and fouled him with 31 seconds left. Hurley bounced up off the floor. He withstood the pressure within the Crisler caldron and sank all 3 free throws. Within 57 seconds, he had scored 8 points and the game went into overtime.

Laettner, who scored 24 points, and Webber both fouled out in the extra period. But Hurley was still around. He made 2 free throws with 54 seconds left, then 2 more with 14.9 on the clock, and Duke had its victory, 88–85.

Hurley had been unbelievable. He played all 45 minutes, scored 26 points, and had 7 of Duke's meager total of 9 assists.

"I think our poise showed in the end," Coach K said. Duke made all 10 free throws in overtime, 31 of 36 for the game. Coach Fisher agreed. Not Webber, however. "The only difference is they got the breaks," he said. "If we play them again in the NCAAs, we'll win."

The first segment of the season had ended. There had been a major scare, but Krzyzewski was more than satisfied. He had hoped to develop the team further, mixing the bench with the starters, but a string of nagging injuries had made that impossible. They weren't anything serious, but Lang, Parks, Laettner, and Thomas Hill had all missed games. The team may have been ranked No. 1, but its progress report was essentially an incomplete.

Still, Coach K had seen enough flashes of greatness to allow himself to think, "Boy, we really have a shot at this again. Our kids hate to lose. Especially Hurley."

CHAPTER 5

WHILE THE PLAYERS WERE HOME over the Christmas holidays, the staff went to the movies. Regularly. Watching tape was Krzyzewski's favorite part of the job. He studied all the players in the program, looking to see what they could do and how they could fit together.

All that tape-watching gave the rest of the Krzyzewski family an idea about a Christmas gift for Dad. In the family room of the comfortable house in northern Durham, "Mole Man" watched game film for hours on end. The nickname resulted from Coach K's solitary video sessions in the wee hours of the night, at home and in motel rooms. So his present from his girls was a massage chair. "This gift is completely unlike anything we usually give him," Mickie said. "The girls and I have been running around saying, 'What's he going to think?' "

Dad thought it was just fine.

The team had no formal practices between the Michigan game on December 14 and their reassembly on the twenty-seventh. The players went through their final exams, then went home with instructions to stay in shape, but to stay out of pickup games. During the time off, Hurley got a chance to watch his younger brother Danny play for Seton Hall, and he saw some St. Anthony's games with his dad on the sidelines. Grant Hill worked out with his South Lakes high school team in Reston, Virginia. Brian Davis had a working vacation, poring over tapes to see why he wasn't getting many rebounds. "I saw I'm not going to the boards enough or being smart enough when I am going. I'm allowing myself to be boxed out, and not using my quickness."

Hurley and Thomas Hill agreed that the long break was a good refresher. "I think everyone should be more intense in looking forward to getting back and playing," Hurley said. "I know I am. I think that's how everybody will react."

"Our team needed that," Hill said. "Personally, I was getting tired. Not tired of playing ball, but I just hadn't had time to sit down and rest my body. This was needed."

During the holiday break, the staff decided there were two areas for major improvement: defensive rebounding and halfcourt offense. Krzyzewski was always looking for ways to get better; he did not share the philosophy of "If it ain't broke, don't fix it?"

"He's always looking to get better," said Mike Brey. "It doesn't matter that we're undefeated."

"It's people that make your system a success or failure, or just average," Coach K said. "If you can in some way instill a positive attitude and a spirit of cooperation and teamwork, some things can happen you don't even plan to happen. I think that's what's happened in our basketball program. We don't go around saying we're going to build a national championship team or a team that's going to the Final Four. You just have to go about the business of making your team as good as you possibly can."

Along those lines, the staff was anxious to get Parks back in action. The 6-11 freshman had been devastating when he had played, but his varsity career thus far consisted of 51 minutes. He had gotten hurt after just 9 minutes against St. John's and did not play against Michigan. Those had been the two quality opponents, so nobody was sure yet how he would fit in when the games got serious.

Parks rehabilitated himself during the holidays and pronounced the injury 90 percent cured before the December 30 game with William and Mary, coached by Chuck Swenson, a former Duke assistant and longtime Krzyzewski friend. Krzyzewski usually scheduled an easy home game for immediately after Christmas to allow the players to get the kinks out after the layoff.

The Indians didn't have a starter taller than 6-8. Duke opened with only one guy shorter than 6-7—Hurley. Coach K's unit that began the game had the double-post duo of Laettner and Parks, with Davis at forward, Hurley, and the 6-8 Grant Hill at guard. It may have been the tallest team in school history.

Laettner took advantage of the setup to go one-on-one down low against the smaller defenders. He scored 15 of Duke's first 20 points and had 21 by intermission. He finished with 25 in the 97–61 victory. Krzyzewski was seeking to establish a seven-man rotation. Hurley played the most minutes, 27; the others—Laettner, Parks, Davis, the Hills, and Lang—each got at least 21.

"Cherokee opened up a lot of things for Christian because of his size and skill level," Davis said. "He was out on the high post and Christian could go one-on-one. When he does that, he's going to score a lot of points."

Now the Blue Devils were anxious to open the ACC schedule. No opponent had been a more accurate barometer of the state of Duke basketball than Virginia. In Krzyzewski's first three seasons, while Ralph Sampson was playing for the Cavaliers, the Blue Devils were 0–7, and the games were not close, capped by a 109–66 thrashing in the ACC tournament in 1983. After that game, Duke freshmen Dawkins, Alarie, Henderson, and Bilas vowed never again to lose to Virginia. Not only did that group succeed, but Duke went on to defeat the Cavs sixteen consecutive times.

More often than not, with each team playing tough man-to-man defense, the games weren't pretty. Terry Holland's teams had trouble finding ways to beat Krzyzewski, but mostly because of problems on the offensive end.

When Holland resigned, he was replaced by Jeff Jones, a former player and assistant coach who became, a month before his thirtieth birthday, the youngest coach in ACC history. His first team got its biggest win when it thrashed Duke, 81–64, in the game that led to the unusual workout back at Cameron and Grant Hill's broken nose. The previous year, also in University Hall, the Cavaliers had snapped that lengthy losing streak.

Duke arrived in Charlottesville for its ACC opener averaging 99 points and leading the nation in field-goal percentage at 58.5. None of that would mean anything; Duke-UVa was just like it always was, a grasp-and-pull struggle, dominated by the defense.

Hurley in particular did not like UHall, the ACC's smallest arena, where the vapor lights somehow seemed to make both sides shoot bricks. The point guard had played poorly in his first two games there.

On this night, Hurley made his first shot. Then he missed 10 in a row, including 7 three-point tries. Duke, shooting a woeful 31 percent in the second half, found itself leading just 61–59, with the clock running down in the final minute. With 26 seconds left, and 2 left on the shot clock, Hurley took another three and swished it. Just like Michigan.

The Blue Devils held on to win, 68–62, although Laettner had been limited to 4 second-half points by Virginia's swarming defense.

Although Hurley made the big shot, Duke's key player was Grant Hill, playing only an hour and a half from his hometown. Hill's numbers were decent enough—16 points, 4 assists, 3 rebounds, and 2 steals. But Krzyzewski saw far more than that. "He stepped up and took big shots, he controlled the ball a lot, and he played defense. He just did everything. You could feel his presence on the court. It was one of the first times in his career that I felt he was our presence. He's been a good player for us, but tonight he was actually the guy holding us together. It was a very important game for Grant Hill."

One of the legitimate concerns the staff had about its team following the break was conditioning. Part of the problem at Virginia, according to Hurley, was "we're in shape, but we're not in basketball condition. The only way that can happen is to play games."

Presto! Three ACC games in six days: Florida State on Monday, an away game at Maryland on Wednesday, and back home for Georgia Tech on Saturday.

Florida State came to Cameron for its first visit as an ACC team, with the Blue Devils legitimately wary. In its first league road game ever, the Seminoles cruised into Carolina's Dean Dome, and even without suspended star Doug Edwards they creamed the Tar Heels. Afterward, FSU ace Sam Cassell delighted many Duke partisans by terming the audience "a wine-and-cheese crowd."

There was a chance something like that could happen at Cameron because the students were still on break. Although the game was a sellout, it wasn't on television, so there would be none of the visual antics from the Crazies that were created with the cameras in mind.

The Florida writers had not had an opportunity to hear the Krzyzewski philosophy before. Coach K appreciated that FSU's reputation was as a football school, and he drew an analogy to that sport.

"I love our sport, the fact that the true champion is decided without a public relations firm. In football, they don't give their teams an opportunity to grow. You have to win right from the start of the season. There are some football teams that finish the year at nine and two and

might have been better than the teams that went undefeated, but if you lose an early game, you might be out of
the national championship.

"That's not going to happen in college basketball. You
can learn from your early defeats. We had seven losses
last year, but we were the best team. We won. We beat
the so-called best team. I like the sports that do that."

Grant Hill made certain that FSU remained a football
school first. In the most sensational performance of his
still-young career, he scored a career-high 26 points,
grabbed 10 rebounds, and added 4 blocks and 5 steals as
Duke led by 18 points at halftime and won, 86–70.

In the first half, Hill smothered a jumper by football
quarterback/point guard Charlie Ward on the baseline,
grabbed the loose ball, fed it to Hurley, and ninety feet
away got a return pass for the most intimidating of his
slams.

Hurley grinned and shook his head. Hill could even
astound his teammates. "I always look for Grant on the
break because he's our best finisher," Bobby said. "He
does some amazing things. He's such a great basketball
player and such a great athlete. To see some of the things
he does is just incredible."

Hill credited the coaching staff. "The coaches noticed
they didn't do a good job getting back. They wanted us to
get it and run."

That was what fooled FSU coach Pat Kennedy. "I
didn't realize how fast they were. They flat outran our
kids down the floor. They run the wings and attack as well
as anybody."

The staff liked the use of the dunk, whenever possible,
because of the intimidation factor. And this team could
dunk better than previous Duke squads.

The Blue Devils were a huge squad. Three of the eleven
scholarship players were at least 6-10; three others were 6-
8. Everybody except Hurley was 6-4 or taller. They were
also athletic. Most of the Duke players could dunk with

pizazz. They liked it and the crowds loved it. The stuff could get the competitive juices flowing.

Against FSU, Hurley was 1 for 8, and now 3 for 20 in two league games, but he keyed the attack. "Thank God we were able to get out and run. That's what won the game for us."

The frightening thing for FSU, and the rest of the league, was how easily the Blue Devils won. Duke made one three-pointer the entire game and didn't make an outside shot of any kind in the second half. Yet the score was 66–41 with 8:21 left. Krzyzewski tried different lineup combinations and ordered defenses that they hadn't been practicing to test the team's adaptability and keep the score down. The rest of the way it was sloppy, not unlike St. John's, with too many turnovers. Still, Duke had won by 16 points despite no outside shooting and an inefficient halfcourt offense. It was an indication of how good the team could be; it had so many ways to win.

As for the Cameron Crazies, their number was relatively small and they weren't at their most creative. They did get in one zinger that even brought some amused smiles on the FSU bench. "You beat Carolina?" the Crazies yelled after another botched Seminole play.

But Brian Davis wasn't satisfied with his team. The co-captain had responded to his VCR homework over the holidays with 9 rebounds to go with his career-high 19 points. But he wasn't pleased with the attitude displayed by the entire squad.

"If we're going out lacking enthusiasm, we don't look like a good team. I wish we could be more excited. We're not having as much fun as we used to. We're not smiling, we're not laughing. We have to provide the fun for ourselves."

With a glance at Krzyzewski, Davis said, "He can't coach and be our enthusiasm. He can't yell and scream to get us excited. It's something we have to do among ourselves. We need to talk about it. We need to do it in practice and not worry so much about making mistakes. We need to go out and just get excited about playing.

"We are very good. We know that. But not all twelve guys are getting excited. I think there are seven or eight having fun. It can take just one or two to spoil it for the rest of the guys."

With that in mind, and with a trip back to his Maryland home coming next, Davis talked to his teammates before practice for the game with the Terps at College Park.

Then, as the team prepared to warm up at Cole Field House, he mentioned it again: "Let's play like Duke. Let's have a good time out there. That means everybody." Davis could lead in many ways, and one of his best was by direct communication. He was a natural spokesman.

One guy Davis didn't have to worry about was Grant Hill. Grant always played hard, and he certainly would before the home folks. He was a major weapon. Maryland was not far from Grant's home in Reston, Virginia, and was close to where his father, football Hall of Famer Calvin Hill, worked as a vice president for the Baltimore Orioles.

Although Calvin was now affiliated with baseball, his ties were still to football. Grant Hill remembered well a recruiting trip to Michigan he was supposed to take in the fall of 1989. The Wolverines were No. 2 in football, and they had a home game with Notre Dame.

It was an exciting prospect, watching two of the nation's most legendary teams, playing before 106,000. One of the Hills was fired up at the prospect of meeting Bo Schembechler—unfortunately, it was Calvin.

"I came back from my recruiting trip to Duke, and I just knew it was where I wanted to go," said Grant, now one of the nation's most versatile basketball talents. "I told my dad that I didn't want to make the trip to Michigan because I had decided to go to Duke, and I just didn't think it was right. He was so upset he didn't speak to me for a week. He really wanted to see that football game."

Calvin Hill, now most often referred to as Grant's father, liked to remind his gifted son, "Don't get too cocky because you only have half the genes."

Janet, his Wellesley-grad mother, was, said her only child, "notoriously uncoordinated. She's nonathletic."

But Grant inherited sufficient talents from his father, the Yale graduate who had a distinguished career with the Dallas Cowboys, Washington Redskins, and Cleveland Browns.

Nobody was quite sure how Grant Hill wound up at Duke after a high school career at South Lakes in Reston, an affluent Washington suburb. "I was always a [North] Carolina fan," he said. "As far back as I can remember, I rooted for Carolina. When they won the national championship in 1982, that's when I discovered basketball." Hill was nine at the time.

Hill's attire at South Lakes was remarkable in its consistency. "Carolina hat, T-shirt, shorts, anything," he said. "They were the dominant team then. I saw Carolina and Georgetown a lot [on TV], and every person in D.C. who was black was a Georgetown fan. But when I grew up and it was time for college, I didn't want to go to Georgetown."

As it developed, Hill didn't want to go to Carolina, either. "The summer before my senior year, Brian Reese and I talked about going to North Carolina together." Reese went to UNC, but remained a friend.

Hill had no explanation for why he chose Duke. "It's not like I had a great time on my visit or anything. It was just that when I got on campus, it fit. Maybe it was a little maturing. But everything I wanted—type of school, campus, coaching staff, style of basketball, opportunity to play —was there. I went back home and I knew I wanted to go to Duke. I think it shocked my parents, my teammates, my friends. To tell you the truth, I think I shocked Duke."

Hill had been impressed by the Duke coaches during the recruiting process. "Coach K was very honest. And they didn't bother me. Other schools were calling all the time, day and night. Duke just checked in about once a week."

It didn't hurt that one Duke assistant, Amaker, was also from northern Virginia, and the other recruiter, Brey, had a background from Maryland private school power-house DeMatha. "I saw how I would fit in at Duke," Hill said. "The pros for Duke just outweighed North Caro-lina's."

Growing up with a famous father was not without its burdens. Especially when you were The One. "Not only am I an only child," Hill said, "but I don't have any cous-ins or aunts or uncles, either."

What he did have was PGA—post-game analysis, deliv-ered throughout his adolescent years by his father. "Sometimes it was for fifteen minutes, sometimes it was an hour," Grant said. "We discussed what Grant did wrong. I never listened and he knew I didn't listen. I'm happy to say PGA has ended."

Perhaps, Grant decided, Calvin was trying to make up for the early years, when the father was playing out his National Football League career in Cleveland. "Even after he retired, he worked for the Browns. Mom and I stayed in D.C. It was hard on him. Mom took me to my games. She was the Little League parent."

Perhaps it was because they played different sports that the father and son got along so marvelously. "I know there are a lot of Little League fathers who live out their sports goals through their sons. But Dad wasn't like that, maybe because he was so successful.

"He never pushed me into sports. He let me find my own way. He encouraged me to do other things, like music. I played various instruments when I was growing up. Basketball was my own decision. The fact that I'm in a different sport has eliminated the comparisons, and maybe that's made it easier."

Calvin Hill liked to tell how when he was still playing, an NFL superstar, he took his son to various functions.

Or when they'd go out to eat, people in the restaurant would stare and say, "That's Calvin Hill." But last year Calvin was in a checkout line at a grocery store when he noticed some kids staring. "That's Grant Hill's dad," they said.

"Now, he's just a proud parent," Grant said. "It's weird. It must do wonders for his ego. The roles are now reversed. But I think he likes to be called Calvin Hill [instead of Grant's dad]."

Calvin was in Cameron for most home games, a baseball cap on his head, seated just a couple of rows behind the Duke bench. "He's got the jock mentality," Grant said. "Basketball to him is now a year-round game. He's probably watching tapes, over and over. He'll call me in and say, 'You know, in the Clemson game, you really defensed your man well.'"

Hill had the pro scouts eagerly anticipating his arrival in their ranks, which won't happen until 1994. For that, Janet Hill deserves some of the credit.

"People talk about turning pro [early]," Grant said. "It never enters my mind. I'll be here four years. When I was a kid, playing on three or four teams, sometimes I'd feel tired and tell my mother I didn't want to play. She'd always remind me, 'Son, you made a commitment. You told them you were going to play.' So I would. Duke has made a commitment to me."

The thought that Hill would play four years couldn't be a comforting one for opponents. He played point guard in high school; he might be a natural NBA wing man. Lithe and swift, Hill can make penetrating so simple, so natural, that he makes the game look far easier than it should be.

Two nights after dispatching FSU with an inside attack, the Blue Devils showed another weapon by romping at Maryland, 83–66, on 8-for-12 shooting from three-point range. And with Brian Davis urging them on, everybody played with enthusiasm.

While opposing coaches were wondering if there was

any way to stop this team, the fans were just eager to mix with the Duke players. Maryland had a sellout of 14,500 in Cole Field House, hoping for the upset. But afterward, it became apparent that they weren't all cheering for the home team.

There is a large, wide runway in Cole at one end of the building. The Maryland locker room was on one side, the visitor's quarters on the other. Both teams entered and left the building the same way.

After the game, Davis dressed and went to look for the numerous family members and friends who were there. He stuck his head out the door. "Brian, there's no way, man," yelled one of the managers.

"I couldn't get to my family," Davis said. "It was incredible. I've never seen a mob like that, screaming and yelling and just trying to get a piece of you."

Hundreds of fans—all trying to get an autograph or souvenir from a Duke player—completely blocked the exit ramp. Finally, after a lengthy wait, it was obvious that the milling crowd was not going to dissipate. Davis, Laettner, Hurley, and Thomas Hill, who had led the team with 25 points and 8 rebounds, climbed out a back window of Cole and scampered for the security of the team bus.

It must have been the first time an opponent exited any ACC gym in such a manner. It really didn't help that much; a large crowd had found the bus and was waiting for the players.

Brian Davis, who grew up a Terp fan, marveled, "I've been to maybe fifty games at Cole, a lot of them when Len Bias was here. I've never seen anything like what happened."

Standing, watching this outpouring of adoration from Duke groupies of all ages, were the members of the Maryland basketball team. It was bad enough that Duke had shot less than 50 percent, missed 15 of 32 free throws, had Hurley and Davis foul out, and still won by 17 on the road. Now they could see for themselves which team was the fans' favorite.

Mickie Krzyzewski observed the stunning mob scene and the dejected Maryland players. "God, no wonder they hate us," she said.

Although the team's popularity was growing everywhere with the fans, it was not without its critics in the media. It was the beginning of an intriguing contrast: while more and more fans rushed to join the Duke bandwagon, some members of the press corps were searching for flaws.

Charles Pierce, longtime writer for the *Boston Herald* and later the now-defunct *National,* scalded the Blue Devils in *Basketball Times.* Pierce's lengthy column took dead aim on a subject that was sensitive to everybody connected with the Duke program—image. He blasted the program's supposed sanctimoniousness.

"You can't like this team simply for the way it plays. You have to like this team because it makes you feel so good about yourself—so righteous, so fundamentally superior, and so clean that you squeak, a ghastly form of moral fascism that allows no one else to establish standards independently of your own because your privileges allow you to remain safe from your own failings."

Pierce went on to say, "Give me the bad guys," noting that "Larry Johnson has more personality in his little finger than the five Duke starters."

While it was the most vicious attack on the Duke program delivered all year, it was far from the only one. Anytime something happened, whether it was wrong or merely perceived to be wrong, some writers attacked with the enthusiasm of feasting piranhas.

Charlotte columnist Tom Sorenson scalded Duke for a supposed change in attitude. "The Blue Devils can wear even on fans who don't care about underdogs. And they have," he wrote.

"They were refreshing when they first emerged as a good team in the mid-1980s. Players were accessible and candid, and not once did they answer reporters' questions as if they were reading from a script. Duke was what happened when academics and athletics came together.

"The Blue Devils won with players who went to class—but not in shiny new booster-provided cars. Players did not sell their tickets or their basketball shoes, and they won anyway. Success, however, can breed arrogance. At Duke, there was a mantra: We are Duke. We do it the Duke way. You are not Duke. You do it wrong.

"What the Blue Devils used to do with a snicker, they now do with a sneer."

Sports Illustrated's Curry Kirkpatrick wrote that there were concerns about Duke's "big-britchedness." One thing was consistent about virtually all of the criticism—it came from people who rarely, if ever, covered the team.

Coach K was stung by the sniping, not because he wasn't thick-skinned and aware that people were looking for things to go wrong, but because Duke worked so hard at not presenting an elitist face, at not coming off as holier-than-thou.

Many in the media saw them that way anyway. When *USA Today* referred to Duke as "the perfect program," coaches, players, and athletic-department personnel cringed.

Laettner was aware of what some people thought. "A lot of our players don't have a lot of money, not like Duke kids do. But people tend to look at us that way. They look at us like we're yuppies, like we're Duke's yuppie basketball team. That's not us. Not even close. We have our own identity. But it's so hard breaking away from the Duke identity."

Krzyzewski constantly pointed out that while Duke ran its program one way, he never believed that that was the only way. It just worked for him at his school. "We're just one program. We've been pretty good, but we're not changing the world. We don't have our noses stuck in the air. My nose is too big to stick in the air, anyway.

"People say we should be the role model for college athletics and I don't believe that. If I'm at a state university, how can I model myself after Duke? We have a different mission than they do. We don't accept all the kids a state university does. Everybody's looking for one way to get it done. There isn't one way. Thank God there isn't. We just want to play ball and have fun. We don't want to be IBM."

None of the Duke players enjoyed the perception that somehow they were better than anybody else—off the court. "With a lot of my friends, we're perceived as almost perfect," Hurley said. "That's how they see us. That's not true. Everything isn't rosy all the time. Nobody on this team is perfect."

Tony Lang recalled the Final Four. "We were the good guys and UNLV was the bad guys. That was the stereotype, and I hated it. I still hate it. We liked UNLV. Their players were good guys. But it's an image thing. Duke has this great image, and some of it is racial. The stars of the team have tended to be white guys like Ferry and Laettner."

Laettner did not think race was that much of a factor in Duke's national popularity: "Everyone thinks it's color. I don't think that's it at all. I think it's how you look and sound. We're on TV so much. People hear us. We don't say 'you know' or 'uh' all the time. Our guys can talk. You hear people who sound reasonably intelligent, and you don't see the color of the person. I think people like us because we can conjugate.

"We're no more genius than anyone. But our guys can speak well. That's the difference. But if people think we believe we're better than anyone else, that's pathetic."

There was validity to Laettner's view. In his scathing criticism of Duke, Pierce recalled the press conference the day before the 1986 NCAA finals, when the articulate Duke players contrasted with the team from Louisville. Pierce wrote that the media's fawning over the Duke players was blatant racism. What he ignored was that three of the five players on the dais for Duke that day were black.

Brian Davis had seen the image problem for four years.

"This is all envy. People think we have too much. Good-looking, good students, good players. That bothers them. We have faults. Everybody does. Some people are happy when they discover ours."

Laettner, who usually enjoyed all the attention he received, understood the criticism. "People just don't think it's fair. They think God is being too nice to us. We shouldn't be perceived as perfect, not in any way. We're not. But we're good. That's the way we should be thought of. We're good people. We have a good team. But we're certainly not perfect, and we don't hide from anybody. Coach makes certain of that. There's a real world out there. He wants us to be a part of it. I think that's good."

If the Blue Devils had any concerns about the crowd at Maryland, they usually had no worries at home. But for the week's final game against Georgia Tech, there was the reality that school was still not in session. Krzyzewski didn't know what the atmosphere would be like against the Jackets, who were 12-2.

He needn't have worried. The students came back a day early, just so they could provide their usual raucous support. Coach K was pleased. "They're our sixth man. I was happy to see them, although I know they just came back so that they could get to class on time Monday."

Crazies saw a team in cruise control. The previous year, Tech had been the unfortunate visitor after Duke's loss at Virginia. Krzyzewski's wrath had gotten his team's attention, and Duke had stung the Jackets by 41. This time, it wasn't quite as bad, but the margin reached 27 points after a 5-minute flurry produced a 23–4 run.

Basketball could be so simple when it was played with precision and joy. For the Blue Devils, this was a pure joyride. One great performance was followed by another. In this case, Hurley took advantage of early foul trouble by Tech's 7-1 Matt Geiger to operate on the Jackets inside. Time after time, he passed the ball to Laettner, who scored 14 consecutive points for the Devils.

Tech had the ACC's most massive front line with

Geiger, 6-11 Malcolm Mackey, and 6-8 James Forrest. But with Geiger benched, the Jackets couldn't guard Laettner. He finished with 33 points and 11 rebounds, the latter a pleasing statistic to his coach. Duke had improved on one of its perceived weaknesses, outboarding Tech, 41–28.

Laettner wasn't the whole show for Duke. Hurley finished with 17 points and 12 assists, making all three of his three-pointers. The biggest one came just before the half; with Duke ahead only 45–41, Laettner spotted Hurley right before the buzzer, and Bobby nailed it from the baseline.

Hurley made his living passing the ball, so he appreciated being the recipient. "Christian has a really good feeling for how much time is left," he said. "He never panics. I just got open and he waited to get me the ball. All I did was shoot it."

The game was such a clinic that the losers refused to be dismayed. "I think they're a lot better than last year," said Tech's Jon Barry, who scored 28 points in the losing effort. "They just play so smart as a team, it really wouldn't matter who's out there."

Krzyzewski and Tech coach Bobby Cremins were the best of friends. "Bobby's no phony," Coach K said. "What you see is what you get. He's really a good guy."

The good guy was in awe of the destruction that Duke had wreaked on his squad. "I wish I could blame my team a little bit. But I really believe that not many people are going to come in here and play them close. It's pretty obvious that Duke is a great basketball team. They are a delight to watch. They are really hard to play against. They are so aggressive and so well coached. They've got the whole package."

Clearly, it had been the best week of the still-young season. Duke's winning margins didn't tell the true story of any of the games because against three ACC teams, the Blue Devils had led by at least 23 points late in every contest.

Krzyzewski was in a unique position. It was still early January; second semester hadn't even begun. Yet his team was just blowing opponents away. He was like a rodeo rider, trying to rein in a wild stallion. "I'm having to put the brakes on," he admitted. "I've never had to do that before."

There was good reason to put on the brakes. There would be tough games to come against these three, two of them on the road. Duke was hot, healthy, and playing at home. Krzyzewski understood there was no need to embarrass anybody.

If there was any trouble in paradise, it was that the starters were doing almost all the scoring. Every regular had at least a dozen points, but only 8 of the 97 against Georgia Tech were scored by the reserves. Considering what the team would face in February and later in the NCAAs, that could be a problem.

The most disturbing aspect was the play of Parks. The experiment with the twin towers had lasted one game. Parks played just 11 minutes at Virginia and had one flat-footed rebound. Thomas Hill, who played almost the entire second half at Charlottesville, returned to the starting lineup.

Parks entered the FSU game after Erik Meek. That was a first. He played 7 minutes against the Seminoles, 9 at Maryland, and 13 against Georgia Tech, almost all of it at the finish when the outcome was no longer in question.

Parks was not the same player who had gotten off to such a rousing start in November and December. He wasn't jumping the way he did earlier. Of more immediate concern to the staff was his frame of mind. He was having problems with Laettner and had retreated into a shell. Unless there was an immediate turnaround, he wouldn't be of much help.

Parks was a direct contrast to the intense, combative Laettner, who utilized his internal drives to make himself a great player. Cherokee was a stereotypical laid-back Californian. An ideal day at home, he said, was to "get up about one, go down to the beach and mess around until about five, go home, shower, and go out for the night."

When Parks got into physical difficulty in December, it also played on his mind. "I had a lot of sprains before," he said, "but this was different. This was in my Achilles tendon. I came back and I wasn't in shape. I couldn't jump. They kept getting on me about not rebounding, and I didn't handle it. It became a mental thing."

In practice every day, Parks worked under the tutelage of Gaudet and Bilas, also a California kid. "At first, Cherokee was killing everybody," Bilas said. "He was great. Then he came back after the injury, and now it seems he's thinking about everything instead of just playing."

Laettner's plan for getting Parks out of his slump was to beat on him harder every day. He would never go individually against the other big freshman, Meek; Erik was a little shorter, but heavier and far more physical than Parks. After every game, he headed for the weight room while the other players were conducting their media interviews.

Meek had not fully recovered from his injuries. He had a lot of scar tissue around his calf that kept him from doing any quick jumping. He had little lateral movement. What he did have was a big body and a fighting spirit. When Laettner whacked on him in drills, he hit back. It wasn't dirty; Meek simply enjoyed the physical part of the game. He became known as Baby Huey, and if Laettner tried to intimidate him, he always retaliated. His attitude was, "If you want to play rough, let's do it. I'm real good at that." Laettner soon left him alone.

Laettner figured it was his job to get Parks shaped up. That meant doing it Christian's way. "I spent a lot of time with Cherokee, trying to get him better," Laettner said. "I pushed him physically, but it was all on the court. I've treated him very gentle in a verbal sense. Maybe that was wrong."

That was, of course, Laettner's viewpoint. By now, Parks had become a typically confused freshman, uncertain of his status, unaccustomed to the demands of a big-time college program. "Cherokee has a confidence problem right now," Krzyzewski said.

Once when the players were on their way to a training meal, Parks asked Grant Hill what it had been like for him as a freshman. "I kind of understood what Cherokee was going through. I just told him, 'Try to kill Christian. Try to beat him every time you play him, and don't worry about what he says,' " Hill said.

But that wasn't easy for Parks. He hadn't been prepared for how intense the college game would be. "It's been really hard. I wasn't expecting to go through so much basketball. I didn't know we'd have all the meetings and the film and the talks and the lectures. Eating with the team was a lot more than I expected."

Especially when Laettner would say to him, "Cherokee, did you see me dunk on you today?"

In Laettner's view, he was doing all he could to enhance Parks's progress. "I talk to him," he said, stressing that he played that role from the beginning. When Laettner was a rookie and Danny Ferry a senior, "Danny didn't really talk to anyone except Quin [classmate Snyder, the point guard]. Later, in January and February, Danny talked to me. I tried to talk from the beginning.

"If I didn't think Cherokee was going to be a good player, or a great player, then I wouldn't pay as much attention to him as I do. I know how good he can be. I've seen it. So when he doesn't live up to expectations, then I will say something to him."

Hurley understood Parks's situation. "Christian is very confident, very cocky. The type of personality Cherokee is, I can see it affecting him. It definitely affected me my freshman year. But you can't let it affect you. Laettner has a lot of good things to say, but some things he says, you just don't listen to him. Cherokee has to learn that."

Parks's confidence was low, and Laettner wasn't about to change. The coaches could see it. "Laettner will stay after practice and work," Brey said. "Here he is, a player-of-the-year candidate, and he's doing the extra stuff to get better. Cherokee works hard, but he goes in when practice ends. If you know Christian, you know he's thinking Cherokee needs the extra work."

One day at practice, Parks became so frustrated that he walked off the court and sulked in the locker room for 20 minutes before returning to the court. "I didn't want to be around him at all," Parks said of Laettner. "He always gets on you. He pisses me off a lot. I don't know if he's doing it to make me play better, but he's always coming at me with all the negativity."

Krzyzewski understood what Laettner was doing. "That's the way Christian would want somebody to talk to him. But Cherokee's not the same guy. I've told him, 'You think anybody wants you to do poorly? They're trying to help you. You've got to grow up and be tougher. Don't take those things personally. These guys have been through a lot. They realize that for us to be good, everybody's got to be good.' "

But for the moment, Laettner's psychology wasn't working with Parks. "I'm not disappointed in Cherokee," Krzyzewski said. "I'm disappointed for him."

Next up for the team was N.C. State, in Cameron, where, to the amusement of the Crazies, the Blue Devils shot lights out—literally. With 2:19 left in the first half, a bank of lights went out. Because there was still sufficient light to play, the teams finished out the period.

"We forgot to pay our light bill," Krzyzewski said after the 110–75 massacre ended. "It was like playing a little late at night on the blacktop."

The lights returned for the second half, and Duke turned up the heat with its most devastating 20-minute session of the season. The result was the widest margin for the Devils in the ancient series in twenty-five years, and it left State coach Les Robinson somewhat in awe. "Frankly, it was just a case of a real good basketball team taking advantage of a not-so-good basketball team. They did it methodically and gradually."

That was a message Mike Brey had been repeating throughout practices: "You can create a blowout gradually. You don't have to do it in spurts. You get a lead and you just add to it."

The problem State had was deciding whom to guard, and how to do it. Double-team Laettner down low? Fine. Hurley hit 4 three-pointers and Thomas Hill made 3. For the game, against a team that specialized in three-point shooting, Duke was 10 for 15.

Defend the perimeter? Laettner, given one-on-one coverage, scored 17 points in the first 13 minutes of the second half, during which Duke shot almost 70 percent.

Worst of all, what happened after turnovers? "In one stretch, they had two or three dunks," said State guard Curtis Marshall. "It's just incredible how Grant and Thomas run. You think you've gotten back, you turn around, and there goes the ball over your head for another dunk."

As good as Duke was against State, it was even better three days later against North Carolina-Charlotte. The 49ers were coached by Jeff Mullins, a former Duke all-America and Hall of Famer who had played in the school's first Final Four in 1963. Mullins brought an 11-1 team to Cameron.

UNCC played well. The 49ers shot better than 50 percent, and their long-distance accuracy was astonishing. Henry Williams, who played internationally under Krzyzewski, and James Terrell bombed away all day. They combined for 45 points, making 9 three-pointers. For the game, Charlotte made 11 of 18 behind the stripe.

It made absolutely no difference. Duke won, 104–82. The Blue Devils shot 60.9 percent. They had 7 steals. They had a season-low 7 turnovers, despite running the fast break the entire game. Five players, led by Laettner with 24 points, scored in double figures. Thomas Hill, becoming more of a force in every game, made 10 of 12 shots and had 23. Hurley scored just 8, but had 11 assists. Everything worked.

The Crazies contented themselves with yelling, "Overrated, overrated," at the eighteenth-ranked 49ers, but it wasn't that UNCC didn't play well. It was just that Duke was overpowering. Alumnus Mullins was convinced. "How do you stop them? You have to give up something, and when you do, they immediately probe that weakness. We had to collapse inside on Laettner because we lacked size, and Thomas Hill killed us from outside. Everybody talks about Laettner, Hurley, and Grant Hill, and they're all great. But do you realize how good Thomas Hill is? He would be a star for just about any other team, and here, he's maybe the number four guy. That's amazing."

The team flew into Boston late Monday for a game Tuesday night against the hometown Boston University Terriers that had been arranged for Crawford Palmer, whose dad taught at BU. Now, though, Palmer was at Dartmouth.

Because of the late arrival, some members of the Boston media elected to seek out Duke's players and coaches on game day. They were turned away. Krzyzewski had only one rule with the media: no interviews on game day by anybody until after the contest was played. Otherwise, the press would be accommodated.

But Boston was a pro town, and Dan Shaughnessy was a pro columnist for the *Globe*. He came to tiny Walter Brown Arena (the overflow crowd of 4,108 for the game was a record) at noon, expecting to talk to the Duke players. When that was not permitted, Shaughnessy attacked Krzyzewski in his next-day column. "We don't want to infer that Coach K takes things too seriously, but the marching orders were that the Duke players would be off-limits all day. The team's shooting practice was closed and the players and coaches were unavailable before taking the floor at night. This is the kind of paranoia and isolationism that makes us glad Chris Ford instead of Coach K is coaching the Celtics. You almost forgot about that, right?"

Krzyzewski was mystified by that bit of sarcasm. He

knew his players were accessible, that his locker room was never closed. He had just this one rule about the media, and because an exception would not be made, he got burned in print.

"Game day is sacred for me," he said. As far as Shaughnessy's complaint, Coach K said, "That's what phones are for." Had the Boston writer called Durham in advance, he would have been told of the Duke rule and when the team was arriving in town. He would have been accommodated that night.

"I don't do TV interviews at halftime, and I never allow TV in the locker room," Krzyzewski said. His only concession to game day was a pregame interview in the locker room an hour before tip-off with play-by-play man Bob Harris. "But that's all part of the Duke program."

Even for big games such as North Carolina, the opposing announcers knew to come to Durham the previous day if they wanted any comments from Krzyzewski.

The Shaughnessy complaint notwithstanding, Duke beat the Terriers, 95–85, despite missing 19 of a season-high 55 free throws.

Wake Forest came to Cameron on Saturday on an upswing and promptly got squashed. The way Duke was playing now, the opponent seemed irrelevant. Grant Hill called his buddy Rodney Rogers the night before the game to exchange pleasantries. Nothing serious, Grant said; "I didn't want to get him mad."

But after an 84–68 Duke win that like so many before was deceptively close at the finish, Hill grinned and said, "Now I can talk some trash."

Home games were becoming reruns: same script, same finish. This time, Duke played well and led by 11 at the half, 45–34. But that was just a tease. The Blue Devils were ahead only 49–41 when Coach K, unhappy with the concentration and work ethic, took a time-out to explain his demands. Result: an 18–6 outburst in the next 5 minutes that settled the outcome.

The lead reached 27 points at 76–49 before the Deacons

got some meaningless baskets at the finish to make it more respectable. Krzyzewski slowed his team down again. Opponents did not appear capable of the same action.

"Duke clearly is the best team we have played, by a long margin. Make that a big margin. And I can see that they will only get better over the course of the season," said Wake Forest coach Dave Odom.

The Blue Devils once again shot better than 60 percent, including 69.6 in the second half. All five starters were in double figures for the third time in five games, led by Laettner's 25.

Two nights later, Clemson put up even less resistance. The highlight of the 112–73 victory was a three-pointer by Laettner early in the second half. That made him the seventh Duke player to score 2,000 points in a career. No other school had as many players who had surpassed that barrier.

It was so easy that the reserves played more minutes than the starters. Parks, in his first good showing since early December, led Duke with 18 points as the Blue Devils placed eight men in double figures. Parks and Lang actually got the most minutes, 24. Marty Clark also benefited from the Tigers' noneffort with an 11-point game.

It was 55–27 at halftime, and Clemson coach Cliff Ellis had given up. He did not take a time-out in the second half. The win was Duke's fifteenth of the season and twenty-first in a row, dating back to the previous NCAAs. That tied a school record held by the '86 team.

The chance to establish a new mark would take place at Tallahassee, and the Blue Devils were eager for the trip to Florida State. Blowouts were fun, but the team was concerned about how it would react under pressure.

FSU had been brought into the ACC to strengthen the conference's football image. That it was certain to do. But Pat Kennedy also had the Metro Conference basketball champions returning intact, and starting with their victory at North Carolina, the Seminoles had been the surprise team of the league.

When Duke arrived in Florida, Krzyzewski hustled off to Kennedy's house for a Special Olympics fund-raiser. Kennedy bought Coach K a Dalí designer necktie as a gag. "Mike's pretty conservative, dark blue businessman's suit and all," Kennedy said. "I just want to see his face when I give it to him."

When Krzyzewski arrived at Kennedy's house, he was already wearing the exact same designer tie that Pat had picked out as a gift. Kennedy just shook his head. "It wasn't a setup," he said.

There was no setup the next day, either. In football-mad Tallahassee, the Civic Center was sold out in advance. The Seminoles even made their first attempt at copying Krzyzewskiville, Duke's famed tent city: some two dozen fans camped out overnight in a cold rain near the ticket office. That, like the size of the crowd, was an FSU first.

The Duke players loved the enthusiasm of the FSU fans. "Pretty neat," Davis said. They got a kick out of the tomahawk chop, which the student body used throughout. "I liked the chop," Laettner said. "I'm sorry I'm a senior and won't get to come here again."

Most of all, the team was happy with the way it responded to a tight game on the road against a quality opponent. The Blue Devils hadn't been tested since they played at Virginia. But this time, FSU played more patiently than it had at Cameron, got back on defense, and generally slowed the Duke attack to a walk.

With 5 minutes to play, Doug Edwards gave FSU the lead at 58–56. It was just the third time Duke had trailed in the second half all season, and the first since Charlottesville. FSU was still ahead, 62–61, when Krzyzewski made a defensive switch. He put 6-8 Grant Hill on the Seminoles' star, Sam Cassell, instead of 6-4 Thomas Hill.

Not only didn't Cassell score again, but the Seminoles didn't either. Duke got the game's final 14 points for a 75–62 victory. For once, the final score was deceiving the other way; it had been much closer than that.

Grant Hill did the job defensively on Cassell, and he had 8 of his 20 points in that stretch run. Hill made the go-ahead basket, and after a Laettner free throw, he stole a pass from Bob Sura and scored on a difficult lay-up when he was unable to dunk.

FSU had no answers for Duke's pressure. Afterward, Kennedy said he would like to freeze the final three minutes and play them again. "We had a legitimate chance to win. But they are simply a great team. They have been in these situations before and have the confidence to pull it out. Their experience helps make them such an impressive team."

Having proved to themselves they could stand the heat, the Devils returned home for the final tune-up before the really tough part of the season, the four-game road trip that would start at North Carolina and go immediately to LSU.

Notre Dame came into Cameron dragging a losing record, but the Irish got everybody's attention by upsetting Carolina in a game at the Meadowlands. But this contest was more a matter of achieving some school records.

The 100–71 romp was Duke's twenty-third in a row overall, and the 17-0 record broke the mark for best season start, held by the '86 team. For the historians, it was Duke's five hundreth win in fifty-two-year-old Cameron. Only five other current buildings had seen that many home victories.

Late in the game, Krzyzewski and Amaker got into an amusing conversation. Amaker was urging Coach K to remove Hurley from the game.

"Is he tired?"

"Yeah, Coach, he's dragging."

Eventually, with 3:27 remaining, Krzyzewski pulled Hurley for the last time. The point guard, who had passed the 1,000-point mark during the game, left with 7 assists. He now had 707 for his career. The record holder with 708? Amaker. Coach K enjoyed Amaker's joke, but they both knew a new mark was only one game away.

The assistant coach wasn't concerned about his record standing long. "Time after time, Hurley's made big shots, big plays for us. It's not even close who's the best point guard ever at Duke, and I think he'll go down as one of the greatest in the ACC."

Hurley was on top of his game. "I got a lot of confidence from the NCAA tournament last year. I'm in control of my game and I'm in control of my emotions a lot better than I have been, and I think I have a better relationship with officials and my teammates. Everything seems to be going well."

Laettner was the unquestioned star. Grant Hill was the greatest talent. But most people who had watched Duke blitz its way through the first half of the season with scarcely a scare considered Hurley to be the key performer. One Durham columnist wrote that if he had to vote for player of the year now, it would be Hurley. There was no question how important he was to the No. 1 team in the nation.

CHAPTER 6

WHEN KRZYZEWSKI HAD PLANNED out his season, he was eager for the four-game road swing that would start February 5 at Chapel Hill against North Carolina. The team had rolled through its opponents so easily that Coach K seriously worried that it was peaking too soon. He knew it couldn't maintain this pace for the whole season, and he almost didn't want it to; the last thing he wanted was to enter the NCAAs without having been tested at the end of a close game.

In eleven days, the Blue Devils would play at archrival Carolina, at LSU with Shaquille O'Neal, at tough Georgia Tech, and at N.C. State, where no squad member had ever won a game. "I'm scheduling us to lose," he had said. But they hadn't lost yet. The next four games would tell a lot.

Coach K always liked to test his team in February, especially against non-ACC opponents. It provided a more accurate reading of how the team was developing. Nonconference games had the flavor of the NCAAs. In addition, Shaq against Laettner might be for player-of-the-year honors.

Krzyzewski was looking for some adversity. He wanted to see how his team would respond. Until now, even though Parks had slumped in January and the reserves were still untested, Duke was dominating everybody. But Coach K knew "it's tough to sprint all the way to the finish. We've been scoring too easily. Nobody's been able to make us run a halfcourt offense, and we're going to need that in March."

Because of the blowouts, Coach K had been unable to put his reserves in situations where they could improve. It wasn't that they weren't getting sufficient playing time, because they were. But because of the nature of the games, the people coming off the bench rarely got to play much with the starters in tight situations. More often, they wound up playing as a unit when Krzyzewski was trying to hold down the score.

Because Duke was ahead by so much, there wasn't the seriousness of purpose the players required to make the time meaningful. And because opposing teams had often cut into those huge deficits against them while they were trying to use the clock, the reserves couldn't develop much confidence. They didn't even have a lot of fan support because even the Crazies wearied with 30-point leads.

Discussing the bench's lack of development with his staff, Coach K said, "I've really screwed them up. They haven't played enough under tough game conditions."

He had done what he needed to do for the team so that it wouldn't think it was too good. But it hadn't helped the bench players improve.

Sitting in his office at Cameron, Jay Bilas told Tommy Amaker, "I've never seen a team play this well. These guys are so good it's scary." Bilas and Amaker had played together in '86, when Duke won 37 games.

The statistics were frightening. In ten home games, Duke's average score was 101–72, despite Krzyzewski's efforts to pull in the reins. In virtually every game, the margin reached 25 points at least once.

Duke was 8-0 in the ACC, and seven of the wins had been by at least 13 points. The average margin was 19.3. Duke had been challenged only three times, and in serious danger of losing only at Michigan.

Hurley made the big points at Ann Arbor, where Duke led by 17 in the first half. He made the key three-pointer at Virginia, where the Blue Devils won by 6. Grant Hill had been the hero at Florida State, where Duke scored the final 14 points. Laettner was already the favorite to win national player of the year. He was looking forward to the face-off against O'Neal on Saturday.

Duke had three players having exceptional seasons. Thomas Hill and Davis were also playing well.

The team was averaging 94.5 points and leading the nation in field-goal percentage. Three-point shooting had been considered a potential weakness, but the Devils were leading the ACC, making almost 49 percent in conference games.

Duke was also going to the free-throw line more than any other team in the nation and topped the ACC in percentage. It was difficult to imagine any team playing better. The schedule had been good, with six of the victims (FSU twice) rated among the Top 25.

But the Tar Heels would be their usual rugged assignment. They were rated ninth in the nation at 15-3.

There was no greater basketball rivalry than Duke-Carolina. Both were among the top five programs in the nation year after year, and they were located less than ten miles apart in the Research Triangle—at Durham and at Chapel Hill.

The basketball rivalry existed 365 days a year and pitted neighbor against neighbor, worker against worker, friend against friend, and often, spouse against spouse. It was the proximity that fueled the combativeness and heightened the tension among the supporters.

Duke had been the No. 1 program in the sixties under

coach Vic Bubas, who had played for and coached under Everett Case at N.C. State. Case had brought fast-break basketball to the state in the late forties and forced Duke and Carolina to get better in order to compete.

Bubas took Duke to the Final Four three times in four years, the last in '66. Then the torch was passed to North Carolina, where a young Dean Smith had replaced Frank McGuire in 1961. Smith began his run to immortality in 1967 with his first Final Four team and never stopped. His teams became the model of excellence by which all others were judged. The Tar Heels won twenty or more games every year; they almost always finished first or second in the ACC; they reached the NCAA round of sixteen every year, starting in 1980; and they won the national championship in 1982 on a last-minute shot by freshman Michael Jordan.

Smith's team played in the Dean E. Smith Center, a 21,500-seat, $33.8 million facility paid for exclusively with private funds and promptly tabbed the Dean Dome.

Duke teams were erratic after Bubas retired following the 1969 season, and no coach seemed able to handle what seemed to be the condition of the job, that no matter what you did or how well you played, you were always going to be No. 2 behind Carolina.

Until Mike Krzyzewski.

When Duke athletic director Tom Butters was seeking a new coach in March 1980, he took advice from very few people. After Bill Foster confirmed the rumors that he was leaving Duke to take the job at South Carolina, Butters got on the phone to Bobby Knight.

"Do you want the job?"

"You couldn't stand having me around," Knight replied.

Butters had called to inquire about Kansas State's Jack Hartman, who was the leading candidate in the AD's mind, although the coach never knew Duke was interested.

Knight told Butters that Hartman would be flattered,

"but I think he'd wait four or five weeks, then say there's no way he can leave Manhattan [Kansas]."

Knight then suggested a couple of his former assistants, Bob Weltlich, head coach at Mississippi, and Dave Bliss, who was at SMU. On that recommendation, Weltlich became one of four people interviewed by Duke. The others were assistant coach Bob Wenzel, Old Dominion's Paul Webb, and Krzyzewski.

Krzyzewski had completed his fifth year at Army with a 9-17 record, his worst. Butters had heard of him through Steve Vacendak, a former Duke basketball player who had just been hired as an assistant athletic director.

In discussing the possibility that Foster might leave, Butters said to Vacendak, "I'm looking for the best defensive coach in America. There are nights when you're going to shoot thirty-seven, thirty-eight percent, and you've got to win those nights."

Vacendak immediately replied, "There's a guy at Army, Krzyzewski, that you ought to look at."

Knowing Krzyzewski had played for Knight at West Point and had coached under him at Indiana in 1975, Butters asked Knight, "What do you think about Mike Krzyzewski?"

"Now there's a guy with all of my good qualities and none of my bad ones," he replied.

Butters believed Knight to be an exceptionally bright guy who would tell you the truth. Based on that evaluation, Butters placed Krzyzewski on the interview list. They first talked at Lafayette, Indiana, where Duke was playing in the NCAAs. After Duke advanced to Lexington, Kentucky, to the NCAA regional, Butters wanted to meet again. He called West Point.

"Can you get to Lexington?" he asked Krzyzewski.

"There's a foot of snow up here, but I'll get there somehow."

On the day before Duke beat Kentucky at Kentucky—Foster's last win at Duke—Krzyzewski met secretly with Butters, Vacendak, Duke chancellor Ken Pye, and vice president Chuck Huestis. Then the four finalists were brought on campus to meet with the search committee, Duke's athletic council.

Everybody was interviewed at Huestis's house in Duke Forest, not far from the campus. Butters placed Krzyzewski last in the sequence.

Following the interviews, the council told Butters, "It's your choice." Meanwhile, Krzyzewski was headed home to West Point. Mickie, who had accompanied him for the first time during the process, was returning to Alexandria, Virginia, where her parents were baby-sitting Debbie and Lindy. They were driven to the airport by Lynn Butters, Tom's wife. Mickie's flight was scheduled to leave 20 minutes before Mike's.

Meanwhile, standing in Huestis's kitchen, Butters turned to Vacendak and said, "Don't let him get on the plane."

"What are you going to do, interview him again?" Vacendak asked.

"No, I'm going to hire him."

Vacendak paged Krzyzewski at the airport and brought him back to Durham. Mickie's plane had already departed. Later, when she had not heard from her husband, Mickie started calling their home at West Point. "After a while, I really got worried. I even called the airlines to see if there had been any problem with the flight. There hadn't been."

Around midnight, Mike finally called his near-frantic spouse. Before she could say anything, he said, "They called me at the airport and they wanted to ask one more question."

Mickie exploded. "Three interviews and now they want to ask you one more question?" Mike let her yell. Finally, when he could get a word in, he said, "Mickie, they wanted to know if I would take the job."

The first three years at Duke were the toughest for Krzyzewski. That first team, featuring Gene Banks and

Kenny Dennard, struggled to a 15-12 regular-season record and was fortunate to get an NIT bid. After Banks broke his wrist, Duke lost in the third round to Purdue, 81–69.

More critical was recruiting. Krzyzewski and his staff went after virtually every blue chipper in the nation. They came close on many, including Chris Mullin, but didn't get a single one.

Krzyzewski was devastated. The staff had spent countless hours seeking out blue chippers. But they had too wide a base. Coach K made two changes in recruiting philosophy, neither of which he ever went back on. Duke would narrow its base, cutting the list of prospects. Most important, only players Mike could fall in love with would be courted. If Coach K didn't have a good feeling about the player and how he would fit in the program, he would simply be dropped from the list. It wouldn't matter how talented he was.

The second and third teams each lost 17 games, the most in school history. But recruiting turned around, with six players signed in the spring of that second year, including key national recruits Johnny Dawkins and Mark Alarie. Those two, who finished their careers as the first- and third-leading scorers in school history, were to become the nucleus of Krzyzewski's first great team, in 1986.

In January of the fourth year, rumors were rampant that Krzyzewski would be fired. It had reached the point where the rumors were affecting recruiting. Butters called Krzyzewski into his office. "I'm going to do something about your contract. I'm going to tear the son of a bitch up." The AD handed him a new five-year contract.

"You don't have to do that," Krzyzewski said. "Yes, I do," was the reply. That night, Butters received three death threats.

That team finished 24-9 and received an NCAA bid. Krzyzewski was voted ACC coach of the year. The Blue Devils have not missed the NCAAs since.

The '86 team set a national record by winning 37 games, was rated No. 1 in the final polls, and reached the NCAA finals where it lost to Louisville, 72–69.

After losing to eventual champion Indiana in the third round in '87, Duke began its string of Final Four appearances the next year. The Blue Devils finished third in the regular season, but won the ACC tournament, upsetting North Carolina in the finals, 65–61. They then upset No. 1 Temple in the East Regional finals as Billy King stifled Mark Macon. Kansas and Danny Manning beat Duke in the semifinals at Kansas City.

The next year, again the No. 2 seed in the East, Duke won once more in the Meadowlands, claiming a victory over top-seed Georgetown in the regional finals as freshman Laettner made 9 of 10 shots and scored 24 points. Duke lost in the Final Four at Seattle to Seton Hall.

The path to the '90 Final Four included another shocker at the Meadowlands, this time on the shot against Connecticut, the third No. 1 seed Duke had beaten in as many years. That led to an upset of Arkansas in the semifinals in Denver, before the crushing defeat by UNLV in the most one-sided championship game ever.

It also led to a weary, unhappy, frustrated Krzyzewski. It should have been exhilarating because of all his Final Four teams, '90 was the least expected. Unlike the other years, there was no superstar. No Dawkins as in '86; no Danny Ferry, as in '88 and '89. But Krzyzewski was very upset that—for the first time in his coaching career—his seniors weren't graduating with their class after four years at Duke. None of the three seniors—Abdelnaby, Brickey, or Phil Henderson—graduated that year.

Coach K was first and foremost an educator—"I'm a teacher and a coach," he often said, and he meant it in that order. He was more than disappointed. He refused to hang the team's Final Four banner from the rafters of Cameron Indoor Stadium. Hanging the banner was a symbol; it was an acknowledgment that this was a special team. To leave it stored sent a message: basketball was important, but no more so than graduation. The banner is still packed away and will be until the two players graduate, if they ever do.

With that as a prologue, Krzyzewski entertained an offer to coach the Boston Celtics. He had had college offers before and ignored them; he had even had feeling-out meetings with a couple of pro teams, but had never seriously considered leaving. But this time was different.

Dave Gavitt, former commissioner of the Big East and the head man of USA Basketball, had gone to work for the Celtics. Krzyzewski and Gavitt were close friends; they had worked together numerous times in conjunction with USA Basketball, where Coach K was on the player selection committee. He had enormous respect for Gavitt; that was part of what made it attractive. Another was the fact that it was the Celtics. It would be a chance to go to a team with a great tradition and great players.

The Celtics needed a coach. Gavitt came to Durham to find out if Krzyzewski was interested. It was mid-June, and they talked for hours at the coach's house in northern Durham.

For the first time, Krzyzewski was having doubts about whether his players understood what he wanted for them. He was no longer sure if he was being effective in his teaching role.

"We had gone to the Final Four," Krzyzewski said, "but things seemed a little bit different. The attention to detail around the program had waned. It was so big. Trying to meet high expectations is never as much fun as when you were first building them. Everyone was taking things for granted. Everything was too serious. We had lost the element of fun."

So Coach K talked with Gavitt, and with his family. Would he enjoy pro basketball, although the financial rewards would be far greater? Would there be a life for Mickie, since unlike at Duke there was no way she could be part of the program?

They talked. Krzyzewski weighed the issues and decided he was where he wanted to be. In the college ranks, where, as a teacher, he could influence lives.

The decision rejuvenated him. He had explored the unknown, the NBA at the very top, and decided it wasn't for him. He determined that Duke was where he wanted to remain and proved his teaching abilities by taking his next team to the national title.

From an extremely modest beginning, Coach K had built a program that was the most successful in the nation. And he never used Carolina as a measuring stick.

Shortly after Krzyzewski accepted the job, he talked with Bubas. During his decade on the sidelines in the sixties, Bubas had been Duke's most successful coach. Krzyzewski had great respect for Bubas. "He should be in the Hall of Fame. It's too bad for basketball that he didn't coach longer."

Bubas told Krzyzewski, "Don't get into the Carolina thing. It will be destructive. They're going to be good. But that doesn't mean you can't be good, too." It was perfect advice and Coach K never forgot it.

This year there were early signs that the rivalry had reached an emotional fever never before seen at UNC, where the team was always expected to win its home games. For the first time, Carolina students had emulated Duke and created their own tent city outside the Smith Center, camping out to get tickets for the game, although it was officially discouraged by the administration.

The atmosphere inside the building for the game was electric. There was not just the feeling of excitement, but also of tension and hatred. Carolina basketball had a lengthy, proud tradition. The Tar Heels did not take kindly to being No. 2 in their own backyard.

Krzyzewski had planned this difficult stretch in the season in search of some adversity. Less than 7 minutes into the Carolina game, adversity found him. Bobby Hurley passed to Thomas Hill for the lay-up that broke the school assist record.

And broke his foot.

Nobody knew Hurley was hurt that badly. "I heard something pop," he told trainer Dave Engelhardt when he came out a minute later during a TV time-out. He returned to action 3 minutes later and played the rest of the game. By halftime, he had 11 points and 4 assists and Duke was leading a ferocious struggle, 39–38.

The training staff evaluated Hurley again in the locker room. There wasn't much swelling. They thought perhaps it was a strained tendon. Later Hurley said, "They didn't know the severity of the injury. Part of me knew. But the guys needed me at that point, and I thought I could play through the pain."

Hurley played the entire second half. He didn't score another point, going 0 for 4 from the field.

Carolina, getting inspired play from its big men inside, scored the first 10 points of the second half and never trailed again.

With UNC leading, 50–43, a technical foul was called on the Carolina bench. Hurley made eye contact with Krzyzewski. He wanted to shoot the free throws. Usually it would have been Laettner, who was No. 2 in the league. But Hurley was shooting better than 80 percent, and his coach wanted to see if that would get him started offensively.

Hurley couldn't push off on his foot. He had made a courageous but foolish request. He missed them both, the only time all year he was 0 for 2 at the line. Two points was Carolina's final margin of victory.

The crowd in the often passive, reserved Dean Dome was noisy and intense. In the six years since the building had been opened, it was easily the loudest ever. Play was physical, brutish. Carolina seven-footer Eric Montross twice left the court for repairs with blood running down his face. Later, films would show he had been accidentally elbowed by teammate Kevin Salvadori.

Salvadori, who came into the game averaging 7 points and 4 rebounds, was the surprise weapon for the Tar Heels. He finished with 12 points and 6 rebounds and helped in Carolina's seven-foot double-team sandwich that formed around Laettner. The Duke star was held to a dozen points and as many rebounds.

Down 72–66 after Salvadori made two foul shots with 4 minutes left, the Blue Devils turned up the defensive pressure. After the teams traded free throws, Brian Davis and Grant Hill each scored inside, and each was fouled. Each missed the chance for a three-point play. Duke, accustomed to the foul shot being a prominent weapon, made only 13 of 20 to 23 of 29 for the Tar Heels. The Blue Devils missed 4 of their last 5.

But with 1:03 to play, Laettner hit a follow shot to tie the score at 73. It was the only time Duke got even after intermission.

When the Tar Heels brought the ball up the court, Krzyzewski called for his team to be in an "11" defense, designed to defend only to the three-point line. The action was away from the Duke bench, and none of the players caught the defensive switch. They remained in "21," a defense that extended to halfcourt.

Hurley, who by now had no quick lateral movement left, fouled Derrick Phelps. The Carolina guard made both free throws and it was 75–73. With 24 seconds remaining, Laettner got the ball inside for one of the few occasions all night. He went up against Montross and missed the lay-up. "It was the easiest shot I had in the game," Laettner said. "I just missed it."

Montross rebounded, but instead of holding for a foul, Brian Reese missed a lay-up and Duke had another opportunity. The Blue Devils came hard on the break, Hurley with the ball, Laettner on the left wing. For one of the few times all year when he got the ball in that situation, Laettner did not try a three-pointer.

Surely, Carolina would not foul him. But Laettner elected to drive. He was contested at the foul line by Salvadori. His shot bounced away, to be corraled by Phelps as time ran out.

"I got a good shot," Laettner said. "I thought for a

second about taking the three, but there was an open lane." He was not going to second-guess himself.

When the game ended, there was bedlam on the floor. The normally blasé Dean Dome quickly became chaotic. The fans rushed onto the court before Duke's players had a chance to get off. Suzanne Gilbert, one of Duke's senior managers, was slightly injured when she was whacked in the head by a TV camera.

It was easy to imagine this happening elsewhere, but not in Chapel Hill. Carolina was known for being cool. Going nuts was something they did elsewhere. At, say, Duke.

When the game ended, Montross and Salvadori joined the growing swarm of students at midcourt, raising their hands in the No. 1 signal. It was an emotional scene.

As Hurley limped off the court, a bearded man sprinted up to him and shouted in his face. Brian Davis looked at the berserk fans, nodded, and clapped his hands over his head. "Okay, you got your win, enjoy it. You had to give them respect. They played a great game."

Far into the night, Carolina students partied on Franklin Street, the main drag in the distinguished college town. That had never happened before following a regular-season basketball game. It seemed now that Duke had become the measure of Carolina's success.

The road trip had gotten off to a rugged start: not because of the defeat, but because of Hurley's injury. Coach K wanted his team to be tested. Now it would be—and then some.

On the quiet bus returning to Durham, Davis sought out Tony Lang. Davis had played one of his better games. He had been Duke's leading scorer with 17 points. But now was the time to be a co-captain. He knew Hurley was hurting, and that Lang would have to play more. Against Carolina, Lang had played 14 minutes with a basket and 2 rebounds. He had been about all there was to the bench. Parks had played 8 minutes, Clark just 3, and neither had a field goal.

Davis called Lang to sit with him. "There's nothing worse than this," he said. "Next time we play them, play your ass off. Right now, we need you to come through."

Davis reminded his teammate that the team never had a goal of being undefeated. "Right now, we just need to stop talking about it and go back to playing basketball."

That was Davis at his best, being a leader, being intuitive. He knew that in the Saturday game at LSU, Lang would be playing before his family and friends.

The phone rang early the next morning at Grant Hill's house. His dad, Calvin, who had come down for the game and was staying at the Washington-Duke Motel, had just heard on the radio that Hurley had a broken metatarsal bone in his right foot. He would be sidelined a minimum of three weeks.

Suddenly, Duke's point guard had grown from a six-footer to 6-8. "Wow, playing point guard was something I always wanted to do," said Grant. But he also felt for Hurley, whose injury would hurt the team. Hill knew the pressure would now be on him.

Calvin Hill took his son, the new point guard, and the injured Hurley to lunch at Chili's. Calvin was concerned about how depressed Hurley would be, and he wanted the two players to talk informally about the nuances of playing the point.

At practice that afternoon, Grant Hill was very, very nervous. But he did well. Krzyzewski had confidence in him, and so did the team.

The team was going to have to change its style of play. The bench had not been productive, and now it would be stripped of its best producer with Lang moving into the starting lineup. That wasn't all bad; when Lang had started as a freshman while Hill recuperated from his broken nose, Tony played his best, most confident basketball. But unless somebody such as Parks or Clark stepped up right away, substitutions on the road swing would be infrequent.

Grant Hill would have to play a lot, perhaps 40 minutes. Grant understood the new position. He had great basketball instincts; he had played the point some in high school and had played it earlier in the season at Boston U. when Hurley was in early foul trouble. But Grant also was the team's best finisher. Having him control the ball would cut down on the number of fast-break attempts.

"Bobby can push the ball all the time. That's something I can't do," Hill said. "I'll have to play intelligently, not try and do too much, and not try to do something that isn't there."

Adversity. Coach K had wanted the team to improve its halfcourt offense all through January, but it was humming along in such high gear that it never had to. Now it would be forced to rely on patterned play more than ever as it faced the toughest stretch on the schedule. This would be when the team learned about itself; where the players learned about their own resiliencies and capabilities. It was just the kind of challenge Coach K relished.

Ever since the schedule had been announced, Shaquille O'Neal had not minced words: forget the SEC. The game he was looking forward to was Duke. He had been badly outplayed by Laettner the previous year in Cameron. This was going to be his chance for revenge. "I've got that date circled in my locker," he said.

Hurley, his foot in a walking cast because of the fracture, accompanied the team to Baton Rouge on Friday. It was a tough time for the ultimate gym rat. "I've never been hurt," he said. "It's going to be tough sitting on the bench." But this was his team, and perhaps he could offer some advice if Hill needed any help.

The team arrived at LSU and found the students camping out at the Pete Maravich Center, something they almost never did. When the team bus parked, the players looked up to see LSU students hanging over the rails of a walkway, hurling typical insults. "Overrated, overrated."

At practice, LSU coach Dale Brown came over to offer his condolences to Hurley. "We've got a great doctor," he said, "if you'd like to see him." That didn't sit well with trainer Dave Engelhardt. It wasn't as if Duke didn't have some pretty good doctors, too.

As the Duke players made their way toward their bus afterward, the LSU students came down off the walkway and rushed at them, hurling more insults. "Have another beer, buddy," Laettner said, waving his hand. As the bus was leaving the arena, some of the students ran up and tossed cups of beer on it, much to the displeasure of the driver.

On game day, as the Duke players walked out to the court to shoot, they heard a loud noise. The elephant doors were opened, and a large cage was brought inside. When the Blue Devils turned the corner, they were greeted by Mike—LSU's 400-pound tiger, who rarely made an appearance at basketball games.

Suddenly, a loud roar came from the rafters, and down from the ceiling dropped a mangled arm, with *Duke* written on the sleeve. The LSU mascot, a student dressed as a tiger, propelled himself from his perch to the floor, revealing the rest of the now-mutilated Duke dummy.

The noise was deafening. LSU, 14-4 and always tough at home, had pulled out all the stops against Duke. Out at midcourt, Coach Brown greeted a couple of former players, Chris Jackson of the Denver Nuggets and Stanley Roberts of the Orlando Magic. It was NBA All-Star weekend, and the pros had come back to see if the Tigers could upset the Devils.

Duke had just lost in the Dean Dome. Now the Devils were going to play in the Deaf Dome. The Maravich Center was appropriately nicknamed.

Krzyzewski was fired up. He was eager to see how Grant Hill and Tony Lang would play in their new roles. The

Blue Devils were the underdogs for once. This game would be a gut-check.

"Our main focus is us," Krzyzewski told his players. "We aren't trying to figure out how to beat Shaq. The main thing is to play the perimeter tough. Their guards aren't good passers. We want to pressure the ball, so they can't pass it inside easily. That's our main defense, play the perimeter tough."

The Duke staff also felt LSU would play a zone, and without Hurley, the Devils would have a lineup of players of mostly equal height, somewhat interchangeable parts. Lang could stay inside, and Laettner could rotate and spot up behind the three-point line.

Hill might have been nervous the night before, but he was ready for the challenge. In the pregame huddle, in which he had never said anything before, he told his teammates, "Never fear, thirty-three is here."

Hill played splendidly. He played the entire game, scored 16 points, grabbed 9 rebounds, and handed out 6 assists. He had just 3 turnovers and played well defensively. Coach K was especially happy that Hill shot from the perimeter, although none was a three-pointer.

In his first start of the year, before a lot of family and friends, Lang did exactly what Davis had urged him to do after the Carolina game: he stepped up his play. He had 12 points and 5 boards in 31 minutes, and made a couple of critical free throws in the last 2 minutes with Duke holding on to a 4-point lead.

But Laettner was the story. He not only played well, he played smart. He had some early shots rejected by the emotional O'Neal, and with a minute left in the first half, he had just 4 points. But he scored two late baskets to give Duke a 34–28 edge at the break.

O'Neal was dominating inside. He had 16 points, 6 rebounds, and 3 blocks by halftime, but the rest of his team had scored just a dozen.

The Tigers, with O'Neal on his way to 25 points, 12

rebounds, and 7 blocked shots, rallied in the second half to take leads of up to 5 points. But with the score 60–59, LSU, the Duke game plan kicked in and worked to perfection. Laettner spotted up and hit a three. On the next possession, he did it again.

Laettner tried a third three-pointer, and as the Duke bench watched in eager anticipation, it bounced away. Some of the staff felt Christian shouldn't have shot, but not Krzyzewski: "My thing with Christian has been that for him to reach another level, he's got to take Bird-type shots—the ultimate, cocky shot by a great player. That was right, to take the third one. Christian just assumed more of the burden."

Even with the miss, LSU was done. The Tigers never got any closer than 4, and Lang took care of that at the foul line. The Blue Devils, used to shooting clutch free throws when weary, made 8 of their last 10. LSU was 3 for 10 down the stretch, with Shaq twice missing two at a time.

Duke won, 77–67. Hill and Laettner played the entire game. Davis was on the floor for 39 minutes. Parks was the only sub of consequence, with 12 minutes of playing time.

Laettner was 8 for 21 from the floor, finishing with 22 points and 10 rebounds. But if O'Neal won the battle of the statistics, Laettner won the game, which was far more important. Christian draped his arm around Shaq's shoulders. "Keep improving," he said. "Just keep improving." He meant it, too.

In the Duke locker room, there was more celebration than usual for a regular-season game. Normally, it was business as usual. "But this was special," Coach K said. "This was just a huge win. Grant's position change was the easiest thing to see, but we got a bonus—Tony Lang." Lang scored a dozen points and rebounded well. Krzyzewski saw that Lang could fit in with his usual starters without missing a beat. He could be that key player from the bench Coach K had been looking for.

The Devils were halfway through the road swing and back on track. They had responded the way their coach wanted. In the most trying of circumstances, they played brilliantly in the closing minutes. That's what Krzyzewski wanted to see.

A disturbing undercurrent to the game went largely unreported. Throughout the game, to the beat of drums accompanied by a tomahawk chop in the rhythm made famous by Atlanta Braves fans, the LSU students chanted at Laettner, "Ho-mo-sexual, ho-mo-sexual." Near the end, with Duke in command, Laettner raised his hand to the crowd. The taunting hadn't bothered his performance.

The whispers had begun in his freshman year: Was Laettner gay?

"I heard it the second semester my freshman year," Laettner said. He believed it started because he walked hand in hand with a male student across campus, his way of protesting the macho jock image. "It was very shocking at first. Suppose somebody said you were from Mars. That can't be. It should be obvious to everybody. That's the way I felt. There was no reason at the beginning," he felt, to deny the rumor.

Intensely protective of his privacy, Laettner said that the incident occurred before he had a girlfriend. Even after he was going with "one of the prettiest girls on campus," the rumors flourished. "She even asked me about it. I said, 'I just kissed you last night.' But I'm very secretive. As bad as it is to be seen with no women, it's even worse to be seen with a hundred."

For a while, Laettner enjoyed the notoriety. "It was somewhat hot, somewhat taboo, and it got you publicity."

There was enough of that, although it started slowly. Right after his junior season began, Laettner told Chip Alexander of the *Raleigh News & Observer*, "I have one best friend, my teammate and roommate, Brian Davis, and I spend ninety-five percent of my time with Brian. I don't want anything else; I don't need anything else. All I want to do is be with Brian, play well on the basketball court, and do well in school. That's it: basketball, school, and Brian."

In an article in *The New York Times*, Davis said on the sexuality issue, "We know we're not gay. We're so mature we know what 'friends' is all about. We can tell each other we love each other."

What occurred at Baton Rouge was a major part of an interesting phenomenon. The media clearly did not know how to deal with the issue. CBS's Billy Packer mentioned an offensive cheer, but didn't identify it. The print media virtually ignored it, as if it didn't happen.

Krzyzewski had his own thoughts. "The media hyped this as Tyson against Holyfield, Shaq against Christian, and it didn't want to let anything stand in the way of its stories."

But the issue of Laettner's alleged homosexuality had been raised before, without ever being dealt with publicly. Whispered for a couple of years on campus, it spread to virtually every place Duke played.

At Maryland, the cheerleaders held up a huge paper sign, a Duke jersey No. 32, with a pleated skirt attached to the bottom. At Florida State, there were repeated isolated derisive cheers directed Laettner's way. But this was the first time a group had done anything in the form of prolonged abuse.

The only writer to address the situation was Seth Davis, a Duke senior and columnist for the school paper, the *Chronicle*. He wrote that if students yelled "nig-ger" or "Po-lack" or "Jew," the administration would halt it immediately. But because the references were to sexuality, nobody did anything.

Writers regularly covering Duke knew Laettner wasn't gay. He had girlfriends on campus and he was presently seeing a player on the women's volleyball team at Georgia. Some writers were uncomfortable with the situation. One told Laettner's mother he wouldn't write about it unless Christian talked about it. But Laettner elected not to make a statement about the situation unless someone specifically asked, and nobody did.

"The whole gay thing is envy, jealousy," Brian Davis said. "What else can people say about him? They can't say he's ugly. They can't say he isn't a good player. If he is gay, then every other player should be mad because he's getting killed by a gay."

Interestingly, although the rumor about Laettner first became public when he talked about his close relationship with roommate Davis, nobody ever accused Brian of being gay.

"It's a stereotype," Laettner said. "People don't think black men are gay."

But the rumors were starting to wear on the team. Even Laettner, who enjoyed the backhanded notoriety for a while, had grown weary of it. "This is getting old," he said. But there was still no statement from him denying the accusation.

Grant Hill's attitude typified the way the team felt: "We knew why they didn't say anything at first. Everybody knew they weren't gay. I don't think they expected it to go as far as it did. It has gotten out of hand. This thing made them even more mysterious, but I don't think they've handled it well." He thought Laettner and Davis should have publicly dismissed the rumors.

The insults didn't affect Laettner's play, however. The cheer at LSU he called "par for the course," then went out and beat the Tigers.

"That does push Christian," Hill said. "It's just something that gets him fired up."

Like his coach, Laettner had his own forms of planned adversity. And when he challenged himself, he usually responded.

Duke's road show next played Atlanta. The big time. Braves. Falcons. Hawks. Olympics. By now, not much new could excite the folks in Hot-lanta. But Grant Hill could.

With Hill leading the way offensively and defensively,

the Blue Devils led Georgia Tech, 28–20, having just scored 11 straight points. The crowd was quiet in Alexander Memorial Coliseum—the Thriller Dome. Then a leaping Davis threw a pass from the right hash mark. It was intended for Hill, but just like the slam-jam against Kansas, the ball appeared headed out of bounds. No human could possibly retrieve it, much less do anything with it.

So Hill leaped, maybe two feet above the rim on the left side, threw out his right hand, caught the ball, and in one motion slammed it through the basket. The crowd sat stunned. Nobody could believe what he had just seen. That ball had been long gone, and like a cobra springing for a strike, Grant Hill grabbed it and jammed it.

Billy Packer, that man of reserve, lost it on TV. "Yo, yo, yo," he gurgled.

Mark Bradley wrote in the *Atlanta Constitution*, "It was the greatest dunk anyone had seen since . . . oh, the beginning of time."

If Hill got a perfect 10 in Indy against Kansas, this one was off the charts. That took all the fight out of the Jackets, who succumbed meekly. There were no thrills for the home crowd in the Thriller Dome. With 6:50 left and Duke ahead, 55–37, they began vacating the joint. The 71–62 final score was again no indication of Duke's domination.

Hill, who once again played 40 minutes, had 20 points, 5 assists, 5 rebounds, and 2 steals. But Grant's defensive job was more astonishing. Travis Best, Tech's star rookie point guard, played 31 minutes and didn't score. Zero. The first shutout of his career.

"I just tried to stay in front of him and get a hand up on his shot. I was thinking to myself, 'Why isn't he taking me?' I think I got two blocks on his shot, and he was real hesitant to shoot it again," Hill said.

Krzyzewski was delighted with his backup point guard. "We were real worried about Best's penetration, so Grant played off of him to try and keep him in front. Grant just put together two exceptional games."

The tempo had been just what Krzyzewski wanted. The Blue Devils worked the clock and were patient, especially once Lang and Davis were in foul trouble. Hill did that perfectly. Duke scored on 17 of 20 possessions in the second half, most of them with their halfcourt offense.

"I got really tired," Hill said, "so I decided to take advantage of our time-outs. I'd sit there to the final whistle before I walked back on the floor. I'm just glad it wasn't a fast-breaking game. When Hurley's in there, we're going to run, run, run. But he's not there and we have to make some adjustments. I'm going to be glad to see Bobby come back, so I can go back to my normal spot."

Duke had now won twice in difficult arenas without Hurley. For the team that had been so overwhelming in January, nothing was coming easy. But Krzyzewski was pleased how they were accepting the challenge. These games counted in ways the blowouts couldn't.

The last game of the road swing was at N.C. State, where Duke had lost four in a row. The Blue Devil players had won almost everything possible, but none of them had ever won a game in Reynolds Coliseum.

The final score was almost the same as against Georgia Tech, 71–63. And just like Tech, it wasn't that close, with Duke leading by 14 points with a minute left. The Blue Devils actually took the lead for good at precisely the same score as against the Jackets, at 20–20, this time on two free throws by Grant Hill.

But it was a different kind of game. Duke was outscored from the field and made just one basket in the last 5 minutes. Good free-throw shooting made the difference. The Devils made their last 9 and 23 of 30. State was a woeful 5 for 13.

What Krzyzewski could see was a tired team, more so mentally than physically. There were telltale signs against the Wolfpack. Duke was in control and good enough to

win convincingly, but the team was not sharp. Grant Hill
played 40 minutes again; since Hurley's injury, he hadn't
been out of a game.

Krzyzewski knew Hill was getting fatigued. "He has a
great understanding of the game. But the responsibility is
wearing on him. Bobby just plays. Grant uses emotional
energy analyzing the game. With Bobby, it's instinctive.
But I'm sure it will be for Grant someday, too."

The Blue Devils completed the road trip 3-1. Krzyzewski's hopes for this stretch of games had been fulfilled,
though in ways he couldn't have anticipated. It was grueling, but satisfying. His team was tired, but he knew it
could play tough under duress. That was a lesson well
learned.

CHAPTER 7

AT PRACTICE BEFORE MARYLAND, the first home game in nineteen days, Krzyzewski wanted to pump up Grant Hill. So he talked to the team about how hard Grant was working because he was so into the game mentally, and then he called Hurley forward.

"Will you tell him you don't think about anything?" The team laughed. Hurley gave his little-boy grin.

"Bobby doesn't get tired because he's not analyzing. He's like a great chef who doesn't use a recipe, he just cooks by feel. But we'll take you the way you are, Bobby, because the best thing you do is win."

Now both of Krzyzewski's point guards had reason to feel good about themselves.

Maryland was a game they figured to win, Hurley or no Hurley, but the staff could see the danger signs in the second half against State. "We're starting not to play well," Krzyzewski said to his coaches. "The thrill of the challenge is starting to wear off. The adversity brought us closer together, but I'll be glad when Bobby's back."

Their lack of depth was still a problem. The starters were having to play too many minutes; with Hurley sidelined, the nation's No. 1 team became virtually a five-man unit. Parks was playing 10–12 minutes per game, but had not been productive. Nobody else had come forward to help out.

Back in the fall, the staff had counted on an eight-man rotation that would include Lang, Parks, and either Clark or Blakeney coming off the bench. Clark had had some big scoring games early against East Carolina and Harvard, where everybody got plenty of minutes and none of the starters played much more than a half. But Clark was struggling now.

Clark had hoped to replace McCaffrey as Duke's outside shooter coming off the bench. But that wasn't the role the staff wanted for him; with Hurley, Thomas Hill, and especially Laettner already in place, more three-point shooting wasn't what they needed. The coaches wanted the eighth man to fit in with the four regulars who were on the court. That meant playing tough defense, rebounding, and feeding the ball into the post. It meant shooting only when wide open, since scoring wasn't a requirement for the role.

As a freshman, Clark had been the fans' favorite. Whenever he was whistled by the officials, the students would yell, "Marty doesn't foul." But Marty was also used primarily at mop-up time, when the outcome was no longer in doubt, and he could shoot with abandon.

His new role was different, and Clark had trouble adjusting to it. Against better teams such as St. John's and Michigan, he had problems defending quick 6-5 and 6-6 opponents. Over a lengthy period in practice, he played himself out of the spot because he wouldn't stay in the defined role. As a result, the demands on the starters increased.

Another factor that was increasing their fatigue was the loss of Hurley's presence on defense. "Unless you really study the films, you don't see what a dominant player Bobby Hurley is," said Krzyzewski. "He puts tremendous pressure on the ball on defense. I sometimes hear announcers say we're playing great post defense when we're not playing great post defense at all, it's just that Bobby's harassing the ball handler so bad he can't even see the post men. When Bobby's out there, the other guys don't have to use up quite as much energy on defense, and that helps us run. It's almost like when you've got a great shot-blocker on the floor; Bobby makes everyone else's job on defense easier, only it's from the exact opposite direction."

With a tired team coming off a road swing that had been difficult both physically and emotionally, the staff was concerned about a letdown. There was always the danger the team could let out a collective "Whew!" and be content that it had gotten over the hardest part of the schedule.

Maryland was a second-division team and in the eyes of the public a one-man squad. Walt Williams, the 6-8 guard, scored well the first time against Duke, but he also had 11 turnovers and zero assists.

That night, it quickly became apparent that the entire home crew thought this win would be easy—not just the players, but also Krzyzewski's sixth man, the Cameron Crazies. He thought the crowd would be wild. Instead, the students appeared bored.

"There's a real closeness between the student body and the team here that's unique," said Krzyzewski. "They're not separate. They're more like parts of a whole. Our fans are really a part of everything we do, and they're usually incredibly sensitive to what we need. I thought they'd be really up tonight because we'd just come off such a successful string of games on the road. I didn't do anything to key them up because I didn't think they'd need it. I was wrong."

Ever since he had first seen Cameron Indoor Stadium

and become aware of the level of student support there, Krzyzewski had worked to make the student body a part of the program.

"The way Cameron is set up is the best way for college athletics and the students," Krzyzewski said. "At some big schools, they have a lottery for tickets, and a student might be able to see just a couple of games. Here, the students don't even have tickets—the student section is all bleachers. They've got the best seats in the house, right down on the floor, and it's all first come, first served. If a Duke student wants to see all of our games, he can. He might have to pitch a tent or wait on line, but he can do it."

Nobody was ever sure how many people were at a game at Cameron. The listed capacity was 9,314, but that was just a number. You couldn't guess by seating capacity because the students never sat. As long as the team was on the floor and was standing up, the students stood up with them. It was one more declaration that they were all in this together.

When Duke refurbished Cameron in 1989, it tore out the old bleachers and added new ones, including two more rows that could accommodate 750 more students. The bleacher benches were so narrow that it would have been too uncomfortable for anyone to sit through a whole game, but that was irrelevant. As far as athletic-facilities manager Tom D'Armi was concerned, the new bleachers served their purpose by letting more students see the games.

Even when the team was bad in Coach K's early years, the students didn't boo. "When we were terrible, they were still there," he said.

For a while, the Duke students were known for being as malicious as they were clever. Alumnus Lefty Driesell delighted in interacting with the students when he was the Maryland coach. He laughed as hard as anybody when the students wore Lefty masks, featuring a gauge in the brain area that read "empty." But nobody thought it was funny when the students threw condoms on the floor at the Terps' Herman Veal, who had been charged with sexual assault.

Krzyzewski worked hard to get the students to support his team, but not get on the players for the opponents. The whole team was fair game, but not one individual. "We've gotten better at that," he said. "They don't throw things as much; they don't get on the other people.

"The game is the show. They have to police themselves. I talk to them like I talk to my team. I'll point out that if they throw stuff, it might be Bobby Hurley that gets hurt. They don't want that. I feel comfortable with the students."

The students could still be hard on the referees to the point of significant vulgarity. When the cry of "Bullshit!" got too frequent, athletic director Tom Butters ordered a stop to it. So at the next game, after a controversial call, the Crazies yelled, "We beg to differ."

Certain chants became almost a custom. On Senior Day at Johnny Dawkins's last home game, when his parents were introduced, the Crazies screamed in unison, "One more kid." The chant was repeated at Danny Ferry's last game, and a few others. And they always knew, and acknowledged, the recruits in the stands.

With more and more games on national TV, many students learned the sight lines of the cameras. They not only painted their bodies, but they knew exactly where to stand. And standing was one of the primary symbols of their support.

But at halftime against Maryland, they sat. They ate and drank sodas, but mostly they sat. Krzyzewski was shocked. His weary team needed the student support and it wasn't getting it. Maryland couldn't stop Duke from scoring; Laettner wound up with 30 points. But it was 52–46 at intermission, uncharacteristically high-scoring for the games since Hurley's injury. After having played so well defensively on the road, the Devils were a step slow.

When Williams drew his fifth foul, against his old buddy

Davis, with 6:49 left, Duke was ahead 82–74. Williams had scored 26 points. It was all over, wasn't it? The crowd relaxed. So, apparently, did Duke.

Kevin McLinton, a heretofore nondescript Maryland guard, was scoring like crazy against Grant Hill. Later, without apology, Hill said, "McLinton played the game of his life. But I was so exhausted, so fatigued."

Every time down the floor, McLinton scored. He had 9 points in 6 minutes, and suddenly it was 88–87. The Crazies woke up. Duke was actually in position to do the unthinkable—to lose in Cameron, where it had been undefeated for two seasons.

But that only helped Maryland. "The crowd getting into it at that point didn't help us," Krzyzewski said, "because they weren't in the game until then. Now Maryland had nothing to lose. The crowd invigorated them and put the pressure on us."

McLinton did it again. His jump shot with 34 seconds left put the Terps ahead, 89–88. The Crazies panicked. "We had the game right there," McLinton said. "The number one team in the country, and we had them."

But Lang saved Duke. Laettner missed in close, but Lang swarmed down the lane and stuffed the rebound.

Krzyzewski made a defensive switch, putting Davis on McLinton. McLinton took a shot in the lane. Davis made it tough on him. Maybe he got a piece of the ball, maybe a piece of McLinton. It didn't matter; there was no whistle. The shot missed.

A Thomas Hill free throw with 5 seconds left clinched it, and after the game ended, Krzyzewski was the first to congratulate McLinton. "He was the story of the game."

Then Krzyzewski unloaded on the student body. Before the game, he had been presented a "Sixth Man" plaque from the senior class in appreciation of what the team had done during their four years. It now felt like a hollow gesture.

"We need to be a lot hungrier here at Duke University and appreciate what the hell is going on. I come out at halftime, I've never seen all the students sitting down before. It was a shock to me. I told my team to get off their butts and start playing better, and I think our students should get off their butts, too.

"You have something very special here because we've worked hard together for it. We've done it together as a university, but I think the students have gotten spoiled. Maybe my team is, too, but I know what real support is. If the students get mad about my saying that, maybe that's good.

"We don't need them to sit. We need them to stand up and be a part of it. They got rowdy and into it the last couple of minutes when they thought we needed it. But a good team has to be able to do it all the time, not only when you need it. That to me is being spoiled. I thought we played a little bit spoiled and we cheered a little spoiled."

The outburst sounded a little spoiled, too, but it was a calculated effort to get the students keyed up for the next game, and the ones beyond that. Krzyzewski usually did a pretty good job motivating twelve basketball players; he didn't mind trying it out on a whole student body.

Duke had been fortunate to win the Maryland game. The feared emotional letdown was evident, especially on defense. The next day, at the staff meeting, Krzyzewski discussed the practice plans. "We're at the end of an energy cycle. The key players are tired. We can knock the hell out of them, which they'll expect, or we can talk to them."

He decided on the second option. It was a beautiful February day, so when the team arrived, expecting to be chewed out, Coach K took them outside. They sat on the steps of the football stadium, the blue sky overhead, and he talked in a positive way. "Let's learn from victory," he said.

Then the players came inside, where, instead of practice, they were greeted with sundaes in the locker room. As they ate ice cream, they watched some tape, mostly of the team playing well. Afterward, Krzyzewski asked his staff, "Was it good? I have no idea. I really have no feel for this team right now."

He got his answer two days later in Winston-Salem. With 5:19 left in the game at Wake Forest, it appeared that Duke was going to beat the Deacons the same way it had been winning games ever since Hurley had been injured.

The Blue Devils were shooting 65 percent from the floor to that point, making 13 of 20 in each half, and holding a 67–57 lead. But it had been a choppy game. Duke had been called for three technical fouls, and Laettner was involved in a way with all three.

After getting a technical in the first half for complaining, Laettner was tagged with his second technical midway through the second half when he was called for hanging on the rim after a slam dunk. It was the only time that was called in a Duke game all season.

It was the third technical that outraged Krzyzewski. In their game at Chapel Hill, Carolina had gotten a technical when they complained about Laettner's touching the ball after Duke scored. Dean Smith pressed the complaint after the game. ACC supervisor of officials Fred Barakat sent out a memo on the subject, and national supervisor Hank Nichols even addressed the issue. For a couple of weeks, it seemed to Krzyzewski that this was the only thing the officials were paying attention to. It was the hot new felony on the college scene, and it was being called whether or not the touch was deliberate or interfered with the next play. It was ridiculous, and Krzyzewski suspected the enforcement wouldn't have been such a priority if Laettner hadn't been the original "offender," or if the original complainant had been someone less prominent.

Against Wake Forest, Dick Paparo called a T on the Blue Devils for touching the ball after a Grant Hill basket. The penalty was for delay of the game. Ironically, the ball that had been touched went directly to a Wake Forest player, who was able to begin the play immediately anyway. As far as Krzyzewski was concerned, the Laettner Rule was in effect. "I felt like, okay, are you guys happy now? You've finally called it on us. You're stamping out this plague on college basketball, and the ref who got us will probably get the frickin' Congressional Medal of Honor. Now can we please get on with the game?"

On the very next play after the Duke technical, a Wake Forest player touched the ball after a Deacon basket and nothing was called. Coach K didn't complain publicly, but he did talk to Barakat the next day.

The technicals were annoying and gave Wake Forest 4 points, but they didn't cost Duke the game. The Blue Devils did that themselves. Wake Forest outscored Duke 15–1 in the last 5 minutes. The Blue Devils, who had only 10 turnovers up to that point, had 5 more down the stretch. They didn't get off a shot in their last four possessions.

Two turnovers by Hill at midcourt hurt, with Trelonnie Owens turning the second one into a three-point play that tied the game at 67. Then Davis missed a free throw and Hill missed two.

Down 70–68 with less than 5 seconds to play, the Blue Devils took a time-out. Krzyzewski set up a final play, with Grant Hill throwing a full-court pass to Laettner. It was the first time they had tried it all year.

Hill threw a curve ball, which Laettner caught at the sideline with just one man guarding him and an open lane to what would have been an easy tying basket. But his toe was out-of-bounds. That ended any hopes for the Blue Devils. The Deacons added 2 points at the end for the 72–68 upset.

"We were awful, and they executed," Krzyzewski said. "It was a complete breakdown. I'm angry about it. That's just not the way we play. If we lose playing the way we can play, no problem. I have a little bit of a problem when we just give away points.

"There's no question we're not at the peak of our game right now. It's been a long month. And without Bobby,

it's a longer month. That's no excuse. The last four minutes is winning time. And you can't be tired in the last
four minutes."

The next day, Coach K was still fuming. He was especially unhappy with Laettner's play. He didn't like the fact
that Laettner had been out near midcourt handling the
ball when the coach wanted him at the foul line.

He had also studied the statistics, and Laettner simply
wasn't doing the job on the boards. In 1991, Christian had
18 double doubles in points and rebounds. Counting the
six games in the '91 NCAAs and the entire '92 season, he
had been in double figures in rebounding in just four of
his last twenty-nine games.

In the locker room before practice, with the team gathered, Coach K unloaded on his superstar. "Last year,
when you were hungry and had something to prove, you
did the job. You were terrific. Now you think you're a hot
ticket. Well, you suck. You absolutely suck."

Then Krzyzewski showed a tape of the final minutes of
the Wake Forest game. It showed Laettner way up high,
having the ball taken away from him. "What are you
doing forty feet away from the basket when we're running
two-three motion [Duke's delay offense]? That's a passing
offense. You think you're going to make a lot of money in
the NBA? Well, no pro team is going to invest in a
six-eleven white kid who gets four rebounds and tries to
dribble."

Krzyzewski was angry with Laettner, but he also needed
to make his star aware of what was happening to him. In
an effort to respond to the team's needs, Laettner had
gotten out of his role. He was trying to do too much and
it wasn't working. It was time for some shock treatment.

Laettner was genuinely surprised to hear about the rebounding numbers because he didn't usually worry about
his statistics; he just wanted the team to win. But Krzyzewski knew how Laettner responded to criticism: he
would go out and prove to his coach that he could go to
the boards.

The week before, Krzyzewski had told Laettner that his jersey was going to be retired before the Virginia game at Cameron, which followed Wake Forest on the schedule. He wanted Christian to be able to inform his family, so that they could make plans to attend.

Now Coach K was in a quandary. He was angry enough to prefer holding Laettner out of the starting lineup; but he knew he couldn't do that after retiring his number. It would be an intentional embarrassment, something Krzyzewski abhored.

He talked with the staff about it, and then he told Laettner, "A big part of me doesn't even want to start you. That's the position you placed me in. If your uniform wasn't being retired, you wouldn't start."

One of the responsibilities of the Duke assistant coaches was to find out how players reacted to criticism. Mike Brey checked with Davis about Laettner. "He's okay," Brian said. "He knows you're right. He can handle it."

"I bet Christian loved it," Krzyzewski told his coaches. "It was a red badge of courage, a macho thing. He could show people that he could take it."

And Laettner could still dish it out, too, as he showed in the next day's practice.

Duke was obviously thin in personnel with Hurley out, and Krzyzewski didn't expect him back until the finale with Carolina eleven days away and maybe not until the ACC tournament.

Early in the practice there was a scary moment as Grant Hill crashed into the ball rack, making a hustling play. It looked bad for a minute, but Hill was all right. Later, though, the scare was for real. Laettner went up hard for an offensive rebound, throwing Cherokee Parks aside as he did so. Parks stumbled and fell over Hill's ankle. Grant hit the floor hard, obviously injured.

Was Laettner taking out his frustrations on Parks, or being especially tough against him as he had all season? Was he trying too hard, driven by someone's doubts, and especially those expressed by the coach he respected so much? Or was it just one of those accidents that happen at practice? Coach K believed the last explanation; Parks was just in Laettner's way, and Christian was going hard to the boards, just as he'd been told to.

Hill was taken to Duke Hospital for X rays, and although practice continued, a pall fell over the workout. First Hurley, now Hill. Was there anyone who could play the point?

If Hill couldn't play, the starting role would have to go to Kenny Blakeney, who was a true rarity: a Duke redshirt. Blakeney, who had played under the legendary Morgan Wootten at DeMatha High School in Maryland, had been held out of action his first year to make certain he was in good shape academically. He practiced with the team that year, but rarely as a point guard. Even now, he was considered primarily a shooting guard, though his real strength was defense.

The next morning, with Virginia coming to Cameron that night, Dave Engelhardt called Krzyzewski at home. Hill had a high ankle sprain; he would be out ten to fourteen days. Things were not looking very comfortable for the No. 1 Blue Devils.

Two hours later, everything changed. Hurley stuck his head in Brey's office and gave the thumbs-up sign. He had a sheepish grin on his face. He had just been for a checkup with orthopedic surgeon Frank Bassett. "Doc cleared me. He said I can play tonight. I'm not sure I should. I haven't even practiced."

Hurley's intense work habits had resulted in an amazingly fast recovery. It began as soon as the team returned to Durham after the LSU game. Day after day, Hurley attacked the StairMaster in the training room. "I couldn't do anything except let it heal," he said. "But I wanted to make sure I got my cardiovascular exercise so I'd be in shape once I got back."

He found competition—something Hurley thrived on —in the training room. Jay Bilas was a fitness fanatic. He worked out almost daily on the StairMaster. "I really like that machine," said the volunteer coach.

Hurley spotted Bilas's record of 759 floors, scored by pumping the exercise machine at the highest level for almost an hour. When Bilas came in the next day, he found a note from Hurley—800 floors.

Not one to turn down an obvious challenge, Bilas pushed himself farther than usual, and when Hurley came in for his next workout, there was another note— Bilas had hiked the mark to 856. "I never could catch that," Hurley said. "Jay got me on that one. But the competition made me work harder."

"I kicked his ass," Bilas said with a wide grin.

But Bilas also appreciated Hurley's endurance and durability. "He's a machine. I played with Dawkins and Amaker, and they could run all night and not get tired. But they couldn't touch Hurley. He'll play forty minutes and you'll never know he's tired until he gets into the locker room. It must be intimidating being guarded by him. Everywhere you go, there he is, harassing you."

Hurley's own goal was to return in time for the Carolina game, but now he was being told he could play immediately. It was just three weeks from the night he got hurt.

Dr. Bassett told Hurley there was a chance he could break the foot again, but that he might actually help the healing by playing and getting the blood flowing. With the medical staff watching, Hurley worked out that afternoon. Then he waited to see how that affected the injured foot. He wasn't sure he could play.

On game days, Krzyzewski went home to nap in the afternoon. He usually rested for a couple of hours, but his sleep this afternoon was interrupted by Hurley, who never called his house and hardly ever initiated a conversation with a coach. It was uncharacteristic, but he was too excited to care. "Yo, Coach, I can play. I want you to know I can play." The call made Coach K laugh. He knew how eager his point guard was to return.

Hurley didn't take early shooting practice. He remained

in the locker room. Coach and player talked. "Bobby, I don't know how much I'm going to play you. Four minutes, six, ten. But I want you to be real honest with me. If it hurts, tell me right away."

The crowd was intense. It had responded to Krzyzewski's criticism about being spoiled and went bonkers when Laettner's No. 32 was retired. The number was presented to him by school president Keith Brodie.

Then the students cheered themselves hoarse when Hurley came out with the team to shoot lay-ups, and the biggest roar of the night came with 6:04 gone and Duke trailing 10–5, when Bobby entered the game.

"I was real smart in how I played," he said after Duke's 76–67 win that clinched the ACC regular-season title. "My shooting suffered because I couldn't push off. I couldn't do a whole lot of things. I had to give my man a few feet on defense."

But he played 26 minutes and contributed 9 assists, many of them to Laettner, with just 1 turnover. More than anything, he had given the team an emotional lift.

"It was kind of weird or coincidental that the game he comes back was one of my best games," said Laettner afterward. "I feel better with Bobby getting me the ball."

Laettner did play an inspired game. He missed 6 of his first 7 shots, then made 12 of his last 15. He had a season-high 13 rebounds. With a couple of seconds to play, he had scored 32 points—matching his number.

Christian always had a flair for the dramatic. He was fouled on the basket that gave him 32 points. The best free-throw shooter on the team missed badly, a brick off the left of the rim. Somehow, No. 32 with 33 points didn't have the same ring.

With seconds remaining, Virginia star Bryant Stith broke his school's record for career points and had to be helped off the floor with a severe cramp. Duke had recruited Stith hard. It came down to the two schools, and Bryant chose UVa. But he had played for Coach K's U.S.

team in the world championships in Buenos Aires. Krzyzewski respected and admired Stith and knew his family was at the game.

As the game ended, Krzyzewski spontaneously grabbed the courtside microphone and presented Stith with the game ball. Later, he said, "I feel really good that we did that. Yeah, that was right. Bryant was one of my guys."

It may have been the first such occasion in college history: on a night when one of its heroes had his jersey retired and another unexpectedly returned to action, Duke gave the game ball to a player on the visiting team.

The Virginia staff appreciated the tribute, and the fans cheered mightily for the classy Stith, who finished his career as the No. 3 scorer in ACC history, right ahead of Laettner.

Having passed one emotional barrier, the Blue Devils now faced another: a cross-country trip to play in Pauley Pavilion. A couple of weeks before the Duke-UCLA game, it looked as if it would be a rare regular-season battle between No. 1 and No. 2. Krzyzewski would have loved it, but the Bruins had lost two straight to fall to 21–3, and No. 4 in the rankings.

Still, it was a very unusual game for so late in the year. Krzyzewski had agreed to the road game to start a two-year series in another example of his creative scheduling. He wanted a tough road game as one last intersectional test before the NCAAs, and it wouldn't hurt to have the game at home next year, when a younger Duke team might need the Cameron crowd behind it. But for now Duke would have to travel without Grant Hill, and with Hurley still not at full strength.

When the team arrived in Los Angeles and headed to UCLA for practice, the bus driver got lost. Bilas had to give him directions; a native Californian, the volunteer coach had been to Bruins games countless times.

The team was to practice at the Wooden Center, adjacent to Pauley Pavilion, where UCLA had already announced a rare sellout. The eventual crowd of 13,023 was an all-time record for the famous court, where so many NCAA champions had played for John Wooden.

Normally, UCLA was a laid-back school, with no outward display of excitement. "A lot of famous people walk that campus and it doesn't stop," Bilas said.

Bilas showed the bus driver where to park, and the team had to use Bruin Walk, which goes past track and softball fields between Pauley and the Wooden Center. It was a beautiful day, full of southern California sunshine, with lots of students lying around on the warm afternoon. But they weren't just sunning themselves; they were camping out for the Duke game. That was unheard of at UCLA.

As the Duke team began its stroll to practice, hundreds of students rushed over and formed a parade line. Some yelled insults at the players, while others were seeking autographs.

Bilas was shocked. That sort of thing didn't happen in California. "I'm not sure if the Lakers had walked down Bruin Walk, it would have caused that much stir."

Laettner was subjected to a lot of the abuse, but so was Parks, a California native who had been courted hard by UCLA. Coach Jim Harrick had been extremely unhappy when Parks committed to Duke and canceled his official visit to Westwood.

As Parks walked down the ramp, the students mocked him. The school paper referred to him as "Cherokee 'I hate UCLA' Parks." That and the welcome startled Parks: "I wasn't expecting that. I don't hate UCLA. I just liked Duke better."

Krzyzewski realized a lot of the experts thought Duke would lose, but he was confident. He thought his team would win. Prior to the game, he encountered Jim Valvano, the former N.C. State coach who was the TV analyst for ABC. They talked in the runway.

"You guys could lose this game," Valvano said.

"It's the type of game Laettner likes to play in," Coach K replied. "I don't think Christian will let us lose."

Some reporters thought that between Grant Hill's absence and the cross-country trip so soon before the ACC tournament, the Blue Devils could lose or would at least take the game lightly.

Laettner and Davis knew better. "I was fired up from the moment I heard about the game," Christian said. Left unsaid was that Laettner loved the challenge of going against another "big white guy," the Bruins' Don Mac-Lean. Individual matchups with highly publicized players intrigued and motivated the Duke star.

Davis was more pragmatic. "I couldn't believe that people said we wouldn't care about UCLA. Just the thought of playing at Pauley Pavilion, with all that tradition, gets me excited. We'll be ready. We're taking this game seriously."

At the beginning, neither team looked like a potential Final Four squad. The shooting was abysmal for both sides, and Duke was having all kinds of ball-handling problems against UCLA's press.

The Blue Devils shot 33.3 percent in the first half. That was bad, but UCLA was worse. The Bruins checked in at 26.8 percent, but the home team got off 20 more shots (41–21), mostly because it forced 14 turnovers while making only 3.

As poorly as Duke played, however, it was within striking distance at 29–24 at halftime, thanks to a three-point play by Davis with 3 seconds left.

Both teams shot much better in the second half. Duke hit a sizzling 58.6 percent, more typical of its nation-leading average. The Blue Devils also forced a dozen turnovers. Duke finally took the lead at 55–54, on a three-pointer by Hurley.

UCLA tied it at 56, and Hurley made another three. Then, with the score deadlocked at 61, Laettner hit a three of his own, Lang stole the ball and made a lay-up, and in 43 seconds Duke went on a 7–0 run that broke the game open.

The Bruins closed to 66–63, but Davis put the game in

Duke's win column with a slashing lay-up with 1:34 left, followed by two free throws 13 seconds later. It ended 75–65. The co-captains had demonstated their leadership by coming up big in the clutch.

The defense did its job. UCLA was one of the best three-point teams in the country, but with hands in their faces all afternoon, the Bruins went 0 for 14. It was the first time in thirty-five games they hadn't connected at least once.

"Laettner won't let us lose," Coach K had said. Christian finished with 29 points and 13 rebounds.

Hurley, still not close to being in basketball shape, managed to play 36 minutes. Eight of his 11 points came with the game on the line.

"It was a not-so-pretty game," Krzyzewski said. "But it was good defense that made it ugly. In the last part, we showed who we were. We played smart at the end of the game."

Krzyzewski realized that the trip to California had been tough for Cherokee Parks, especially the walk on Friday, when the crowd that gathered around would alternately insult him and then ask him to pose for a picture. Back in Durham, Krzyzewski decided to have a talk with the big freshman.

On a lovely March afternoon an hour before practice, they sat on the steps outside Cameron for a heart-to-heart.

Krzyzewski asked him how he enjoyed Duke. "Coach, I love it here," Parks said.

"How do you feel about basketball?"

"I'm not doing as well as I can."

"Why not? Is it how you're reacting to Laettner?"

Parks was quiet at first, then he said, "Christian never says anything positive to me."

"It wasn't frustrating to you early when you were playing well. You tell me if this makes any sense. What would you think if I came home frustrated one day and Lindy said something to me, and I took it out on her. Would that be fair? Lindy wasn't the reason I was upset.

"You haven't taken responsibility in dealing with Christian. Would you be playing better if he wasn't on you? You need to be more mature and work harder.

"When you were playing well, nothing Christian said hurt you. Christian thinks you're a good player. He wants you to be really good."

"I understand that," Parks said. "I just wish he'd be more positive."

"I'll handle that. All three of us want the same thing. You just worry about playing. You handle that, and we'll be fine."

So Krzyzewski talked to Laettner. "What you've been doing with Parks isn't working now. You need to change your approach. Say really positive things to Cherokee." Laettner immediately agreed.

"He was really nice to me after that," Parks said later. Krzyzewski's request paid dividends. Nearly every minute Parks played the rest of the year was a productive minute.

Duke had one more road game left, on Wednesday at Clemson, a team the Devils had thrashed by 39 points at Cameron. Initially, Krzyzewski planned to charter down on game day, but he changed his mind. The team flew commercially the day before and would charter back immediately after the contest. He wanted them to get some rest. The staff knew this was a dangerous game; before its only sellout crowd of the year, Clemson would have nothing to lose.

On the surface, Duke had nothing to play for; the Blue Devils had already achieved their regular-season goals. They stood around early in the game, and Clemson made them pay. Not only were the Tigers hot, shooting 65 percent for the half, but Duke got in its worst foul trouble of the season.

Laettner, Hurley, and Thomas Hill all had three fouls. That left the scoring up to Davis. In the last 10 minutes before halftime, he scored 18 points to keep Duke close. He had 20, already a career high, at the break, but the Tigers were ahead, 52–47. The Devils were a step slow throughout in their poorest defensive period of the season. It was clear that they weren't ready to play.

In the second half, things went from bad to worse. Clemson was playing a fabulous game and Duke couldn't stop the Tigers. Krzyzewski was furious. With Duke trailing 68–51, Coach K made a shocking decision. Without a word to his assistants, he looked down his bench and pointed. "Cherokee, Marty, Kenny, Erik, Christian," he yelled. "You go in. Get those guys out of there."

So the nation's No. 1 team, which had not trailed by double figures all season, was suddenly represented on the floor by Parks, Clark, Blakeney, Meek, and Ast.

As the surprised starters walked to the bench with their heads down, Krzyzewski said to Amaker, "They don't deserve to be in there."

If Duke was going to lose, it would at least do it playing hard, playing with emotion. But Krzyzewski was prepared to lose by 30. That would shake some people up.

The deficit reached 19 points, but then freshmen Meek and Parks combined for a quick 8 points and the lead was coming down. The reserves took advantage of their unexpected opportunity, and on the bench, the once-solemn starters were enthusiastically cheering on their teammates. Coach K thought the change in their demeanor earned them another chance.

Laettner promptly hit a three-pointer. Then another. Davis scored again, and suddenly Clemson led by just 7. In less than 5 minutes, Duke wiped out that enormous deficit and took the lead on another three by Laettner.

There was still 7:29 to play. Surely Clemson would fold now in the face of that onslaught. But the Tigers regained their composure and even took the lead several more times.

Finally, Laettner's fourth three-pointer in as many tries gave Duke the lead for good at 95–94 with 1:37 left. Even then, the Blue Devils had to survive a miss by Corey Wallace with 6 seconds remaining to escape with a startling 98–97 victory.

Davis finished with 30 points. "He was placed outside his role because the other guys were in foul trouble," Coach K said, "and he came through." It was further evidence of just how far Davis had progressed in a basketball career that had started so modestly.

As the team was dressing for the trip home, Bilas and Tommy Amaker walked out of Littlejohn Coliseum, heading for the Duke bus and the fifty-mile trip to the airport. What the coaches saw was stunning. "There must be five hundred people out there," said Bilas, retreating into Littlejohn. "It's a mob scene. There's no way to get to the bus. And they're all Duke fans!"

A girl came up to Grant Hill and asked him if she could touch his ear. Startled, he said yes. She kissed his ear.

Clemson trainer Reno Wilson came to the rescue. He got on a forklift and drove it down the ramp into the tunnel that led into Littlejohn. He was followed by the bus, which backed down the ramp after Wilson had cleared away the crowd.

The team boarded and the bus inched its way up the ramp. Krzyzewski ordered the driver to stop. He went to the door, thanked the screaming crowd for their support, and told them the players had to catch a plane and couldn't get off the bus. He told the fans that if they wanted something signed, "just write to Coach K, Cameron Stadium, Durham." A few feet farther up the ramp, he had to open the doors again and repeat the message. His summertime mistake had become school policy.

When the bus arrived at the Greenville-Spartanburg airport around eleven-thirty, a carload of people pulled up beside it at the gate to the runway. It was a family who had followed the Duke bus for an hour. Once again, Krzyzewski thanked them for their support and told them to mail their requests to him.

Back on campus, Krzyzewskiville was growing every

day. That was the name for the tent city that began outside Cameron and weaved its way down the sidewalks, past Card Gym, along and beyond the tennis courts. The handwritten sign projecting the population of Krzyzewskiville changed daily. As the game with North Carolina neared, it had passed 160 tents. With up to ten students per tent, that meant there were more than 1,000 already in line on Thursday for the Sunday game.

This was one of the traditions that made Duke basketball unique. The students camped out, in this case for up to seventeen days, before the game with the Tar Heels.

Krzyzewskiville's residents would get the best places to stand in Cameron. Many of the students were aware of where the television cameras were placed and sought out the best angles for the possibility of appearing live on ESPN or a network telecast.

When the doors opened, the students were moved into a roped-off area in small groups, their IDs were checked, and they were permitted to enter the gym. They'd keep coming until athletic-facilities manager Tom D'Armi got the word from the security police that the place was full.

There were strict rules about Krzyzewskiville, which were enforced by the students. The tents were varying sizes, from one-person pups up to elaborate units that could sleep several. Some had portable generators for TVs and refrigerators. No more than ten people could be registered in any tent, and at least one person always had to be there. That required significant juggling of schedules, since all of the students were going to class while they were camping out. Good weather, bad weather, it made no difference; Krzyzewskiville sprang up to some extent for any big game, but reached a peak when the Carolina game coincided with Senior Day. This year, the weather had been mild, and the students were lucky.

Krzyzewskiville had been around for years, but had grown recently with the success of the basketball program. Television and radio stations did live broadcasts from Krzyzewskiville. Newspaper reporters came regularly to interview the students. It was the nation's longest-running outdoor party.

The coach loved the enthusiasm. It meant a lot to the team. The players laughed daily at the new signs; this year, most of them were directed at UNC center Eric Montross, who, besides having turned down Duke to become a Tar Heel, had said the Blue Devils weren't even the best team he'd played against this year. Montross did not identify the team that was better.

Krzyzewski sent pizza and soft drinks to the tents late in the week. He had gotten in a large supply of shirts from adidas, with whom he had his shoe contract, and gave them out to the campers.

On Saturday night before the Carolina game, it was his custom to invite the Krzyzewskiville residents into Cameron, where he usually showed game film on the large screen and gave them a scouting report. This year was different. The largest crowd ever showed up. The students entered the bleachers, but another fifteen hundred or so interested fans were in the upper deck. Krzyzewski just told stories and talked with the students. The atmosphere was jovial.

He talked about having the proper attitude for the Carolina game. It was a big game, obviously, but considering the status of the Duke program, it wasn't the only game. He told the students not to throw stuff on the floor —"Keep the tennis balls in your pocket"—and not to direct their derision at a single opposing player. "Your responsibility is to help us. You're our sixth man. Be positive."

When Coach K criticized the students after the Maryland game, he had gotten almost no negative reaction. Instead, many student leaders had written to ask, "Tell us what we can do."

So now he did. "All of you in the stands, all you know is Final Fours. It would be easy to think that we have some right to go to the Final Four. Nobody does. On our team, it's up to the seniors and juniors to tell the younger players what it's all about. They explain things. As coaches, we can't teach everything every year. The players do that. It should be the same way with you students.

"If the upperclassmen teach the underclassmen, you'll always recall when we were eleven and seventeen and you helped us build the program with your support. You can never lose track of that. It's up to you to pass on the tradition of Duke basketball."

Later, Mike and Mickie agreed about the gathering. It was the best ever.

The Carolina game was also Senior Day, the last home game for Duke's three seniors, Laettner, Davis, and Ron Burt. Senior Day was an important tradition to the Krzyzewskis; it was a chance for the seniors to reflect back on their time at Duke, not just for the players but for all the seniors in attendance that day.

Senior Day begins with a Friday-night dinner with the Krzyzewski family, usually out at a restaurant, but always someplace quiet, or with a private room. This time, Laettner, Davis, and Burt ate with Mike and Mickie and daughters Lindy and Jamie at Parizade. They relived old times and then got their instructions from Mrs. K. She told them the order in which they were to be introduced.

As usual, they wanted to know what to do. "It's your moment," Mickie said. "Whatever you do will be fine." (While that was true, some players milked the moment better than others. Gene Banks had brought an armful of roses out onto the floor with him, and he spent several minutes tossing flowers to the crowd. "He wasn't one of our recruits," Mickie said, laughing. "Our guys are usually a little more humble.")

The game-day crowd at Cameron was raucous and included recruits Chris Collins and Tony Moore. Also in the audience were author Stephen King, Chicago Bears quarterback Jim Harbaugh, and NBA analyst Doug Collins, Chris's father.

Before the game, Coach K told Amaker to ask Laettner

and Davis to come up to the coaches' locker room. It was a tradition of his to spend a private moment with his four-year seniors before their last home game. He told them how special they had been. "I love you guys. You've been great. Let's make this one our best." After an emotional three-man hug, the players returned to the locker room.

The visiting team was always alerted to the plans for the ceremonies in advance, and they always retreated to their locker room to wait for the start of the game. These moments were for Duke, and Duke alone.

One at a time, the seniors were introduced over the public address system at Cameron. First came Ron Burt. As was the tradition, Burt went out to center court, and applause washed down over him. He turned to all four sides of the court, acknowledging the thanks of the fans, and expressing his own gratitude to them, too.

"It's a very emotional moment," said Mickie. "There's no microphone or anything; the players don't give speeches before the game, and we don't bring the parents out onto the floor. The moment is just for our students, the ones who are in the stands and the ones on the team. It's really a reaffirmation that they're all together, they're all a part of the team and the program. It's the last home game for a lot of fans, too. We want this to be their moment as well as the players'."

Burt moved to stand over by the free-throw line, and only then was Davis, the next senior, introduced. The cheers for the co-captain were a little longer than they had been for Burt; he, too, turned to all four sides in thanks. When the applause had gone on long enough, he moved over to join Burt at the line, and then Christian Laettner was introduced.

The cheers rang out loud and long for Laettner, a good two minutes' worth. Laettner took his time, soaking in the emotions of the moment, turning as the others had in all directions, and then waved for Davis and Burt to join him for a last salute in the center jump circle. Finally, the whole team came running out to midcourt, slapping backs and exchanging high fives with the seniors, and then the whole team went off together to the locker room.

Only then did the spotlight turn to the players' parents, who were introduced in turn and saluted until they acknowledged the applause. Burt's parents were not in attendance, but Davis's mother and stepfather were cheered, and then when it was George and Bonnie Laettner's turn, the Cameron crowd began with the chant of "One more kid! One more kid!"

Unlike at many other schools, Senior Day did not affect the starting lineup. "We're honoring our seniors," Krzyzewski said, "but we've got a game to play, too." So Burt was in his accustomed seat on the bench for the tip-off against Carolina.

The game was predictably fierce. Krzyzewski got an early technical, and along press row there was immediate speculation that Dean Smith would get one shortly. Sure enough, Dick Paparo soon did the honors on Smith. Once again, Krzyzewski felt the officials were more uptight than the contestants.

Duke pulled away down the stretch to win, 89–77, despite a fantastic game by Hubert Davis, who scored a career-high 35 points for the Tar Heels including 6 of 8 three-pointers. "It was one of the top five performances against us in Cameron since I've been here," Krzyzewski said in congratulating Davis.

Laettner finished his home career with a big game. Officially now the second-best three-point shooter in the nation, the 6-11 center made 5 of 8 from behind the stripe. He finished with 26 points. Hurley, still recovering, scored 19, and Thomas Hill added 18. As an added bonus, Grant Hill played 21 minutes in his first outing since his injury. Originally, it had been projected he would be out until the ACC tournament.

After the game, there was one last Senior Day tradition to observe. The players went to the locker room as usual, but after dealing with the postgame interviews, they returned to the court, still dressed in their uniforms. By this time the crowd had poured out onto the court—that's how they leave Cameron anyway—and the players shared the court with their fellow students. It was a big mob scene, with the players at last getting a chance to speak to their fans via a hand-held mike.

"It's such a neat scene," said Mickie. "The players are surrounded by their peers. A lot of people who don't know the tradition just leave at the end of the game. I've never seen the scene on TV, and I've never seen anything written about it in the newspapers. There's no reason the media couldn't cover it, but they haven't. And that's nice, too, because the students aren't being kept at a distance by a bunch of cameras and notebooks. They're right there with the players."

Krzyzewski was delighted with this year's Senior Day. "It was unbelievable. Our fans were the best because they cheered for Duke, not against Carolina. It was the Cameron of old. I want to thank the students who camped out for two weeks. The senior class of students can pass on the legacy of how it's supposed to be to the other classes."

The Blue Devils finished the regular season at 25-2. In four years at Cameron, Laettner and Davis were 56-2. Ahead of them was one last shot at one of the few things they hadn't accomplished yet: an ACC tournament championship.

CHAPTER 8

AFTER THE CAROLINA GAME, Krzyzewski congratulated his team in the locker room. "It was a great game. I'm proud of you guys for not losing your focus because of Senior Day."

Then he wrote some numbers on the blackboard:

25-2—"This is what we've done. So first, let's enjoy that." Then he drew an arrow to 0-0. "This is where we are now," in reference to the ACC tournament. And another arrow to 3-0. "This is where we want to go next."

The ACC tournament was always important, but also kept in focus because the NCAAs, which followed, were the season's main goal. But this time it was different.

An ACC tournament championship was the missing jewel in the Seniors' career crowns. They had won everything else: national championship, three regional championships, back-to-back ACC regular-season titles. But Krzyzewski never brought up that point; he and his coaches knew the players would do that themselves. As competitive as Laettner and Davis were, they would get ready to play and they'd make certain the team was, too.

Davis understood Coach K's thinking: "We get tired of hearing 'You can lose every game as long as you win the two against Carolina.' That's not championships to me. We want to beat them, but we want to beat everybody. Carolina is a big game anytime, but all ACC games are big games.

"Making Carolina out to be the only game, the biggest game, that's for the fans. Carolina's just another game if they're the team in the way of our goals. We want championships, man. We want hardware."

There was a more practical concern among the staff. Since Hurley's injury, the Duke team that had been so dominating in January had not been intact. First Hurley, sidelined for six games; then Grant Hill, out for three. "I haven't had my team for five weeks," Krzyzewski said. "And when players come back after an injury, they are never at the level they were when they got hurt. Never."

The players partied Sunday night at Hurley's apartment, their one concession to having concluded the regular season with the No. 1 seed in the ACC tournament and the No. 1 ranking nationally. After this one social gathering, it would be all business again. The team wanted to get back to what it had been in January. If they accomplished that, the players were convinced everything else would fall in place.

There was no Monday practice, and Laettner and Davis conducted more mass interviews with the media at Cameron. Both talked about the need to get the team back in gear again; that was much more important than the tournament itself.

The ACC tournament was the one all others were judged by. The league was formed in 1953 by seven schools dropping out of the Southern Conference. Virginia became the eighth entry the following season.

The Southern had always held a tournament because it had so many members—once more than twenty—that not all the teams played each other. A tournament was considered to be the best way of crowning a champion.

The ACC maintained that tradition, although in the late sixties and early seventies it was excoriated by the national media for doing so. Quite often, the regular-season champion lost in the tourney, and since only the tournament champion qualified for the NCAAs, the ACC's best team would have to stay at home.

In an unusual circumstance that lasted until a second-place Duke team reached the NCAA finals in 1978, the ACC never won a regional when its regular-season champ didn't also win the tournament, while never failing to make the Final Four when its No. 1 team was the qualifier.

Eventually, when the NCAA expanded its field and allowed multiple entries from the more powerful leagues, almost every conference began to hold its own tournament. None has achieved the status of the ACC.

Even though five or six of the ACC teams are assured of an NCAA bid before the league tournament, fan enthusiasm has never waned; if anything, it has increased.

The tournament is a huge revenue-producer. There is no public sale of tickets; the number of seats is divided by nine, and only contributors to the various booster organizations and a handful of students get to purchase them. At some schools, with Duke and Carolina as the leaders, it took a lifetime contribution of many thousands of dollars just for the right to buy ACC tickets.

While most schools sold almost all of their tickets to boosters, Duke permitted students to buy one-tenth of the available seats. Slightly more than two hundred of the Cameron Crazies would be on hand in Charlotte.

People planned to stay for the entire event, whether their team won or not. In 1990, on a lovely Sunday afternoon, Georgia Tech and Virginia played to a sellout in the first-ever ACC finals that didn't feature one North Carolina team. There was almost no scalping because nobody went home.

If the coaches were unsure of the value of the tournament, the fans and players loved the competition.

Duke decided to make a change. Even though Grant Hill was back, Tony Lang would remain in the lineup, with Hill coming off the bench as the sixth man.

On Tuesday before practice, Coach K spotted Hill walking down the hallway. He motioned to Grant to join him on the Cameron court.

"How's the ankle?" he asked.

"It feels great. I'll be ready to go."

"I'm not going to change the lineup," Coach K said. "You're not ready yet, and besides, you know who you are. It's not like you need to start."

That was fine with Hill. He knew he was still recuperating, and Lang was playing better than ever as a starter. Hill and Lang were roommates and close friends. Hill had seen for himself that Lang responded better as a starter than as a reserve; he'd first noticed it their freshman year, when Lang moved into the lineup after accidentally breaking Grant's nose. During that period, Lang played his best basketball of the season.

Hill's ego didn't require that he start, and he knew he would play just as many minutes and be in the game at crunch time. If starting Lang helped him and the team, Grant was willing to come off the bench.

"It's fine with me," he said. "I get to see what's happening and I have an idea of what I want to do. I've never done this before, sat and watched what happened at the start of the game. But right away, you can see things develop. You have a different perspective than when you're starting. Then you just play. This way, you develop something of a game plan. I think I'm a little more offense-minded in this situation."

Thursday in Charlotte, Duke was practicing at the coliseum where that night Maryland would play Clemson. During a brisk scrimmage, Davis had the ball on a two-on-one fast break. He saw Thomas Hill out of the corner of his eye. He faked, then flipped the ball to Hill. But

Thomas wasn't expecting it and the ball went out-of-bounds. "Hey," yelled Coach K. "Let's go! If we play like this tomorrow, we'll get our asses kicked. We're here to win this thing and it starts right now."

Davis wanted desperately to win the ACC. He wanted to complete his career report card. But he wasn't concerned about the sluggish workout: "It was natural. We had been on the bus for three hours. We just woke up. But you're not going to say, 'Hey, Coach, we just woke up.'"

Now that everyone was back, the coaches wanted the team to remember how good it had looked when it was blowing everybody away. They wanted the players to see the joy they'd played with, the pride they'd taken in their trust and communication on the court. At the team meeting Thursday night, the players watched an 8-minute videotape in which they blitzed a good Georgia Tech team in Cameron. It may not have been the best they had played all year, but it certainly typified what had happened in January, when, as Coach K said, "we were in an all-out sprint."

The players saw a sensational transition game, fast break after fast break, with their smiles clearly showing their enthusiasm for the way they were playing. The staff wanted them to see how well they played when they could depend on one another. Now that everyone was back in action, that was the goal.

Maryland on Friday turned out to be one of those "almost" games—almost close, almost a blowout, Duke played almost well. Playing at noon with the crowd still streaming into the Charlotte Coliseum, the Blue Devils cranked up their scoring machine and found it a trifle rusty. Duke never dominated the Terps, who had beaten Clemson the previous night in the first play-in game in ACC history. But the Blue Devils were never in serious trouble, either.

Duke won, 94–87, and one play typified the whole afternoon. Hurley came barreling down the middle on a fast break, flipping a perfect no-look pass to Hill. Grant instantly flicked a touch pass to Davis, just the way they did it in January, when nobody doubted who was No. 1. It was a beautiful, daring play. Then Davis blew the lay-up. The team knew what it wanted to do, but execution was lacking this time. Still, the play energized Hurley. "That was the main thing that made me so excited," he said, that they would try that kind of play again.

Krzyzewski told the media it might be two weeks before Duke returned to midseason form, "But it's coming faster than that," Hurley said. "I can see us doing it more. It's right there."

Hurley had 16 points and 13 assists, and it could have been more. But Duke managed only 13 points out of 15 first-half transition opportunities, not the completion efficiency the team was seeking. But as far as the point guard was concerned, it was just a matter of time until the running game was there.

Laettner and Davis showed they were serious about becoming ACC champs. Christian matched his season high with 33 points and added 16 rebounds, his best board effort of the year. Davis scored 17 points and did a terrific defensive job on his old buddy Walt Williams. It took the Wizard 29 shots to get his 9 field goals, and he praised Davis's defense.

In the semifinals, an 89–76 victory over NCAA-bound Georgia Tech, Duke carried its regeneration a step further. This time, the Blue Devils did it with their defense. In the first half, Tech big man Malcolm Mackey was 5 for 5, but he might as well have been playing by himself.

Three Tech starters—Matt Geiger, James Forrest, and Travis Best—didn't even get a shot in the opening half. Other than Mackey, the Jackets were 4 for 25. Not surprisingly, they trailed, 43–25. "You can't get intimidated," Mackey said. "That's what we did—we got intimidated. You can't let Duke do that to you."

Tech's star guard, Jon Barry, had another interpretation. "That's that Duke mystique. People back down.

They don't believe they can win. The last three minutes [before halftime] is when Duke just puts you away. They go on one of those runs, and it just messes with your confidence."

That was exactly the message that Krzyzewski wanted his team to deliver. "When you're playing hard on defense and they're missing their shots and you're getting the rebounds and you're running, that just makes you want to do it more and more," Hurley said.

By fiercely defending and hitting the boards hard, Duke fit another piece into the puzzle, but the Devils weren't yet back to January form. They relaxed defensively in the second half and Tech scored 51 points. But despite some mistakes in transition, the offense continued to come together; Duke shot nearly 60 percent from the floor and missed just 2 of 27 free throws.

The team arrived back at its Charlotte hotel before it learned that Carolina had registered a mild upset by beating second-seeded Florida State in the other semifinal. It would be the championship game that the fans and media wanted.

"Let's not get caught up in the Duke-Carolina thing," Coach K said. "But I realize you guys are smarter than that. Just go out there and play like champions."

Krzyzewski knew the Duke players always wanted to beat Carolina, but the game was never played up over any other. Few of them were from North Carolina, so while they could feel the fan- and media-fueled hysteria, it wasn't the biggest game of their lives. If nobody believed that but the players, so be it. The emphasis this week was on doing something this particular team hadn't done— winning the tournament. But Krzyzewski wanted to make sure his players didn't feel that if they won, they had achieved something so huge it would detract from the larger goal—the NCAAs.

On Sunday, the Tar Heels came out firing. In the first 12 minutes, they pushed the ball downcourt and inside for eight straight baskets. They led, 26–21. But then the trapdoor opened and the hangman's noose tightened. Duke turned up the defensive pressure, strangling the Tar Heels and particularly Hubert Davis.

After having a career day at Cameron the week before, Davis couldn't score because Brian Davis wouldn't let him. It was 9 minutes before he could get off another shot, 13 minutes before he scored again. By that time, Duke was in complete control. "That's the most fun we've had playing defense in a long time," Hurley said.

When Duke had the ball, it was exceedingly efficient. Carolina couldn't figure out a way to guard Laettner on the perimeter. Christian hit 3 three-pointers in the first half, including 1 with 9 seconds left that was a back-breaker, creating a 44–36 lead. It was exactly the kind of play the Blue Devils ran so well when they were on top of their game during January.

"We were going to run a different play," Laettner said. "But I crossed halfcourt and no one was on me." That surprised Hurley, who made the pass. "I can't understand why they don't guard him out there. Montross tried, but he can't do it." The seven-foot Montross didn't have the agility to defend outside against Laettner.

Laettner finished with 25 points and 5 three-pointers in a 94–74 blowout that was almost an exact reversal of the score in 1991. He was the tournament MVP. "Like everyone said a million times before, this was something we hadn't gotten," he said. "We're going to put it under our belts. That's where it is already because I'm looking to the NCAA tournament."

Hurley had 11 assists, establishing championship-game, tournament, and career ACC records. He would have a chance to add to them as a senior.

But most pleasing of all to the staff was the play of Grant Hill, recovered from his ankle sprain. Hill didn't miss a shot of any kind, scoring 20 points and handing out 7 assists with just 1 turnover in a solid 27 minutes. Laughing, assistant coach Mike Brey said, "We're a pretty good team if Grant Hill isn't good enough to start."

Meanwhile, Lang started, played 22 minutes, and contributed 11 points and 4 rebounds.

Duke played a brilliant 28 minutes, outscoring the Tar Heels 73–48 after that initial deficit. It was easily the best the team had played in over a month.

When it was over, Laettner said to his roommate and co-captain, "B, we've got to cut down the nets."

"No, we don't need to do that," Davis replied. They discussed it with Coach K. "Do we have to cut down the nets?"

"Yes!"

Laettner was the next-to-last man up the ladder. He looked down at Davis and offered his best smile. Then he cut the last two strands and descended to the floor with the net in his hand.

Davis went up the ladder anyway, pulling away a lone string that was still attached to a hook. Had Laettner forgotten his buddy? "No," Davis said with a knowing grin. "He was just being an asshole."

Dean Smith marveled at Laettner's three-point shooting, 19 for 29 in the past six games. "Most people would like to see a six-eleven guy shoot three-pointers," he said. "Bird couldn't shoot sixty-five percent in this league."

The postgame talk immediately switched to the NCAAs. Laettner promptly dismissed the idea that Duke was invincible. "They said that about UNLV last season. I've always had fun times in the NCAA tourney, and if we play extremely smart, we're hard to beat."

That was the message Krzyzewski wanted to deliver. He couldn't have said it any better: have fun and play smart. That was Duke basketball.

Krzyzewski was proud of his team, and what it had accomplished. He'd created obstacles in the February schedule, and then the injuries created even more of a challenge. But to date, the team had met all the goals. It had started the year No. 1 and never dropped from that spot because on the week of the loss to Carolina, No. 2 Oklahoma State and No. 3 Kansas were also beaten, and when the Devils lost at Wake Forest, they were the ninth team in the Top Ten to lose that week. Duke was the first team since Carolina in '82 to begin the year No. 1 and finish it that way in the national polls, which ended with the regular season. It was the first team since Indiana in '76 to remain on top all year. Both of those teams won national championships.

As the team bus rolled toward the Holiday Inn in Lexington, North Carolina, where the team would eat its postgame meal, Krzyzewski stood and talked about the differences a year could make. "It's a little different from last year," he reminded the players. But he had the same message: "We're going to win the national championship."

Last year, perhaps some of them didn't believe him. This time, there were no doubters.

CHAPTER 9

THE MOOD ON THE BUS after the ACC tournament was light and happy, but as the players looked forward to watching the NCAA pairings, Bobby Hurley felt increasingly uneasy. Hurley knew that for the first time in seven years, the NCAA East Regional wasn't being played at the Meadowlands, Seton Hall's home court. Tournament rules prevented a team from playing in a regional at home; Hurley understood that the shift meant that Seton Hall, regular-season champs of the Big East, might be placed in the East, where the Blue Devils were a certain top seed.

The one thing Hurley did not want was a potential pairing with Seton Hall because his younger brother Danny played for the Pirates. Hurley had no desire to have to play against Danny.

When the team arrived at the Holiday Inn, it was taken to a private room where there was a big-screen television and a buffet line. And a crowd outside. Somehow, a lot of fans had found out where the team was going to eat. They weren't allowed into the room, so they did the next best thing: as the Duke players strolled through the chow line, the fans pressed their noses to the windows, watching them. Nobody knew how the fans knew where they would be at that time, but it should have been no surprise. It was just another example of the rock-star fervor that had followed the team around this season.

The families of the coaches were there, as were the Hurleys, Bob Senior and Chris, and daughter Melissa. They had dropped by to visit with their eldest son.

When the NCAA pairings show came on, there wasn't the sense of anticipation there had been the year before. The team knew it would be the No. 1 seed in the East and play at Greensboro. Mike Brey told the players they would probably play Campbell, surprise winners of the Big South Conference. Because of their religious affiliation, the Camels couldn't play on Sundays, so they had to go to a site where the games were on Thursday and Saturday. Greensboro was one of two, and it would have made no sense to move Campbell to the West. Brey was convinced the Blue Devils would be paired against the Camels from Buies Creek, North Carolina.

That prediction was accurate. Duke would play Campbell Thursday evening. After it disposed of the sixteenth-seeded Camels, it would play the winner of Texas-Iowa. But Hurley's fears were realized: when the TV screen showed the pairings for opening-round games, he immediately spotted that Seton Hall was the No. 4 seed in the East, matched against La Salle, also at Greensboro. If Duke and Seton Hall each won twice, the teams would meet in the third round at Philadelphia's Spectrum. Hurley's parents weren't pleased. Neither was Bobby.

Krzyzewski wasn't about to reveal his feelings to his team. But when he and his coaches discussed the pairings, they felt it was the most difficult bracket they had faced since they began their run of Final Four appearances.

Forget Campbell. That would simply be a great story line for the media. But either Iowa or Texas would be

dangerous in the second round. And Coach K thought
Seton Hall was the best team in the Big East. Usually, if
you had to play the top club from that powerful conference, it wouldn't be in the Sweet 16; it would come in the
regional championship or the Final Four. Duke had met
a Big East team in that situation the previous three years.
But this pairing would be an emotional one in many ways.

Seton Hall's P. J. Carlesimo and Krzyzewski had been
selected as the two college coaches on the U.S. Olympic
squad, the Dream Team. Their relationship went back to
Coach K's days at Army, when Carlesimo coached at
nearby Wagner College. They worked together in 1990,
coaching the U.S. team in the Goodwill Games. A matchup with Seton Hall would be difficult for more than just
the Hurleys. P.J. was a great friend. His mother, Lucy,
said, "If P.J. has to lose, I hope it's to Mike." The Krzyzewski family loved the Carlesimos.

Kentucky was the No. 2 seed in the opposite bracket.
The Wildcats had been moved out of the Southeast Region, even though they had won the Southeastern Conference tournament, because that regional would be
played at Rupp Arena.

Many in the media were saying and writing that the
East was the easiest bracket. Nobody on the Duke staff
felt that way.

Something new was added Monday to the notebooks
the Duke players always carried with them. It was a
bracket for the NCAA tournament. Come tournament
time, in office pools and locker rooms all around the
country, even casual basketball fans carry around a sixty-
four-team chart of the draw so they can follow their picks.
The Duke team's brackets were different. They contained
just four teams: in huge letters, Duke-Campbell and Iowa-
Texas, then Duke versus the Iowa-Texas winner.

Fans could enjoy the tournament as a broad tapestry, a
huge hoops feast being played out all over the place. But
for Krzyzewski and his players, the focus was narrower:
three four-team tournaments, one each week. Win one,

then move on to the next. As always, Krzyzewski wanted his players to focus on what *they* had to do, and not to worry about anyone else.

Davis and Laettner, the co-captains, helped set the tone at Duke's media luncheon on Monday. "Our method is simple," Davis said. "We have three four-team tournaments left—Greensboro, Philadelphia, and Minneapolis."

Although Duke had won the previous NCAA tournament and had just finished the season as a wire-to-wire No. 1, the media attention for the opener was not on the Blue Devils. From the moment CBS showed the Duke-Campbell pairing, the phones never stopped ringing in tiny Buies Creek, located approximately one hour from Durham.

This was the first NCAA trip for the Camels, and their colorful coach, Billy Lee, became an instant celebrity. "When we got the news we were playing Duke, we were shaking like a wet dog in the wind," said Lee. "I'm as nervous as a cricket in the henhouse."

Lee loved the attention, and national media poured into Buies Creek, which has one stoplight and no restaurants. "Duke has all those McDonald's all-Americas," Lee said. "We can go to McDonald's, too. But we have to travel to Lillington."

The biggest hit was a T-shirt that read, "If you can't run with the Camel, stay out of the Creek." Requests for any kind of shirt with a camel on it came pouring in from all over the nation.

Krzyzewski, reflecting on the "We want Duke" signs that had been prominent all season, said, "I guess, 'We want Campbell.' " Certainly the players did. They realized that if they were successful in their pursuit of this title, they would establish their place in basketball history.

Although Duke had been to four consecutive Final Fours, this NCAA was different. "This is the first time we know we can win the national championship," Davis said. "In the past years maybe there has been some apprehension. There have been some other good teams. But we know how it's done. We know how to get there. All the things that are needed, we can provide."

Krzyzewski wasn't concerned about being the favorite. "There has been so much so-called pressure on this team all year long. But we don't look like a team under pressure. We're excited about the opportunity to do something that's special, that's unique. I don't see why that should be pressure. It's a fantastic opportunity for us."

Tuesday's practice was short and to the point. There was no need to overwork the team now. The concentration would not be on the opponent, but on Duke. The scouting report on Campbell was brief and succinct. Krzyzewski looked at his players, seated on the bench at Cameron, and said, "Campbell is not a talented team. They're not nearly as good as we are."

But the Camels certainly were enjoyable. Coach Lee and his squad delighted in the attention they received at the Coliseum practice on Wednesday, and some of their fans stuck around for the Duke drills.

The Blue Devils met first at Cameron, where they watched a highlight tape, walked through the Campbell scouting report, and departed for Greensboro at five. The Duke practice was set for seven P.M.

When the team got off the bus 20 minutes before their practice time, the Coliseum was almost empty. Then, almost magically, within moments there were more than five thousand screaming, shrieking fans, all eager to get as close to a Duke player as possible.

This was far more people than had seen a Campbell game at any time in the season. It was typical of the reception that Duke got on many of its road trips, but it was the first time the North Carolina media had seen it for themselves. The sports information and promotions people were barraged with queries. The answer was always the same: "You should have seen what happened at Buffalo, at Maryland, at Clemson, at UCLA. This is the way it was on most of our road games."

Duke opened the hour-long session just as it had during the '91 NCAAs, with a dunking exhibition. The audience reacted as if it were a New Kids on the Block concert. The heartthrobs, as usual, were Laettner and Hurley, even though the earthbound Hurley could only envy his soaring teammates' stylish jams. But all the players drew cheers from the growing audience.

Cameras were everywhere. Flashbulbs popped incessantly. Dunk after dunk brought louder and louder noise, with one fan holding a sign, "10," after every slam. The noisier it became, the more vigor the players put into their slams.

"It got a little crazy there for a while," Krzyzewski said. "I just told them to go out and have fun. You have to remember, this tournament, it's still fun."

Until it came time to leave. Fans were pounding on the door where the players would normally exit. There was a mob scene outside the door, so Coliseum authorities had to sneak the nation's No. 1 basketball team out the back way.

Duke was staying at a motel near the airport. To the delight of the Hurley family, Seton Hall was also staying there. Bobby and brother Danny got to hang out together. Hurley also spent time with his former high school teammates Terry Dehere and Jerry Walker, now stars for Seton Hall. The atmosphere was very relaxed.

The odds makers had made Campbell a trillion-to-one shot to win the NCAAs. Lee wanted to know how many zeros there were in a trillion. He also said his concern was not whether his team would win, but if it would get off a shot.

The Devils showed their intensity right from the opening tap. The ball went inside to Laettner against Campbell's sagging zone. He flipped it out to Thomas Hill, who made a three-pointer. Laettner then forced a steal on Campbell's first possession and Hill turned it into a lay-up. Panic was setting in quickly for the underdogs. The Camels couldn't get the ball across halfcourt in the required 10 seconds. Laettner made a three-pointer. Just like that, in less than 90 seconds, it was 8–0.

At halftime, Campbell was shooting 18.8 percent and had 14 turnovers. Duke led by 20 and cleared the bench early in the 82–56 blowout. Krzyzewski got just what he wanted—a solid performance and a game to build on.

Earlier in the day, Seton Hall rallied in the last minute to defeat La Salle. Bobby Hurley wasn't sure how he felt; he wanted Danny to do well, but he still had no desire to play against the Pirates. "I hope it doesn't happen," he said.

The Hurley parents were also uneasy. "I'm devastated at the thought of them playing against each other," said Bob Senior, who coached both sons in high school. "We've always dreaded that this might happen," said mother Chris. "In my heart, I don't want to see that game."

The assistant coaches stayed to watch Iowa break through Texas's pressure defense to shoot lay-up after lay-up. They were somewhat surprised because the staff had felt the Longhorns were dangerous. But for the second year in a row, Duke would be playing the Hawkeyes in the championship game of their first minitournament.

That meant Duke had avoided one brother matchup. Lamont Hill played for Texas. Unlike his teammate, though, Thomas wanted a shot at his brother. "He doesn't think we're that good," T. Hill said.

There would be no surprises against Iowa. The Hawkeyes returned their entire starting five and most of their bench. They pressed and were good rebounders. In '91, Duke had taken charge by beating the pressure and then attacking shot-blocking center Acie Earl.

Duke-Iowa II was different. Brian Davis, who had made 6 three-pointers all season and was shooting 20 percent behind the stripe, began the game with a three. Laettner hit a couple of lay-ups. Hurley made a three-pointer. Just like that, it was 11–2.

Davis, who normally had his toe on the three-point line when he shot from outside, made his second trey, the only time he hit two in a game all year. That made it 19–5. The rout continued, even though the Blue Devils were missing regularly on their jumpers. But Duke was hitting the boards relentlessly in its best offensive rebounding performance of the season.

At one point it was 41–15, and the Duke students were yelling, "Campbell was better." It reached 48–22 with 2:08 left, and even though the Blue Devils didn't score the rest of the half, they had still doubled the score on the startled Big Ten team.

All this was accomplished despite 37.8 percent shooting, Duke's worst percentage of the year. But 14 offensive rebounds and 13 Iowa turnovers made it a blowout. Davis, usually the team's No. 5 scorer, had 17 points.

The Blue Devils didn't maintain that intensity, but it was still 59–37 with 11:13 left after a Grant Hill dunk. But 2½ minutes later, Iowa had scored 14 consecutive points, the lead was down to 8 points, and the crowd was buzzing. Only then did Coach K call a time-out. He had let Duke play because he wanted to see how they'd react. "I got my answer," he said later. "Badly."

Davis began the sinking spell with a couple of wild shots. Brian had scored just one field goal in the half after that big start, and he got carried away. With its lead, Duke didn't need to be shooting that quickly, especially with nobody underneath to rebound.

That was bad enough, but Iowa's pressure was starting to bother Duke, which turned the ball over three times. The Blue Devils usually destroyed a press; that was when Hurley was at his best. But not this time.

Suddenly, the ball didn't seem to be important to Duke. The players weren't coming to meet it, and that caused the careless giveaways. Krzyzewski could see that his team didn't yet have the staying power to play a complete 40 minutes. With the big lead, Duke quit thinking on the floor. That was uncharacteristic.

Laettner screamed at Hurley to come get the ball against the press, and Hurley yelled back at him. They ran down the court, openly bickering. Laettner pointed at Hurley, who shouted back, "Don't put your finger in my face."

A furious Krzyzewski called an immediate time-out. As they were seated on the bench, he grabbed his two stars by their jerseys. "God damn it, what are you guys doing? If you play like that, we're going to lose. I hope we do lose." Then he walked away, letting them think about what had happened.

The team had fallen into a trap. They had begun to play as individuals, not as a unit. Davis's shots were dumb, but the on-court confrontation between Laettner and Hurley was dangerous.

Coach K returned to the huddle. "Can you guys play together?" he asked. Hurley was still mad at Laettner and wouldn't look at the big center. But Laettner always did what the coach asked. He gave the point guard a playful pat on the back of the head. He knew he was wrong, and he was ready to play it Coach K's way again.

During the uncharacteristic 14–0 run, Duke was disintegrating because nobody was leading. Hurley needed to come to the ball more, and Laettner needed to do a much better job of inbounding against Iowa's pressure.

After the time-out, Duke regained control. Laettner made two free throws. Hurley hit a jumper, then fed Christian for a baseline basket. Hurley drove for a lay-up. Laettner made 2 steals, a lay-up, and a free throw, and then two more foul shots.

Between them, they scored 13 consecutive points as the Devils resumed command by 17 points. The final was 75–62. In less than 7 minutes after Krzyzewski's blast, Laettner scored 9 points, had 2 steals, blocked a shot, grabbed a rebound, and took a charge.

Laettner and Hurley were veterans. The Duke program was built on communication and trust, and for a moment they had forgotten about that. Krzyzewski got them back on track, and the result was obvious. If Duke was going to win, then everybody had to play together.

In the second game, Seton Hall played a great second half and crushed Missouri. Bobby and Danny would be on opposite benches at the Spectrum on Thursday night.

The brothers had enjoyed Greensboro. They went go-cart racing along with Kenny Blakeney and Seton Hall's 7-2 Luther Wright. "Danny and I really went after each other," Bobby said. "We were trying to knock each other into the wall, and for a while I thought they might kick us out of the place. But we never really talked about playing against each other."

Philadelphia would be another matter. Bobby had all kinds of mixed emotions going into the game. In the summer, he had played for Carlesimo in the World University games and the U.S. had won. "I know his offense and his defense," Hurley said. "Maybe I should give the scouting report."

Coach K had mixed emotions of his own. The thought of competing against as good a friend as Carlesimo was difficult for him. "You have to be professional about it. I'm happy for them they advanced this far. You want your friends to do well. That's good. The fact that one of you has to lose is bad. Real bad."

The workout on Wednesday at the Spectrum was similar to Greensboro, with one notable exception. Perhaps it was the Jersey influence, but the horde that tried to touch every available Blue Devil was primarily interested in Hurley. One young lady was emphatic: "I want to marry Bobby Hurley."

Duke put on its usual dunking exhibition for the picture-popping audience, and Hurley got so carried away with the enthusiasm directed his way that he attempted a slam. Coach K had made a point of trying to get Bobby into the spirit of the dunkfest. "I knew that playing against

Danny was preying on his mind," he said later. "I wanted the energy of the crowd to help get his mind off it. Before his turn he looked over at me, and I just laughed and told him to go for it."

The year before, at one of the tournament dunk sessions, the seniors Koubek and Buckley had held down the breakaway rim so Hurley could throw one through. This year, with all the attention Bobby was getting from the crowd at the Spectrum, Davis's and Laettner's attitude was, "Hey, kid, you're on your own." He came up short, but received a huge cheer just for trying. "I was pretty close today," he said afterward, although that was strictly his viewpoint. "I'm kind of excited about how close I was today. I didn't think I could get that close. If I had bigger hands, I might have been able to throw it down."

One issue had been decided: Bob Senior and Chris would sit on the Duke side. "Bobby is the older son," his mother said. In a more practical vein, Bobby noted, "I got them the tickets."

Duke–Seton Hall didn't begin until well after ten P.M. on Thursday night, and it was Friday before the Blue Devils prevailed, 81–69. The Pirates never led and were deadlocked only at 2–2, but the game justified Krzyzewski's—and Hurley's—worst fears.

There was nothing easy about it. Both teams played great defense. Seton Hall swarmed all over Laettner, limiting him to 16 points, but to do that, the Pirates had to give up something—Tony Lang. Lang tied Laettner for Duke's scoring honors with 16 points and led the team with 7 rebounds. He was continuing to produce as a starter. Grant Hill, despite being plagued by a sinus infection, added 13 more points.

The main problem for Duke was Hurley. Carlesimo played Danny 18 minutes against his brother, far more than he had averaged during the year. Although Danny didn't score, it was a smart move; Bobby had just one basket in the first 39 minutes and turned the ball over 6 times.

"When my brother was out there, it was a weird situation," Bobby said. "It was really distracting. It was the hardest thing I had to do this year. My whole game is concentration and intensity. Running the team was hard for me with my concentration and intensity not up to the level it normally is."

Hurley's normal frame of mind was, I'm going to kill this guy. Against Danny, he couldn't do that. "It was a no-win situation," he said. "If I did well against him, that's hurting my brother. If I did bad, it's bad for my team. For the most part today, the matchup was a negative for me."

Hurley finished with 4 points. He was obviously distracted, so Carlesimo kept Danny on the court, even though the freshman wasn't scoring.

But Duke's defense was every bit as good as the Pirates', and its offensive balance was far better. Five of the Devils had at least 13 points, while only Dehere and Gordon Winchester did much scoring for Seton Hall. The Blue Devils made 24 of 31 free throws while the Pirates were only 8 for 14.

The locker rooms of the two teams were side by side in a narrow hallway. As Carlesimo was talking with a few members of the media after he departed the press interview room, he spied Mickie Krzyzewski. He went over immediately, hugged her, then cried on her shoulder. Later, as the press corps walked back from the interview room, there was Mike Krzyzewski seated next to his friend P.J., consoling him. It had been a difficult game for everybody.

The Blue Devils were just one step away from another Final Four. But now they would be in a matchup that had everybody at CBS smiling. It would be the No. 1, top-seeded Blue Devils against the second-seeded Wildcats. Even in a city with a great basketball tradition such as Philadelphia, you couldn't get much more tradition than Duke versus Kentucky.

Krzyzewski knew it would be tough. Kentucky was unpredictable. The 'Cats made their reputation by shooting three-pointers, but they had eliminated a good UMass team despite 3-for-18 outside shooting.

Rick Pitino was a great coach and sophomore Jamal Mashburn a great player. But what Coach K really liked about Kentucky was the seniors—John Pelphrey, Richie Farmer, Deron Feldhaus, and Sean Woods. With their program in turmoil when Eddie Sutton was forced out as coach, those players stuck around. They were veterans, older than the Duke players, and tough mentally. That was a characteristic Krzyzewski admired.

In three NCAA games, Duke had never trailed, just as it had led all the way against Kansas in the '91 finals. But that streak ended in a hurry against Kentucky. Running its offense flawlessly, the Wildcats surged into a 20–12 lead, making 4 three-pointers. But Duke didn't back down, outscoring Kentucky 15–2 to gain a 27–22 lead. After that, the teams matched baskets in an elegant offensive display that concluded with the Blue Devils holding a 50–45 halftime advantage.

Krzyzewski reminded his team in the locker room that Kentucky was a team with nothing to lose. "You've got to stick with them on the perimeter. They're running their offense well, and all of their guys are shooting with confidence." As halftime speeches went, it was nothing big; the coaches felt Duke just had to play its game and not keep turning the ball over.

With Laettner converting every time he shot and Hurley hitting well from outside with 5 three-pointers, Duke led by as much as 12 points at 67–55. But the Wildcats battled back behind Mashburn, and with 8:24 left, the lead had been cut to 73–68.

Then came a play that would be replayed and discussed for the next week. Kentucky freshman Aminu Timberlake came under Laettner and fouled him, falling to the floor beneath Christian. Laettner lost his balance, and while regaining it, he did something stupid. He tapped Timberlake on the chest with his foot, collecting an immediate contact technical from the officials.

Timberlake, the rookie, had caused the senior all-America to lose his cool. The Kentucky player bounced off the floor, laughing. He wasn't hurt, and Laettner was one step closer to fouling out. Under the rules, a contact technical counted against the personal foul limit of five.

Coach K called Laettner to the sideline. "That was a dumb thing to do. We have the game in hand and you do something like that. What were you thinking about?"

Laettner didn't respond. He knew he had made a mistake. Then Coach K reminded him that the play also counted against his personal-foul total. He now had three. As usual, Laettner was ready to play his best after getting chewed out.

On the CBS telecast, analyst Len Elmore said, "I don't know whether Laettner did that intentionally." Play-by-play man Verne Lundquist replied, "Oh, yeah, that was intentional."

The play was never mentioned again during the telecast, and neither coach made any comment about it afterward. For the people who were in attendance, it was not a major topic of conversation. The reaction would come later.

Duke led 81–72, but Kentucky scored 9 points in a row to forge the first deadlock since 20–20. These two heavyweights slugged it out until Kentucky took a 91–89 lead on a three-pointer from the corner by Dale Brown.

Moments later, with Duke on top, 93–91, Feldhaus worked free for a lay-up with 33 seconds left and the crowd was roaring. Duke held for the last shot. Hurley didn't execute on the final possession well and ended up taking a runner in the lane that missed. Overtime!

David Gladstone, Duke '91, brought his nine-inch TV set with him Saturday to his job as manager of the Triangle Dinner Theatre at the Radisson Governors Inn, located near the Raleigh-Durham Airport. Gladstone knew the Duke-Kentucky game would end about the time of inter-

mission for Pump Boys and Dinettes, *which had attracted a near-sellout crowd of 150. Some 30 seconds before the end of the first act, regulation time expired in the Spectrum.*

When the audience heard the score, there was a mass exodus. Most of the crowd went downstairs to the bar, where there were three TV sets, to watch the overtime.

Others, including waiters and actors, crowded into Gladstone's office to watch on the tiny TV set. There was no interest in starting the second act on time. Intermission would be extended until the game ended.

Kentucky twice took the lead in the first few minutes of the extra period, but Laettner's two free throws tied it at 98 with 1:53 left. In the first 4:28 of the 5-minute period, each team scored 5 points. Each would score at least that many in the next 32 seconds.

With 31.5 seconds remaining, Laettner fought through a double-team to bank in one of the most remarkable shots of the season for a 100–98 advantage. But at the other end, the bullish Mashburn broke free down the baseline, made a lay-up, and was fouled on the arm by Lang, who was beaten on the play and should have let him go. When the Kentucky star converted, the 'Cats led 101–100 with 19 seconds to play. Kentucky called time.

When action resumed, Grant Hill made the inbounds pass to Hurley, who threw inside to Laettner, operating inside the foul line. As Laettner spun right, he was grabbed on the arm by Mashburn. Five seconds of playing time after his three-point play, Mashburn had fouled out.

Christian made both free throws just as he had against UNLV the previous season, giving him 10 straight for the night. Duke led, 102–101. After his miss against Arizona as a freshman, Laettner never again missed a key foul shot.

Woods dribbled the ball up the floor and passed to Pelphrey, who was still outside the circle. Pitino didn't like what was happening. With 7.8 seconds on the clock, Kentucky called time-out. The capacity crowd was standing.

Farmer inbounded to Woods, who was guarded by Hurley at the left side of the key. The Wildcat senior drove right, down the foul line. Hurley was floored by Pelphrey's solid screen, but Laettner flashed out to throw his hands up as Woods shot over him. The ball banked off the backboard and swished through the basket.

Kentucky led 103–102. Duke called an immediate time-out. There was just 2.1 seconds on the clock. It appeared the experts who believed it was impossible to repeat were correct. Duke's Final Four streak was about to end.

Mike Gminski was seated on the end of the Charlotte Hornets bench, where the twelve-year NBA veteran had been for most of the season. Gminski, who played in the NCAA finals for Duke in 1978 and was a three-time all-America, had missed three months of the pro season with a cranky back. The Hornets were playing the Washington Bullets in the Capital Centre, where a surprising late-March crowd of 17,522 was watching the home team romp in what would be a 113–97 victory.

Gminski, recently returned to active duty, had not played in four or five games. He was satisfied to be three seats away from a fan who was watching the Duke-Kentucky game on a portable TV. He was able to get constant updates. Apparently, many in the audience were also watching the college game because the periodic roars had nothing to do with what was happening on the court.

With less than 4 minutes to play in the Duke game, but in the third quarter for the Hornets, Charlotte coach Allan Bristow inserted Gminski into the game. Since it was a blowout, the game action was less than scintillating.

Updates on the score of the Duke game were carried on the Cap Centre scoreboard, and the crowd reacted every time the numbers changed. Most of the players did not know what was causing the seemingly strange fan reaction.

As play continued, there was a huge roar from the crowd. Gminski peeked at the scoreboard, which showed Kentucky ahead, 103–102, with 2 seconds left. "Oh, well," he thought, "it had to end somewhere."

While the Kentucky delegation was hysterical and Duke's fans noticeably dejected, Krzyzewski was angry. "Damn," he thought to himself, "we can't lose this game on a lucky shot." With his team huddled around him, he looked at each player intently. "We're going to win," he said. "We're going to win!"

The players listened. Krzyzewski knew that execution was vital, but a positive mental attitude was imperative. There could be no negative thoughts in the huddle. So instead of just assigning roles, Krzyzewski began by asking them if they could do what they were supposed to, looking for a positive response.

"We need a three-quarter court pass. Grant, can you make the pass?"

"Yeah, Coach, I can do it."

Yeah, I can. That was the frame of mind each player needed.

"Christian, you're going to flash from the left corner to the top of the key. Can you catch it?"

Laettner nodded.

There wasn't time for further conversation, so Coach K reviewed the other assignments and received confirming nods in reply.

Lang would be stationed at halfcourt along the sideline, with Hurley at the top of the key on the same side. Tony would set a pick for Hurley, then run to the basket. Hurley was the second option, but there really was no second option. "If you can't throw it long, get it to Bobby at midcourt," Krzyzewski said. Hurley would have to improvise from there.

The primary option was the long pass to Laettner. Thomas Hill would be positioned at halfcourt on the opposite sideline from Lang; if Laettner couldn't catch the pass, he would try to tip it to Hill, who would be racing toward the basket.

The mood in Bravo Pitino's had been upbeat all week. On Tuesday in the Kentucky coach's restaurant, located a three-point shot away from Rupp Arena in Lexington, the owner had predicted Duke would not win the NCAAs.

Rick Pitino's radio show was always broadcast from his restaurant, and the building was jammed. Pitino told his audience his team had a chance to win, and Saturday night, when Woods banked in the shot that put the 'Cats ahead, the place went bonkers. People were screaming, jumping on tables, hugging and kissing strangers.

Nobody defended the inbounds passer. There were two Kentucky players assigned to Laettner, but Pelphrey, who was stationed at the top of the key, had his feet parallel to the baseline rather than perpendicular. He couldn't see Christian until Laettner rushed past him from the corner.

Hill's pass was perfect. Laettner was bumped slightly by Feldhaus, but caught the ball cleanly directly behind the foul line. Then all the work in practice and all the times he had seen and been in situations like this in his four-year career paid off. Christian didn't rush. He faked to his right, his back to the basket, taking one dribble. On the bench, Jay Bilas watched in agony: "Why is he taking that silly juke move?"

But Laettner knew what he was doing. He knew how much time was left, and he knew what that time meant. He pivoted back left, with Pelphrey falling away to avoid fouling, and shot a seventeen-footer over the 6–6 Feldhaus. Krzyzewski saw the ball leave Laettner's hands. He didn't see it go through the basket, but he had seen that shot so much in practice, he didn't have to. "I knew it was in."

The shot, taken with 0.3 seconds on the overhead clock, was perfect. Laettner danced wildly up the court, Grant Hill and other teammates in hot pursuit. Lang fell on his back underneath the basket. Thomas Hill put his hands to his head and cried.

Pandemonium broke out. Laettner was buried in a pile of players on the floor, and the Duke faithful went wild.

With Charlotte in possession and bringing the ball up the floor, Gminski heard an even louder roar. Even though his team had the ball, he glanced at the scoreboard. It showed Duke had won.

While Charlotte was attempting to run a play, there was Mike Gminski, professional basketball player, with both arms in the air, fists closed, celebrating the result of a college game.

He wasn't the only Duke alumnus there that night. Mark Alarie, who missed the entire season because of injuries, was seated in street clothes on the Washington bench. Alarie had played for Duke in the '86 NCAA finals. After Gminski saw the final score, he looked for Alarie. Mark gave him the thumbs-up signal. It was a big night for the former Dukies.

Krzyzewski's initial feeling of elation was over in the blink of an eye because the first person he saw in the midst of the mayhem was Kentucky senior Richie Farmer. "My heart broke for him. I saw his pain and I felt I was responsible for it. It was a weird feeling. Instead of feeling joy, I felt . . . well, guilty."

Coach K went to Farmer and put his arms around the young man who had played his last college game. Words were insufficient.

. . .

The fans in Bravo Pitino's were still celebrating when Grant Hill threw the pass to Laettner. As the shot went through the basket, it was like nerve gas hit the room. It became dead silent. You could hear yourself sweat.

The people stood where they were, motionless, awaiting the TV replay. Had that ball really gone in? Did it beat the clock? Wasn't there some way the goal didn't count?

The replay produced mass agony. Kentucky had really lost. People began weeping. One woman had to be carried from the place after becoming hysterical.

As the celebration continued unabated on the court, Krzyzewski went to the sideline where the various radio networks were recapping the incredible final moments of the great game they had witnessed. Instead of heading to the Duke network, he walked to the Kentucky table, where Kentucky legend Cawood Ledford had announced his last Wildcats game after thirty-nine years.

Krzyzewski wanted to say something to the Kentucky fans about how well their team had played. "Please," he said to the listeners along the Wildcats' network, "be proud of your team. Give them the welcome home they deserve. They've represented you in the best possible way."

In the interview area, a solemn Pitino said, "We won, too." Krzyzewski agreed.

Laettner's game had been a perfect "10." He was 10 for 10 from the floor and 10 for 10 from the foul line. He scored 31 points, 6 of them in the last 31 seconds.

For the second time in three regional championship games he had produced a buzzer-beater that sent his team to the Final Four. Both of them were in overtime. But it wasn't all a matter of luck; Duke constantly practiced end-of-game situations. As Vince Lombardi said, "Luck is the residue of design." The play worked because of practice, and because the players believed in it, and their coach.

Duke was going to the Final Four again, for the fifth year in succession.

When the Triangle Dinner Theatre audience and cast finally reassembled, the show's lead walked out, understood the murmuring and mood of the crowd, and raised his hands.
"Duke has won. Let the second act begin."

Philadelphia columnist Bill Lyon captured the feeling of the media. "The best basketball game ever played," he wrote. Not many would disagree.

The Duke charter that headed home to Durham carried a happy, boisterous crew. The Blue Devils had just won a game for the ages. If it wasn't the greatest game ever played, it was certainly one of the nominees.

Laettner assured himself of NCAA immortality with his heroics. "I can't believe it happened again," he said as he and Davis rode the bus to the plane. "If I'm dreaming, don't wake me up," said Hurley. Pete Gaudet whacked him in the head.

The entire flight was one constant congratulations. Radio play-by-play man Bob Harris's call of the end of the overtime was played over the plane's PA system not once but twice. Everyone went crazy both times as if it were all happening all over again. The mood was buoyant, jubilant, glowing, as all but one person on the plane excitedly relived the team's amazing triumph.

That one man kept his feelings to himself, but as Krzyzewski looked around the plane at all the happy faces, he thought, "Holy shit—*this is a real problem.* How am I going to reverse this? Everyone's talking Kentucky, Kentucky, Kentucky—no one's even thinking about the fact that we've got a Final Four to play. How am I ever going to get them back to where we are, and where we still have to go?"

"It's such a catch-22 for a coach," Krzyzewski said later. "You always want to get on to the next thing. That's easy when you lose, but how do you do that after a win like this? It was such a great win, but it's almost like an obstacle, too. Our goal wasn't to beat Kentucky, it was to win the whole tournament. Everybody was so happy with the win, and I wasn't going to throw cold water on that. But I knew we'd really have to work to get their focus back to the real goal."

Coach K was already thinking about the hot Indiana team they'd have to face in a week in Minneapolis. The Hoosiers had disposed of Shaquille O'Neal and LSU in the second round, cruised by Florida State in the next game, then destroyed UCLA 106–79 in the regional finals.

The last three times Bob Knight had been to the Final Four, he had won the national championship. There would be a lot of discussion about Knight-Krzyzewski, which would be another distraction if Coach K permitted it.

Krzyzewski knew that with a week of preparation time, Knight's team would be ready. He knew Laettner would get special attention, because the IU plan, as always, would be to eliminate the opponent's perceived strength.

By Sunday, another concern was thrown into the mix—Laettner's little tap dance on Aminu Timberlake's chest. The incident, which had scarcely been mentioned Saturday night during the press conference and interviews following the Duke-Kentucky game, was going to become an issue. To the people who were there, it hadn't seemed important; that included Tom Butters and C. M. Newton, athletic directors of the two schools and both members of the NCAA Basketball Committee.

But a furor was growing. The Timberlake incident was being replayed countless times on television. It was constantly discussed on sports talk shows. The Black Coaches Association made it an issue because of an apparent discrepancy between how Laettner and Rod Sellers, who is black, were treated for what they saw as similar offenses.

Laettner had been involved in '91 when Connecticut's Rod Sellers tried to shove his head through the floor. Nothing was called by the officials, who apparently didn't see it. But the Basketball Committee, with Butters not participating because his school was involved, reviewed the play and decided in April that Sellers would be ineligible for the first NCAA tournament game in '92. Connecticut didn't appeal the decision until February, when it was too late. Sellers sat out the Huskies' first-round win over Nebraska.

Krzyzewski disagreed with the Sellers suspension, which had only been announced the week before the NCAAs began. He thought the Committee made a mistake and said so: The game was over, no penalty had been assessed at the time of the incident, and Coach K didn't approve of setting a precedent by penalizing a player that long after the fact.

The situation in the Kentucky game was far different. The officials saw what happened and Laettner was penalized. It had been a dumb play, one that hurt the team as well as Laettner. It could have cost Duke the game. The Kentucky athletic director felt the situation had been properly handled and said so. He didn't think any further action needed to be taken.

Still, the NCAA Basketball Committee held a conference call Monday morning. Neither Butters nor Newton could participate. It took longer than Krzyzewski thought necessary to reach a decision, but finally the word came: there would be no additional penalty for Laettner. Case closed.

The Black Coaches Association asked for a meeting in Minneapolis with Roy Kramer, chairman of the Basketball Committee. Rudy Washington, director of the coaches organization, insisted that their concern wasn't racial, but rather was over "the consistency in the way the Committee handles punitive actions."

Mail flowed into the basketball office at Duke. The letters from Kentucky were predictable; many of those people wanted to find a way to explain the loss. But many others, from all parts of the nation, blasted Krzyzewski for not immediately benching Laettner or for not taking other action. It was the most mail the office staff had received over any incident. Krzyzewski answered every letter.

In Minneapolis, Washington met with Kramer and came away appeased, even though he and almost all NABC members felt Sellers also should not have been penalized. But the talk kept up all week, and as the Laettner family was driving in a van to Minneapolis, they heard the hosts of a sports talk show insist that Christian should be suspended. It was just one more thing for Duke's lightning rod to deal with.

Earlier in the week, at a pre–Final Four press conference in Durham, another rumor was finally put to rest. A Minneapolis writer asked Laettner directly, "Are you gay?"

"No," he replied. It was that simple. When asked why he had not answered the question until now, Laettner said, "No one asked me."

Back at Cameron, Krzyzewski met in the players' lounge with Hurley just before practice on Tuesday. He was concerned about his point guard's play in Philadelphia. During the '91 NCAAs, Hurley had been phenomenal. He handed out 43 assists and had just 10 turnovers in six games. In the two games at Philadelphia, Hurley had 14 turnovers, including a season-high 8 against Kentucky.

Part of the problem had been Seton Hall, playing against Danny. But there was no explanation for the Kentucky game. Although Hurley played all 45 minutes and scored 22 points, he had several uncharacteristic floor mistakes, and when Duke held for the last shot at the end of regulation, he botched the play.

By his own admission, Bobby hadn't pushed himself

since returning from his broken foot. He had been under orders at first, but now the problem was mental. Coach K understood. Despite his impish look, Hurley was the hardest worker Krzyzewski had ever coached. He attacked drills, much as he attacked the StairMaster while he was recuperating from his injury. But not lately. He had not been prepared during the regional, and it had shown up in his play.

Krzyzewski showed him a tape. It was a highlight and a lowlight. It showed Hurley in earlier games, brilliantly orchestrating the offense and getting in the face of opposing ball handlers. And it showed him making silly mistakes in the Spectrum.

Hurley watched intently. "I can't believe I did that," he said after watching another bad play.

"Last week you didn't work hard," Coach K told Bobby. "This week, you need to work the hardest. You need to set the tone. We'll win the national championship if you play well. Does that put pressure on you?"

Hurley looked at Krzyzewski. "No, I'm fine."

"Are you sure?"

"Coach, I'll be ready."

Krzyzewski needed Hurley at his best. He believed that a team followed a collective energy cycle. When everyone is healthy, you can read their mood and energy level. But when someone gets injured, others have to step up and do more while the injured player recovers. That threw a team out of sync. Laettner and Davis had done more than expected during Bobby's absence, and that had worn them down. So had Grant Hill, but his own injury gave him some rest, while further wearing down the seniors.

When Hurley returned, he needed time to get back into top form mentally and physically. But now Krzyzewski needed Hurley at his best. While the other players might still be thinking of the unbelievably emotional win over Kentucky, the coach knew Hurley wasn't satisfied. He hadn't played up to his own standards at the Spectrum. Hurley would have to be the leader in this Final Four.

There was no Monday practice, but at the team meeting, Krzyzewski handed out a motivational message to the coaches and players. It was the same message he had given each one in July, when in Krzyzewski's mind the quest for the second title had begun. It started: "Perhaps there should be a point in our working life where we feel our contributions have been such that we're entitled to take it easy from that point on."

And it closed, "Like anyone who coasts, there's only one place for them to go—downhill. Keep alive, keep challenging yourself until the day you quit. When growth stops, decay begins." That had been his philosophy all year. This was a reminder.

At the same time, the players also received the itinerary for the week. It included at the end, with no comment:

Sunday, April 5. 1:45 P.M., press conference. 4:30 P.M., practice.

Monday, April 6. 11:30 A.M., team meeting. 4 P.M., pregame meal. 8:22 P.M., Duke versus Cincinnati/Michigan winner.

Tuesday, April 7. 10 A.M., TWA charter to Durham; welcoming at Cameron.

There was no question. Duke planned to win. In '91, Coach K talked to his team all week about playing 80 minutes. The Sunday-Monday-Tuesday schedules were to reinforce the idea that the Blue Devils were going to beat Indiana, then win the championship.

Practice Tuesday and Wednesday was intense. Krzyzewski set the tone early by screaming at Brian Davis. "For the last three weeks, you've been one of our best players. Now you're doing all that individual bullshit." Davis knew that the message was intended for everybody. Seated in the bleachers, Portland Trailblazers scout Keith Drum said, "The captain's got his game face on." Krzyzewski was known as the Captain, in reference to his Army rank, and to his association with Knight, who had been dubbed the General.

Nobody practiced harder than Hurley. On defense, he made things miserable for everybody. In transition, he made great decisions. This was the old Hurley. "Last year, things were very easy for me," he said. "I understood my role very well. But this year, things have been different."

The Kentucky game and the meeting with Krzyzewski had gotten Hurley's attention. "When you realize you've almost lost something, it really wakes you up."

When the team arrived in Minneapolis, Krzyzewski discovered that the NCAA-designated lodging was even farther from the city and the excitement of the tournament than had been the situation in Indianapolis. Obviously, the authorities didn't agree with him that the competing teams should be housed downtown.

The next morning, Laettner and Coach K had to make the lengthy trip to the downtown hotel where the NCAA officials were staying. Christian was awarded the Adolph Rupp trophy as the Associated Press player of the year.

He left that presentation and went into another room, where he and Coach K taped a video for the Naismith Award banquet, to be held in Atlanta. Laettner was the player and Krzyzewski the coach of the year for that group.

Later in the weekend, Laettner was honored by the NABC and the U.S. Basketball Writers Association as their top performer. He was in constant demand for TV appearances tied to one player-of-the-year award or another.

It had been a tumultuous period, even by Laettner's high-profile standards: the retired jersey, Senior Day, the ACC championship, the shot against Kentucky, the furor over the Timberlake incident, and now all of these awards.

Krzyzewski didn't think it would bother his star. He had been worried about Hurley, but Laettner? Never. Nothing affected him. Coach K didn't give a moment's thought to Christian's state of mind; he had always thrived on such attention before.

During the interviews at the Metrodome, where the teams held their traditional one-hour open workouts, many in the media were more interested in the other three teams.

Knight had talked about "cerebral reversal" for a week, and his one-liners with members of the press corps provided many writers with an easy story. A flap over a photo of Knight jokingly "motivating" a player with a bull whip made for a week's worth of copy.

The Michigan story was obvious. The Fab Five, most of whom were willing to offer the most outrageous quotes, drew the largest gathering in the interview area.

Cincinnati received attention because it was the one significant underdog. The Bearcats came out of the Midwest, where all of the favorites were eliminated early. Only their regional writers knew much about them. Also, it was their first Final Four appearance since their string of five straight from 1959–63, a string now matched by Duke.

Krzyzewski didn't care what the reasons were; he was happy to have some of the attention deflected from his team. His players had been in the spotlight enough this season.

Friday night, the team had its traditional dinner with the coaches' families at Kincaid's. The atmosphere was jovial. Everybody was in a good mood.

Less than twenty-four hours later, Krzyzewski was not nearly so buoyant. He had planned to rest rather than attend the pregame meal, set for four P.M. at their motel. Then he got a telephone call from an NCAA official. The women's NCAA semifinals were running long in Los Angeles. They were also being telecast by CBS. It was the first time the network had attempted the four games in a day, and it was being punished for that decision. Coach K was told that the men's games would be delayed 30 minutes. He was incredulous. "This isn't going to happen," he said. But it did.

Krzyzewski contacted trainer Dave Engelhardt, who

was in charge of the team meal and their transportation. Engelhardt delayed the bus for 30 minutes. It was the first —and probably the last—time the NCAA men's semifinals had been set back by other basketball games.

While Coach K didn't like playing the nightcap of a doubleheader, this time he felt it was an advantage: "I really feel for Cincinnati and Michigan. They'll be at the arena waiting for the okay to get started. It's too late to change their plans now, and there's nothing worse than sitting around, wondering when you're going to play."

The bus got caught in traffic going to the Metrodome, and as a result, the Blue Devils were the last to arrive. They were the last to arrive once the game started, too.

Duke got off to a slow start. Indiana, running its offense to perfection and dominating the backboards at both ends, threatened to make a rout of the second semifinal. (Michigan had eliminated Cincinnati in the first game.)

The Hoosiers swarmed all over Laettner, who missed a couple of lay-ups and was 1 for 6 in the first half. Freshman Alan Henderson and sophomore Damon Bailey were cutting Duke's defense apart. The Hoosiers, supported by a majority of the crowd of over fifty thousand, ran to a 39–27 lead with 2:15 left in the period.

Duke had only one answer: Hurley. With Laettner smothered down low, Bobby took on the scoring load himself. Every time Indiana appeared ready to make it a blowout, Hurley made a three-pointer. With the deficit at a dozen points, he made his fourth shot from behind the line.

Duke played well only in the final minute before intermission. Hurley made two free throws. Thomas Hill hit a jumper and made a foul shot. It was 42–37 at the break. Hurley had kept the Blue Devils close, scoring 16 points while the starting front line was combining for a mere 7.

The scene in the locker room at halftime was intense, but this was not the time to rant and rave. Krzyzewski looked at the players and said, "We haven't played well.

We're going to lose unless you pick your level of play up to Hurley's."

The players didn't need any further explanation from their coach. They knew that if it weren't for Hurley, Duke might be down 15 points. But the margin was only 5. Everybody listened and drew inspiration from their smallest player.

There was an almost palpable sense of determination as Duke took the floor for the second half. They knew what they had to do to win. They gathered together and pledged to play harder, and they knew that Hurley would show the way.

The second half was nearly 6 minutes old before the Hoosiers scored, on a three-pointer by Greg Graham. By that time, Duke had scored 13 points. Counting the last minute of the first half, the Devils were on an 18–0 run.

Indiana looked helpless. The Hoosiers couldn't run their screens. Duke took away the passing lanes. The fouls piled up, including a technical called on Knight.

Midway in the period, the Blue Devils held a 13-point lead at 60–47. They had outscored Indiana 28–5. Bailey fouled out with more than 10 minutes to play. Three more Hoosiers would follow. But Duke was not without its own problems. Davis, who had begun to play well in the second half, sprained his ankle when an Indiana player rolled on him going for a loose ball. Although he returned briefly, he was obviously hobbled.

Grant Hill fouled out with 1:44 left, hitting Graham on a three-point try. With Davis in the locker room, Coach K sent in sophomore Marty Clark, who had played only briefly over the past several weeks. Clark got a rebound, then made two foul shots with 1:27 left. After an Indiana turnover, Hurley made two more free throws. Duke appeared to have the game in hand with a 9-point lead, 73–64, and less than a minute to play.

Two people contributed to make it close. One was Todd Leary, who came from the end of the Indiana bench to make three shots in a row from behind the three-point line in a span of 25 seconds. The other was Christian Laettner.

Laettner grabbed the ball too quickly after each Leary basket. The Hoosiers had just one time-out left, and Duke wanted the clock to run, but Laettner acted as if his team were in a hurry and needed to get the ball inbounds instantly. Being slower would have allowed more time to run off the clock.

Still, after Indiana took its last time-out, Duke seemed safe when Clark made the first of two free throws, his fifth straight in the last minute of play, to make it 78–73 with less than 26 seconds to go. He missed the second try, however, and on the rebound, Laettner fouled Matt Nover.

While the other mistakes were bad, this one was shocking—almost a freshman kind of mistake. With Indiana out of time-outs, even if they had gotten the rebound cleanly and rushed up the court for a quick three, by the time Duke had to inbound again, a good 10 or 15 seconds would have run off the clock. Laettner's foul not only gave Indiana ninety-four feet and two free throws, but it stopped the clock and let them set up their press after the foul shots. It was the worst kind of play—a horrible mistake made by an all-America in crunch time that showed Krzyzewski his superstar was running on empty.

Nover made both of his free throws and it was 78–75. Then, as the inbounds passer, Laettner stood still when he should have run the baseline, and practically handed the ball to Hurley, whose foot was on the end line. Turnover! Incredibly, with 24 seconds left, Indiana had the ball under its own basket with a chance to tie.

But the basketball gods and his own teammates kept Laettner from going from ultimate hero to ultimate goat in one week's time. Jamal Meeks missed a hurried shot from the corner, and Lang got the rebound and was fouled. With 13 seconds left, he made two free throws for an 80–75 lead. Nover sank the first three-pointer of his career with 7 seconds left to make it 80–78, but 6 seconds ran off the clock before Duke threw the ball inbounds to Parks. Cherokee was fouled instantly just before the final horn. He made one of two for the 81–78 margin.

Indiana, which took 16:30 to score 13 points at the start of the second half, scored 14 more in the final 52 seconds. But Duke had helped. Krzyzewski realized Laettner was on a down energy cycle, but he felt certain Christian would pull himself together for the final. Nonetheless, Laettner's performance was proof that you could wear out anybody. All that time spent carrying the team was taking its toll.

Reflecting on the Final Four months later, Krzyzewski realized he had made a mistake by taking Christian's competitiveness for granted. He hadn't given Laettner the support that he needed. Because Coach K had been so certain of Christian, he had overlooked the possibility that his star might need some help. Coach K had been so sensitive to Hurley, and not the least bit sensitive to Laettner. For the first time in four years, Laettner had not been involved in a major Duke surge. He took only two shots in the second half, finishing with a season-low 8 points. Hurley scored 26, including a school-record 6 three-pointers.

After the game ended, Krzyzewski and Knight, those longtime friends, headed toward midcourt for the traditional postgame meeting. But there was no embrace as there had been in 1987 when Duke lost to Indiana in the Sweet 16. Knight offered a quick handshake, then moved past to put his arm around Col. Tom Rogers, his old assistant from his days coaching the plebes at West Point. Coach K was visibly shaken; he had been expecting a warm congratulations, and instead Knight's action was decidedly cold and distant.

"I'm happy for our players," Krzyzewski told reporters after the game. "Certainly there is empathy for Coach Knight and his staff. It was a tough loss, but I'm happy for our guys." Knight had no explanation for his attitude.

Both coaches agreed that if it hadn't been for Hurley, the game would have been over at halftime. "We'd have been down twenty points," Krzyzewski said. "Bobby carried us."

Clark had also been a key. He had played well early in the year, but then was relegated to the bench. "I hadn't been in a game in a meaningful situation in more than two months," he said. "But I was always prepared. Coach asked me if I was ready and I said yes. You just need a rhythm on free throws. I shoot them every day in practice. I just tried to relax and get my rhythm."

So now Duke was 40 minutes away from ending the pursuit and winning the national championship again. But it was an entirely different situation from the previous year. At Indianapolis, there had been the emotion of upsetting UNLV. The adrenaline was flowing, and there was no way the players would let anything stop them after beating the top-ranked Rebels. This time, instead of ending their semifinal on an emotional high, the final minutes against Indiana displayed a Duke team that was weary and hurting.

This NCAA had been harder than the last, going back to the second half against Iowa. Last year, the Blue Devils dominated in their regional; this time, it had been emotionally and physically more difficult. Seton Hall. Kentucky. Now Indiana. It had been a long tournament.

Brian Davis was on crutches. He was doubtful for Monday night's rematch with the Fab Five from Michigan.

Krzyzewski looked at the tired faces still in the locker room long after the Indiana game ended. "This is our time," he said, reiterating what he had told them the previous year. "This is our time. We're playing for *us*." When you're fresh, Krzyzewski believed, you can do things for your school, your family, your country. But when you're tired, you have to find the motivation within yourself, and as a part of a group. When a team was at the end of a long road, it needed to play for itself; that was its strength, its bond. That was what could hold it together for the one game remaining in its lifetime.

The two teams that would meet on Monday night couldn't have been more different. The Wolverines were young, brash, eager to spout off. They were constantly told how remarkable they were, how they could win four national championships, before they'd even won one. The Blue Devils were more mature, with a greater collective sense of purpose.

The contrast was clear in statements by the teams' two point guards. Asked by CBS to describe their frames of mind, Michigan's Jalen Rose said, "We're approaching this game like it's a pickup game," while Bobby Hurley said, "We would put ourselves in a class by ourselves in basketball and in what people accomplish [by winning]." The choice was between a team on a lark and one on a mission. Krzyzewski knew which he thought was the more appropriate way to face a national championship game.

When the team met to talk about Michigan, Krzyzewski issued the orders: "The last time we played them, they were talking and you were talking back. Both of you are going to need that energy. If you talk back, you are using energy foolishly. And if you don't talk, that might distract them. They feed off that stuff. Don't help Michigan. Don't play their game. You are not allowed to talk to Michigan.

"There will be times late in the game when you can rationalize. Part of being a champion is not having anything to rationalize. This is our only time. Make them rationalize, 'Well, three national titles wouldn't be that bad.' " Krzyzewski hated the thought of rationalizing defeat. He believed that if, when things weren't going right, players were willing to accept that it was great just to have gotten this far, they stood no chance of winning. His team would have no such thoughts.

CBS was delighted with the matchup. Duke-Michigan in December had been the highest-rated TV game of the season. There was a great story line either way: back-to-back championships, or five freshmen winning the NCAAs.

Krzyzewski wasn't convinced the Michigan players understood where they were, what they had achieved, or how hard it was to get there. They were new to this. His players had been here before. This was their third championship game in succession. They knew what it took to win.

Whatever happened Monday night, the winner was going to make history. Duke understood. Did Michigan?

Davis skipped the Sunday press conference to continue therapy on his ankle. So did Grant Hill, nursing a bruised knee. It was left to Tony Lang to place the game in perspective.

"We've taken a lot of punches, and we have to take one more. Guys like Christian and Bobby, it's been very, very hard for them. Bobby and Thomas Hill have played in the national championship game each year of their careers. Christian is supposed to be this perfect guy who never misses a shot or a free throw or anything. I mean, we're pretty much just kids, and sometimes it's weird to think that it would be this major, major disappointment if we don't win the national title."

"This time we're going to win," Michigan's star rookie Chris Webber said. "It's payback time," said the 6-8 point guard, Jalen Rose.

That was Michigan's focus: they talked about revenge. Several players mentioned that the Wolverines had eventually defeated everybody who beat them first. Duke was the last team the freshmen hadn't beaten. In Krzyzewski's view of revenge, that was just reminding them that they had lost, planting the seeds of doubt.

Practice on Sunday in the Metrodome was in stark contrast to the previous year. All the Blue Devils did was shoot. There was no doubt about the team's focus. The press was still paying more attention to the Fab Five than to Duke, which suited Coach K fine.

Krzyzewski was loose, more relaxed than he had been a year ago. He didn't need to say much to the players; he simply appealed to their maturity, reminding them once again, "This is our time."

He did not talk specifically to Laettner, although in watching the tape of the Indiana game, he said to the staff, "What the hell is he doing? He doesn't make those mistakes." But he still dismissed the notion that Laettner was worn down. Christian was Christian; he'd be there for the final.

One player who was getting a lot of help was Davis. Because of the severity of his ankle injury, there was no way he should have been able to play against Michigan. But Dave Engelhardt, who had taken over for the critically ill Max Crowder, spent hour after hour working with Davis. The trainer spent Sunday night with the co-captain, treating the ankle every few hours. The same procedure continued all throughout the long day of waiting.

"If it hadn't been for the national championship, I wouldn't have considered trying to play," said Davis, the only one of Duke's top seven players who hadn't missed a game because of injury.

At midafternoon Monday, Engelhardt told Krzyzewski that Davis could play if he didn't have too much pain when he warmed up. Davis was hurting, but there was no way he was going to sit this one out.

The mood in the Duke locker room before the game was unusually quiet. There were no fiery speeches, not much joking around. The two captains had enough concerns of their own; Laettner was trying to marshal whatever energy reserves he had left, and Davis had spent the last two days just trying to get in shape to go out on the court at all. Still, there was no indication that the team wasn't ready to play; Krzyzewski read the quiet as an indication that the team was ready to take care of business.

The players wandered out to the court to shoot around before going back to the locker room. They went out on their own and returned in a group. The passageway from the locker room to the court was narrow and ended at a flight of stairs that led to the floor level. As the players returned, the Michigan team was standing at the stairs, and they refused to move to make room for the Blue Devils. As the Duke players squeezed by, the Wolverines had some words for them. "We're gonna get you." "It's payback time." Typical playground stuff.

The Duke players just shook their heads. "Can you believe that shit?" they said. "Is that supposed to scare us or something?"

"Don't talk to Michigan," Krzyzewski reminded them. He believed strongly that his team's maturity would be an enormous advantage in a big game.

Defense had carried Duke against Indiana, and it would have to do it against Michigan. Battered and weary, the Blue Devils once again had to adjust their lineup with Davis hobbled. Grant Hill moved back into a starting role, which would reduce Duke's ability to make adjustments with substitutions.

The first half was a nightmare for Laettner. He started the game with a turnover. Then came another, and then another. A lazy Laettner crosscourt pass was intercepted for a Michigan lay-up. Three times Krzyzewski pulled him out. The first time, he told Christian just to relax, to make easy passes, not to look only for scoring passes. The next time, Coach K chewed out his star to see if he could get a response. The last time, he just talked to Christian to find out what the problem was and if he could help. Nothing worked.

Laettner passed the ball to Michigan more than he did to his own team in the first half. He had 7 turnovers in 16 minutes of action, and only 5 points. Almost half of Michigan's points resulted from his mistakes. Davis wasn't much better; he didn't start, but played 6 minutes. He took one shot. It was an airball.

Michigan could have put Duke away, but the Wolverines were feeling the pressure, too. Unless Duke turned the ball over, Michigan had trouble scoring. Each team made only one basket in the final 3 minutes of the half, which ended with the Wolverines holding a 31–30 lead.

Krzyzewski couldn't wait for the intermission. He hurried to the locker room, his face contorted in anger. His two seniors, who had taken the team to such heights, to the biggest game of all, were completely out of sync. He stood in front of them and screamed.

"Christian, you've just played the worst half of your life. And Brian, you're playing just to play, not to win. You guys don't want it. You're not putting yourself on the line.

"Christian, you suck. You don't give a shit. It's incomprehensible for me. We're playing for the goddamn national championship. You're supposed to be the leader of the team, and you have seven turnovers. It's bullshit! Brian, we'd be better off if you were not out there. This is for the national title and you guys have let us down completely."

Then, with measured aim, he took his forearm and annihilated the blackboard. It came tumbling off its stand. "Shit!" said Coach K, and then he left the locker room. The last time Krzyzewski had attacked a blackboard had been in 1991 in this same Twins' locker room, during the halftime of the NCAA opener against Northeast Louisiana.

Coach K's outburst was experience talking. He remembered the 1986 final. His team had been equally tired at halftime against Louisville, but Krzyzewski didn't know how to make them forget how tired they were. Five Final Fours since then had not gone by without lessons learned. He was trying to channel his emotions in a way he hoped would benefit his team. His angry outburst at his seniors was well-timed. His players needed to get over being tired or hurt or mentally drained, or whatever was stopping them from reaching their goal. They needed to focus on the team's needs, not their own. If they did that, those individual needs would be satisfied.

The players were left to themselves. Hurley, who had

listened to Laettner for three years, now turned the tables. Bobby was rarely a talker; he was a doer, and the
players derived their confidence in him from his demeanor rather than his words.

But after Krzyzewski stormed out, Hurley was so fired
up, so emotional, that he couldn't hold back. "We're playing for the national championship. How can we cheat
ourselves by playing this way? If we're going to play like
this, we might as well stay in the locker room." He was
looking right at Laettner.

Thomas Hill also spoke: "What do we need to do to win
this thing? What are we doing out there? Our turnovers
are terrible." He, too, looked directly at Laettner.

Hurley and Hill set the tone for the rest of halftime.
The players were shocked and surprised by what had happened in the first half. They knew they were better than
Michigan. They just had to start playing like it. Rather
than talk about what had gone wrong in the first half, they
now focused on what they had to do to win. And Hurley
and Hill were taking command.

"We can't play any worse than this and they're just one
point ahead," Hill said. He and Hurley agreed; if Duke
played like Duke, they wouldn't have to worry about
Michigan.

Duke basketball depended on leadership. Laettner and
Davis had taken over last year before the tournament and
carried the team to the title. Now, at halftime in the Metrodome in the locker room, the mantle of leadership was
being passed again.

Hurley's leadership was more than just talk. On the first
sequence of the second half, Duke came down on a fast
break, Bobby with the ball, Grant Hill and Lang on the
wings. Either could have scored. Hill was the team's best
finisher. But Hurley flipped the ball over his head to the
trailing Laettner for a lay-up. Bobby got Christian jump-
started.

Seconds later, Hurley looked for Laettner again. There
he was, squared up behind the line. Hurley got him the

ball, and Christian swished the three. Duke never trailed again.

Michigan hung tough. The Duke lead was 4 at the second TV time-out with 11 minutes to play. Coach K set up a play for Laettner, who took the pass from Hurley and nailed a three-pointer to put Duke up 46–39. But Michigan cut the lead to 4, and with 9 minutes left, Hurley picked up his fourth foul—"A really dumb foul; he missed the third of our three shots on one possession and he just slapped down at the rebounder," said Krzyzewski later. To everyone's surprise, Coach K left Hurley on the floor for one exchange, setting the defense in a zone to protect him, and only then took him out of the game. "I was taking a risk on his fifth foul," Krzyzewski said of the unusual move, "but I didn't want him to dwell on his mistake. We were going to need him soon, and I wanted to give him a chance to do something positive before I took him out."

With 6:51 to go, the Duke lead was 3, and the Blue Devils had missed their last 5 field-goal attempts. Michigan was struggling, too, but everyone could sense the momentum shifting their way. Duke had had chances to put them away and hadn't done it. Even though a TV time-out was due on the next stoppage of play, Coach K couldn't wait. He called his own time-out and put Hurley back in the game.

Krzyzewski's instincts told him that this was the biggest possession of the game. Both teams were tired. After the time-out, Krzyzewski knew his team would come out fresh and focused on this possession. With clipboard in hand, he started diagraming a side out-of-bounds play.

The play was going to start with Grant Hill throwing the ball in. Suddenly, Krzyzewski just *knew* that the play should go to Laettner. He had hit so many of those shots before; Coach K was certain Laettner would hit the shot again.

Krzyzewski stopped and looked at Laettner. "Do you feel it?"

"Yes!" was the co-captain's response.

It would be essentially the play on which Laettner had beaten Connecticut with The Shot in 1990. Laettner would make the inbounds pass, then get it back immediately. "Nobody will be guarding you," Coach K said. "You shoot that sucker. You're going to make the three."

The pass came inbounds to Grant Hill, then directly back to Laettner. Only Christian fumbled the ball. The quick-shot opportunity gone, he drove for the basket, only to fumble the ball again as he went to release the shot. Somehow, he twisted underneath the basket and willed the ball to go in. There was no grace in the execution, but the points were beautiful just the same.

"From then on, we were beautiful, almost perfect," Coach K said later.

The Blue Devils spent the next 6 minutes mostly running the halfcourt offense they'd worked so hard to improve. *They scored on their last twelve possessions.*

After a Grant Hill score, Michigan, obviously rattled, took a time-out. The teams traded a pair of free throws, then the hardworking Thomas Hill missed a shot, claimed his own rebound, and put the ball in the basket.

On that play, Krzyzewski leaped into the air, punching with a clenched fist. "Yes!" It was no Polish ballet, and it was completely out of character. There was still 4:26 to play, and the score was just 56–47. But his coaching intuition told him the game was over.

His leap was like a release. For nearly twelve months now, since he had met with Laettner the previous April, his mind had been focused on the pursuit of the championship. Hill's basket was the clincher. In his mind, the pursuit was over.

The coach who never smiled during a game, who was always thinking ahead, permitted himself this one moment. Krzyzewski's reaction was for himself, and only himself. It was his moment, his reward. A year of being No. 1, a second national title, an unbelievable sense of fulfillment; the lifetime that was this season had lived up to all its promises.

Michigan knew it was finished, too. The freshmen were looking for leadership, and there wasn't any. In the second half, the Wolverines scored 20 points. It was the second-lowest point total in a half of any NCAA final since 1949. They couldn't do anything against the Duke defense.

When Thomas Hill looked at Jalen Rose, the Michigan point guard had that look of disbelief, as if there was nothing he could do to prevent what was happening. Hill knew how much strength Duke took from Hurley's positive front. "When you depend so much on your point guard, like we did and Michigan did, Rose's look told me it was over. He didn't think they could win. If the point guard thought it was over, it was over."

The spectacular Grant Hill provided a punctuation mark with a reverse dunk that made it 58–47. The youthful Wolverines were in full retreat. With 1:45 to play, and the Duke lead at 13, Michigan called a time-out to try to gather its emotions for the end.

Everyone on the Duke bench was laughing, happy, slapping hands and going crazy, with one exception. Christian Laettner just sat in his seat. When Krzyzewski looked in his eyes, he saw that his star was dead tired, completely drained by the emotional load of the long season.

With 13 seconds to go, and the score 71–51 (which would be the final), Coach K cleared his bench. In went Ron Burt, Christian Ast, Erik Meek, Marty Clark, and Kenny Blakeney. Out came Hurley, Lang, Laettner, the Hills. The first to greet Laettner with a big hug was Cherokee Parks. Laettner and Davis looked exhausted but ecstatic: their year-long mission was accomplished, and the teams they led had won back-to-back titles.

As the game ended, Hurley reached under the bench and grabbed a T-shirt. He and Davis had sneaked some there before the game started. On the front, it read, "You can talk the game, but can you play the game?" On the back, "Duke, we can play the game."

As he headed up the runway to the Duke locker room, Hurley giggled as a fan noticed his change of clothing. "It's my favorite shirt," he said. The Duke players had listened to all of Michigan's talk. And now Michigan had seen Duke play.

Hurley's halftime message had been well received. Laettner scored 14 points with zero turnovers in the second half; he was the game's leading scorer with 19. Davis had been instructed by Coach K that his role would be to give Thomas Hill and Lang 30-second breaks, nothing more. Davis responded, "Whatever we need, Coach, that's what I'll do."

Hurley, who went 0 for 5 in the last half and finished with modest numbers, was chosen the most outstanding player, just as Coach K had forecast a week before. The media made the right choice; it just didn't know why. Bobby's leadership had been more important than his scoring.

The scene in the locker room was different from in '91. Then, they were giddy. This time, they had started the year on top and finished it the same way. The players knew they had achieved something very special, something for the history books.

They were tired and battered. But there was an enormous sense of satisfaction. They had set out in pursuit of a goal, and now they had achieved it. There was an uncommon feeling of pure ecstasy. They hugged each other. They congratulated each other. "We did it. Way to go!"

While Laettner, Hurley, and Grant Hill joined Coach K in the interview room, Davis sat on the training table, his throbbing foot propped on a chair.

"We weren't destined to win," he said. "It's by choice, not chance. This is as sweet as last year. Last year we overachieved. This year we knew we could do it. It's something we planned on. No matter what happens now,

this team will always be great. We're great because we do
things the old way—we work hard.

"It was tough [being injured for the final]. But I got to
play a few minutes. I didn't score a point, but people will
always know that I was on this team. Sometime down the
road, I'll go into a town and people will remember that I
was on the team that won back-to-back championships.
They'll want to talk about that. They won't care that I
scored no points."

Over in the interview room, his fellow captain reflected
on his last college game. "I definitely did not want to go
out having a poor performance, but if I had eight or ten
points and we still won, no one could have taken that
away from me." About the halftime conversations, Laettner added, "[Hurley and Hill] just said the team was playing poorly. They didn't actually call my name, but they
should do that. They won't get a chance to any more."

The next day, thousands welcomed the team back to
Cameron. Laettner spoke, and so did Davis. Then it was
Hurley's turn: "The best thing about back-to-back for me
is that *I'll* be back." The next team would be his team, his
and Thomas Hill's. They had made that clear at halftime,
and they already had a title to show for it.

As for Krzyzewski, he looked up to where the first national championship banner hung from the Cameron
roof, where it would soon be joined by No. 2, and said
with a wide grin, "I may be crazy for saying this, but I
wonder where a third one would go."

EPILOGUE

IN THE MONTH THAT FOLLOWED Duke's victory over Michigan, Christian Laettner demonstrated that his ability to break NCAA records was surpassed only by his ability to attract controversy.

Christian was the first player ever to start in four Final Fours. Duke's NCAA record during his career was 21-2. He and Davis played in more tournament games, and more winning games, than any other players in history.

Against Michigan, Laettner participated in his 148th college game, breaking a tie with Danny Manning of Kansas for the most career contests. Laettner wound up as the NCAA tournament career scoring leader, surpassing Houston's Elvin Hayes, and he also set standards for most free throws attempted and made, to go with his championship-game record of 12 for 12 against Kansas in '91.

Laettner also became the record holder in a new category: most times on late-night TV. During the season, he appeared on Roy Firestone's "Up Close" twice on ESPN, but that was just the beginning.

Shortly after Duke won in Minneapolis, Laettner was a guest on the "Arsenio Hall" show, and later in the summer he would appear on the "Tonight Show with Jay Leno" and "Late Night with David Letterman."

It was the appearance with Arsenio Hall that started a flap back in Durham and demonstrated how far an innocent remark could be blown out of proportion.

During his conversation with Arsenio, Laettner referred to the *Durham Herald-Sun* as a "little" newspaper. Although he was technically accurate—the *Herald-Sun* had the lowest circulation of the state's major newspapers —it would have been better if he had said "small."

Somehow, this slight misstep by a twenty-two-year-old appearing on a national television show became a major story back home. Laettner was even criticized by the newspaper's higher-education writer for failing to attend the Duke celebration in downtown Durham, which would have meant turning down Arsenio. That set the stage for an even larger issue, one that gained national attention.

Ten days after Duke won the NCAAs, Bill Nichols of the *Winston-Salem Journal* wrote a copyrighted story that ran at the top of the newspaper's front page. It said that Laettner had an agreement with GQ to keep a diary during the season for publication in the fall, and that might constitute an NCAA violation. The headline on the story suggested Duke might even have to give up its national championship. The story was displayed more prominently than the NCAA title game had been.

Laettner, Krzyzewski, and Duke officials were outraged. Even though Nichols received mixed signals from a former GQ editor and an NCAA official who was asked a hypothetical question, the reporter had not contacted either the player or the coach—and still hasn't.

Nichols also did not speak to Mike Cragg, Duke's sports information director, who had received the initial contact from GQ the previous summer. If Nichols had talked to the SID, he would have discovered that Duke had gone through official channels and received clearance for Laettner's diary before the player ever knew of the request.

Cragg had contacted Chris Kennedy, Duke's compliance officer. Kennedy followed proper channels and reported the request to David Thompson, the ACC compliance person, who then talked with Amy Privette in the NCAA office.

Only then was Laettner told about the GQ request and how it had to be handled. He did not sign a contract with the magazine and he did not receive any money. "Did people think we were stupid?" he said weeks later. "Did they think I would do anything illegal, or that Duke would do anything illegal?"

But the story persisted for three days, receiving headlines all over the nation, until the NCAA's Jim Marchionny said publicly that what Laettner had done was all right. "He kept a diary. That's all he did," Marchionny said in announcing there was no investigation. In fact, Laettner hadn't even kept up his diary after the first couple of weeks.

Krzyzewski was so upset at the way the story was treated that he referred to it in his opening remarks at the team's basketball banquet on April 20. "It just stinks, it really, really stinks," he said of the media's handling of what should have been a nonstory.

But when you have the kind of success that Duke has enjoyed, you live under a media microscope. Anything negative that happened to a Duke player was sure to make headlines.

Bobby Hurley, celebrating the end of exams with some friends, was stopped at a roadblock and charged with driving while impaired after he blew 0.10 on a Breathalyzer. Hurley was fined and had his license suspended for sixty days. He volunteered to make personal appearances at schools. Many students were caught by the roadblock, set up just off campus to catch those who were celebrating the end of their exams; only Hurley had to read about his arrest in the daily papers, in type usually reserved for natural disasters.

The best indication that Duke stories could be blown out of proportion came when Laettner failed to graduate with his class in May.

Because he had played on the Pan-Am team and the Goodwill/World team under Coach K instead of going to summer school, Laettner carried five courses, an overload, in the spring semester of his senior year. He made a D in one of the courses, and thus came up one credit short, although he did participate in graduation ceremonies.

The story made headlines around the nation. Some writers asked if Krzyzewski would take down the team's national championship banner and Laettner's retired jersey from the Cameron ceiling. The coach still refused to hang the 1990 Final Four banner because of the seniors on that team who hadn't graduated.

Coach K had no intention of doing any such thing. This was an entirely different situation. What many in the media insisted on making a negative, he viewed as a positive.

"I think it's remarkable that Christian is within one credit of graduation in four years, considering all of the things that he has done during his career and all of the demands on his time," Coach K said.

Even more important to Krzyzewski the educator, "it shows that the system works." Coach K was delighted that Laettner's professor didn't just give him the C that he needed; if Christian Laettner wouldn't receive something he didn't deserve academically, that was proof that nobody would. Laettner took his remaining elective in summer school and graduated.

It was left to Coach K to sum up the turbulent aftermath of the second NCAA title. In those same opening remarks at the team's year-end banquet, Krzyzewski reflected on the furor over Laettner's "little" comment and the GQ flap and said, "There were times, because of all these things, and all the autograph requests and the people saying, 'You gotta do this or that,' that it flashes through your mind, 'Jeez, if we were sixteen and twelve, nobody would give a damn. Maybe if we were just mediocre, we could be normal.' But if that's what it takes, we don't want to be normal."

And just to show that his coach's mind was already moving forward, he added, "And you can bet your *Winston-Salem Journal* that this team will challenge for the national championship next year."

Not defend; challenge. A new lifetime had already begun.